RUSH HOUR

IAIN GATELY was raised in Hong Kong and studied law at Cambridge. He is the author of four books including *La Diva Nicotina: The Story of How Tobacco Seduced the World*, and *Drink: A Cultural History of Alcohol*. He lives in Hampshire with his partner, Vanessa, and their family.

Iain Gately

RUSH HOUR

How 500 million commuters
survive the daily journey
to work

HEAD
ZEUS

Contents

Crossing No Man's Land

6.55 a.m., Monday, 13 January 2014. I'm standing on platform one at Botley railway station in rural Hampshire, waiting for the 07.01 train to London Waterloo, about to take a ride on a commuter service for sentimental reasons. Three years ago to the day, I'd waited on the same spot for the same train, en route to a new job that required me to wear a suit and work from nine to five in an office in London, seventy miles distant in a straight line from my home, but two and a half hours away via a combination of car, train and tube. I'd been nomadic for much of the prior decade, and saw the return to commuting as a challenge rather than as submission to a gruelling regime. When the alarm went off at 5.55 a.m., I leapt out of bed with fire in my veins.

Back in 2011, my journey to work would begin at an ironing board, squeezing wrinkles from a shirt. I found it a curiously anodyne activity at first, although compelling too – I hadn't ironed in years and felt that once I had begun I should do my best to lay down faultless creases. It was also an opportunity for contemplation, not least of the mystery of why shirts should be ironed in the first place. Are we in secret thrall to stiff fronts? Does it have deep roots in our culture?* My conclusion – a week into my new commute – was that we iron to make ourselves look young again. We try to convey the same messages with our clothing as we could with our flesh before we had wrinkles. That it also makes us appear neat and businesslike is incidental.

With shirt ironed, face shaven, shoes shined, and swaddled in a suit and overcoat, I was ready to go. At 6.20 a.m. I'd start the car, turn on the blowers and wipers, and dash back and forth from the house with pans of tepid water to clear the ice off its windows. At 6.24 a.m., I'd plug in my seat belt and head off into the lanes. There was still snow from December's blizzards in the fields and banked up under the hedgerows, and snowmen built over Christmas lived on in front gardens. As soon as I passed fifty miles per hour my windscreen re-froze and was coated inside and out with a lattice of ice crystals that shattered and refracted oncoming headlights into a million little rainbows. I'd scrub a hole the size of a diving mask in front of my eyes through which I could see trees and hedges, hung with needles of ice, glittering along the verges. If the night had been cloudless, the road too might shimmer at its fringes, and then I knew there was black ice about, which made me drive as if on tiptoes. It caught me out a week into my new job, but I got control back just before the car buried its nose in a

---

* The desire to smooth and flatten our garments has been present in Britain since the days of the Vikings, whose graves contain whalebone 'smoothing boards' (sometimes with sinister-looking beasts carved into their backs) that are thought by archaeologists to have been used by Viking maidens, in conjunction with bun-shaped lumps of glass, to press pleats into their linen. It's been practised more or less continuously ever since.

hedge. The adrenaline rush was tremendous. There wasn't time to think. It was only afterwards that I remembered you're meant to steer *with* the slide not against it if you lose control and wondered if that's what I'd done.

The next challenge on my daily odyssey was whether I should waste a minute or two to see if there was a parking space free at Botley station. It wasn't a problem if not: the Railway Tavern over the road had plenty at £4 per day, but since there was a chance of paying nothing and being on the right side of the road for the drive home I'd try the station first. A frisson of paranoia always touched me as I turned in. Botley has room for only twenty cars – and that's if people park considerately. There's an aggregates plant at the end of the car park, and lorries waiting to weigh in often blocked the last free space. The plant usually cleared them quickly so it was worth hanging on, although only until 6.51 a.m. at the latest, when one had to bolt for a slot at the pub in order to leave enough time to make the train.

Botley station per se, a handsome four-square Victorian building, with loos, a waiting room and a wooden canopy on cast-iron pillars over platform one, was demolished in 1963. Now the dot on the map consists of a ticket machine, a fibreglass shed, and a chain-link fence between the car park and the platforms. A plastic information board beside the machine, co-sponsored by South West Rail and Hampshire County Council, announces various non-existent facilities including a waiting room and wheelchair access. On the other side of the car park, a drinking fountain commemorates Queen Victoria's Diamond Jubilee, and an adjacent stone marks the spot where John Diggins of the

Talbot Fencibles was gibbeted for the murder of Thomas Webb, a travelling man, whom he robbed then stabbed with his bayonet and left in a ditch to bleed to death on 11 February 1800.

There were usually about a dozen or so other people waiting with me for the 07.01, clustered in pools of orange light along the platform, puffing out clouds of condensation with each breath. Everyone was wrapped up tight and some paced to and fro, halting now and then to stare at the LED display mounted on a steel pole that streamed details of the next three trains that were due to arrive. Loudspeakers under the display sometimes announced contradictory information: perhaps pressure sensors on the tracks prompted a computer to play a pre-recorded message. The announcer's voice was female, calm and conciliatory: Big Sister on the Tannoy. She was often guilty of double-speak: 'The train about to arrive on platform one is the 07.01 service to London Waterloo via Basingstoke, stopping at Eastleigh, Winchester, Micheldever... This train has five coaches' she would tell us, although the display indicated that the 07.01 was now expected at 07.26, and then she would warn us to 'stand well clear of the platform edge as the train approaches', while the station was still wrapped in silence and gloom.

The rails started to hum when a train was really imminent. The next indication of its approach was its headlight, visible from a quarter of a mile or so out. On frosty mornings a vortex of white specks like dandruff hovered around its beam as it whirled up ice crystals from the tracks. It seemed to pull up impossibly quickly. From where I stood in the middle of the platform the first two carriages appeared to flash by, the third crawled, and the fourth halted at my feet and juddered. Then the lights around the door buttons flashed, a signal pinged, and it was time to enter the capsule. On my first day back on the rails, I had to kill a childhood superstition before climbing aboard. I'd grown up in Hong Kong and the 07.01 had the number 4444 stencilled on its carriages, which corresponds to Death Death Death Death in Chinese numerology. Only more 4s could have made it unluckier.

Although we commuters at Botley were few, the seconds we spent getting into the train were fraught. There were rituals and pitfalls that took time to learn or to avoid. People formed informal queues for the carriages, and in order to be at one of their heads it was crucial to stand at exactly the right spot on the platform, which varied by a yard either way each day. If one too many got on before you, the journey ahead might be less tolerable.

As soon as we were through the train's doors we'd dash left and right down the aisles in search of a seat, as if we were playing at musical chairs and the music had just stopped. The interiors of the Standard Class carriages of the 07.01 made it feel all the more like a game. They had the same bright colours and rounded edges as the diversions in a children's playground – or a primate enclosure at a zoo. The levity that these conveyed was spoiled by the rash of warning notices on their walls, doors and windows: Don't Smoke; What to Do in Case of an Emergency; Quiet Zone. Perhaps two-thirds of the seats had stickers on their backs that designated them as priority, implying that a statistically unlikely number of us were pregnant or disabled.

Each carriage had a row of twin seats on one side of its aisle, and clumps of three facing three on the other. The forward-looking window seats of the twins were the most prized, because the view through the window came towards you rather than running away, and also because they minimized contact: you were pressed against someone else only on one side. Initially, I found the desire to cocoon surprising and wondered why my fellow adventurers seemed to have a mutual longing to keep each other at arm's length, as if they were meeting in dreams, and would melt if they tried to touch or kiss each other.

Indeed, during my first month back on the rails, I felt like a relapsing alcoholic, facing up to the dangers and pleasures of drinking again. As both outsider and insider, I became curious about other commuters on the train. Why had they chosen to pass so much of their lives in motion? I'd started commuting again for the simple reason that work was so much better paid in London that it made sense to go there, like Dick Whittington, for the gold. Were they, like me, travelling for the money – because higher pay outweighed more hours spent in transit – or something more or less: were they the restless scions of a noble line of adventurers, with wanderlust in their blood, or devotees of a dying art, who belonged to the industrial rather than the information era?

Commuting, in the sense of using some form of transportation to separate one's places of work and rest, is – in theory at least – a rational exercise. It allows people, if not to have the best of both worlds, to achieve the best of all compromises: a rewarding job and a pleasant home. The travelling itself is the price that has to be paid to realize these two goals. It requires commuters to surrender their liberty to the operators of public transport, or to congestion on the roads, while they cross a kind of no man's land, whose interim stations or junctions are measures of their progress – no more – and which they'd probably never visit for their own sakes. In consequence, it's perceived as a kind of purgatory, which lies between the poles of production and recreation that cap our days. This is a true picture in so far as commuting is indeed a world of its own: it's an unexplored part of our lives that influences our behaviour beyond rush hour, and which has had, and continues to have, a significant impact on our culture. It's also far more fascinating than its reputation, offering freedoms and even pleasures to its participants that they may not enjoy at either their offices or homes. I've commuted on trains, buses, trams, underground, in cars, on riverboats and inter-island ferries, sometimes quickly – it's been over in less than twenty minutes – though at other times I've passed nearly a third of my waking hours commuting, and the exercise has given me pleasure as well as boredom or pain. My journey to London via the 07.01, for instance, was more stimulating and satisfying than the work I performed at my destination, which consisted of writing corporate control procedures in management-speak. The driving was fun, the paranoia over whether or not there might be a parking space at Botley station was, after a fashion, invigorating, and on the train I could read, write, sleep, or watch the imprint of the changing seasons on the countryside as it flashed by.

Indeed, although now quotidian, commuting was once radical, and represented both a break with the past and the key to a new way of living. For most of its short history people have thought well of it: on balance it's been seen as something to aspire to rather than an exercise in asceticism. On a global basis, it still is. When commuting began in the first railway boom of the Victorian era, it stood for freedom of movement, and opened up fresh horizons to those brave enough to accept its challenges. It even carried a whiff of danger in its early days. The very first commuters thought they were taking their lives into their hands on their very first commutes. But as the transportation revolution gathered pace, the few became multitudes and altered – amongst other things – our patterns of work, settlement and leisure, and the concept of time itself.

In Part I of this book I'll explore how commuting progressed from being an experience as futuristic as private space travel to a commonplace practice for over half a billion people around the world. In Part II I'll look at it in the here and now – at the challenges that commuters face on their daily journeys, how they overcome them, and whether their persistence is justified or not. Although commuting is accused of causing a host of problems, both physical and psychological, including stress, obesity, hyperactivity, impotence and heart disease, by many measures commuters are life's winners. Together, they gather most of its gold, live to ripe old ages, and set their children off to the best of all starts. In Part III, the final part of the book, I'll examine the future of commuting. Will it be made redundant by the 'great digitization' that is changing our world, and will the work rather than the worker do the travelling? Might it be abandoned as an anachronism, which wastes both people's time and the planet's resources? The answers aren't clear-cut. Indeed, the auguries suggest that it won't end in a hurry, and the time spent travelling to gather fuel to keep the home fires burning isn't all squandered or lost. Commuting, after all, lets us lead double lives: we can be lovers and parents and rebels at home, and pinnacles of efficiency in our offices, respected for our detachment, calm and reason. Travelling to work gives us time 'to prepare a face to meet the faces that you meet', and enables us to escape being bound to the soil or trapped in a city. Perhaps rather than lamenting the commute we should revive the pioneer spirit that inspired the first generation of commuters, to whom the practice represented both the chance to escape the drudgery that hitherto had characterized their existences, and the freedom to remake their worlds.

◆ ◆ ◆ ◆ ◆

PART I

THE BIRTH, GROWTH AND TRIUMPH OF COMMUTING

CHAPTER I

The Man who Went to London Twice in One Day

The late Dr. Arnold, of Rugby, regarded the opening of the London and Birmingham [railway] line as another great step accomplished in the march of civilisation. 'I rejoice to see it,' he said, as he stood on one of the bridges over the railway, and watched the train flashing along under him, and away through the distant hedgerows— 'I rejoice to see it, and to think that feudality is gone for ever: it is so great a blessing to think that any one evil is really extinct.'

Lives of the Engineers, Samuel Smiles, 1862

'The office is one thing and private life is another. When I go into the office, I leave the Castle behind me, and when I come into the Castle, I leave the office behind me.' So speaks John Wemmick, a lawyer's clerk, considered by some literary critics to be the most modern character in Charles Dickens' *Great Expectations* (1861), perhaps because he displays a very modern schizophrenia: at work he's ambitious, worldly, and steals the 'portable goods' of those about to be hanged; at home, in his self-built castle, he's pleasant, eccentric and loving. He represents a dilemma that more and more people had to address in the first half of the nineteenth century. Work and home had become distinct worlds where sometimes contradictory standards prevailed. Rather than coinciding with your place of rest on a farm or forge, where you were the same person night and day and kept the same company all the time, your place of work could be an office or a factory, where you might have to dress and act very differently.

While moral arguments for the separation of one's places of work and residence were compelling, they took second place to sanitary considerations. The Dickensian London from which Wemmick had retreated was a series of factories and slums astride a sewer. There were cholera epidemics every other decade, the average family lived five to a room, and adults, smaller than their grandparents, had a life expectancy of only thirty-five. Dickens made his reputation – in part – by writing lurid stories about inebriated paupers who bred criminals and lived in cellars next to open sewers while London rained soot on them from its coal fires and furnaces. As it happened, the truth was worse than fiction, and was just as bad in the other British cities that were being transformed by the Industrial Revolution.

In 1832, James Phillips Kay, who studied medicine alongside Charles Darwin at Edinburgh University, published *The Moral and Physical Condition of the Working-Class Employed in the Cotton Manufacture in Manchester*. The book was a bestseller, and its scenes of urban filth, disease and degradation both awoke his middle-class readership to the blight within a short walk of their front doors and gave them page after page of reasons to flee the cities as soon as possible. In Manchester's Parliament Street, for example, Kay reported that 'there is only one privy for three hundred and eighty inhabitants, which is placed in a narrow passage, whence its effluvia infest the adjacent houses, and must prove a most fertile source of disease. In this street also, cess pools with open grids have been made close to the doors of the houses, in which disgusting refuse accumulates, and whence its noxious effluvia constantly exhale.' Even Edinburgh, his alma mater, the so-called Athens of the North, had ghettos composed of 'masses of rotten, rat haunted buildings' that were packed with human misery.

The desire to separate hearth and hunting ground – to live somewhere healthy and work where it was most profitable – intensified as the nineteenth century advanced. When technology in the form of steam-powered transportation made such a separation possible, commuting budded and then bloomed. It was part of a greater development, labelled 'locomotivity', that began in the 1830s and transformed Britain within the next fifty years: the coming of the railways set the nation in motion.

Although, in the first instance, railways were built to transport freight rather than passengers – coal from the pitheads to the foundries and the cities, food from the country to the towns, cloth from the mills to the docks – as they came into service from 1833 onwards, their operators found a huge and spontaneous human demand. When, for instance, the Stockton and Darlington Railway, built to link coal mines in County Durham to the factories of Stockton-on-Tees, introduced steam trains in 1833, the local interest was immense: more than 500 people climbed aboard its inaugural service, which consisted of twenty-one empty coal wagons and a single carriage designed for passengers named, appropriately, *Experiment*. Huntsmen raced it on horseback; and a crowd of ten thousand met it at its destination. By 1838 the Stockton and Darlington was carrying 200,000 passengers per year, and its ticket receipts far exceeded its income from freight. Similarly, the Liverpool and Manchester Railway was established to transport raw cotton to Manchester and finished goods to the docks at Liverpool. The barons of industry who financed it wanted to end their reliance for transportation on canals, whose operators squeezed them on price and couldn't offer a service if their waterways froze in winter or became too shallow for navigation in dry summers. In the event the goods-only railway had 400,000 passengers in its first year, and its income from fares 'ran at twice the level' of that from freight.

In some cases, however, the railway companies were pushed into carrying people. The London and Southampton Railway* was diverted from its ambitions to ferry fuel, fish, cattle and imported goods between the capital, the hinterland and the coast by the intervention of William James Chaplin. Chaplin was nicknamed the 'Napoleon of Coaching' and his firm owned sixty-four coaches, 1,500 horses, and ran ninety-two daily services to and from London. He was one of the principal operators in what was then a national business. Prior to the railways, horse-drawn coaches were the only

---

* It changed its name shortly afterwards to the London & South Western Railway (LSWR) and built Botley station in 1841.

form of land-based, long-distance passenger transport. Britain had an extensive and – given its inherent limitations – efficient network that could carry a traveller from London to Edinburgh in a mere three days. But in comparison to trains, coaches were slow and small. The 'Wonder Coach' that ran between London and Shrewsbury won its nickname by averaging 12.1 mph. To achieve this newsworthy pace, 150 horses were used over the 158-mile journey. Like most other coaches, it carried only eight passengers plus baggage. Chaplin foresaw that the railways would kill off his industry. He sold up, and invested the proceeds in the LSWR. He was rewarded with a seat on its board of directors, and a say over its behaviour. Experiments with passengers were carried out on its partially completed line shortly afterwards, including a service to Epsom for Derby Day in 1838. Five thousand people turned up at its London terminus in Nine Elms before the gates opened at eight in the morning, and more and more arrived, faster than trains could carry them away, until 'amid the shrieks of the female portion of their number, the mob broke over the booking counter, leaped through the windows, invaded the platform and rushed pell-mell into a train chartered by a private party'.

While the experiment had been messy, it was also profitable, and was repeated for the Ascot races. In the space of three months, the LSWR took nearly 100,000 fares before it had carried a single bullock or sack of coal. By the time that the company celebrated the completion of its initial track from London to Southampton in 1840 with brass bands, a 21-gun salute, and a banquet hosted by the Duke of Cornwall, Chaplin was its vice chairman. A sermon preached to mark the occasion, which took its inspiration from

Daniel 12:4 – 'many shall run to and fro, and knowledge shall be increased' – indicated that his vision of the company's future as a passenger service had prevailed.

Ceremonies similar to the LSWR's opening extravaganza were enacted the length and breadth of the nation as the railway boom gathered pace. Banquets, banners, brass bands, sermons and massed choirs of schoolchildren seem to have been obligatory. The peak year of the boom was 1846 when 294 Acts of Parliament were passed, creating new railways with nearly 9,500 miles of lines on paper, few of whose principals had anything in the way of a 'track record'.* Boom turned to bust the following year, ruining investors great and small in the process. Two out of three Brontë sisters lost their savings dabbling in railway shares, and the pain was felt in manor houses and rectories throughout the nation: 'no other panic was more fatal to the middle class… it reached every hearth, it saddened every heart in the metropolis… Daughters delicately nurtured went out to seek their bread. Sons were recalled from academies… homes were desecrated by the emissaries of the law.'

Although the losses were great, the railway boom left tangible assets behind after its bubble burst. Over 6,000 miles of track were completed in the 1840s. Steam trains became a feature of the British landscape, and it seems that when people caught their first glimpse of one of these iron monsters painted in lurid colours rumbling through fields, disappearing into hills, crossing rivers, belching out fire, panting like animals, but faster than any pair of lungs, they all wanted a ticket to ride.

---

* The phrase originated in the railway boom.

There were many, however, who resented the railways. Their tracks had sliced into Britain's class system as well as its soil, and the losses suffered in the post-boom bust rubbed salt into the wounds. At a protest meeting against a new line through Northampton, it was predicted that they would 'Spoil our Shires and ruin our Squires' by, in the first case, defiling natural beauty spots and ancient monuments, and, in the second, by providing the squires' tied labour with the opportunity to escape from drudgery.

The charge that railway lines injured the landscape was valid: nothing was sacred if it stood in their path. In Lewes, for example, tracks were routed through the ancient altar of St Pancras Priory, and in Shap in Westmorland they crossed a prehistoric stone circle – in both cases the antiquities were demolished to make way for progress. The railways soon became the pet hate of the Romantics, the environmentalists of the era:

Is then no nook of English ground secure
From rash assault?

asked William Wordsworth in an 1844 poem, 'On the Projected Kendal and Windermere Railway', and the answer, it seemed, was no. The Great Western Railway even planned to lay a line right through the middle of Stonehenge. The scheme only failed because Parliament decided that the route itself was unnecessary, rather than that the monument was more important than having another railway line.

A similar vandalism occurred in the cities. In London, various Roman, medieval and Elizabethan buildings were flattened to create train stations. Iconic views were interrupted with elevated railways. The prospect of St Paul's Cathedral from the Strand, for instance, was obscured by the Ludgate viaduct, described later in the *Imperial Gazetteer of England and Wales* as 'one of the most unsightly objects ever constructed, in any such situation, anywhere in the world'. The destruction continued well into the 1860s, when more than 200 Bills were put before Parliament, seeking permission to build 882 miles of new track in London. *Punch* magazine suggested, not entirely tongue in cheek, that St Paul's itself be turned into a station: 'what else will it be fit for when every railway runs right into London?'

Slums as well as monuments were razed to build new termini, and while romantics shed few tears for them, their destruction forced tens of thousands of workers to find new homes. Indeed, as well as enabling people to travel, the railway boom forced many to relocate. The railways also made enemies among workers in the countryside. Farmers complained that their hens had stopped laying, their sheep's fleeces had been blackened, and their cattle driven mad by the din and smoke of the iron monsters that rocketed through their pastures.

Steam trains were thought to derange humans in addition to livestock. Their opponents warned that their unnatural velocity might have serious consequences for the sanity of their passengers. An 1836 article in the *London Saturday Journal* prophesied that the new freedom of movement, which had 'set the whole world a-gadding' at indecent speeds would have disastrous results: 'Grave plodding citizens will be flying around like comets... it will encourage flightiness of intellect. Veracious people will turn into the most immeasurable liars: all their conceptions will be exaggerated by their magnificent notions of distance.' It was better, surely, that everyone stayed put.

Aesthetes, led by John Ruskin, also believed that people should eschew the railways. In Ruskin's opinion, the speed and convenience they offered dehumanized their passengers:

> The whole system of railroad travelling is addressed to people who, being in a hurry, are therefore, for the time being, miserable. No one would travel in that manner who could help it – who had time to go leisurely over hills and between hedges, instead of through tunnels and between banks... The railroad... transmutes a man from a traveller into a living parcel... he has parted with the nobler characteristics of his humanity for the sake of the planetary power of locomotion. Do not ask him to admire anything. You might as well ask the wind.

In the event, those prejudiced against the railways were sidelined as the new freedom to travel that they had created was embraced. The opportunities they opened up were summarized in a popular anecdote from the 1840s about the man who went to London twice in one day. His point of departure varied with the county in which the story was told, as did the purpose of his journey, and indeed any other details of this futuristic individual. Some claimed he was a speculator, others a bigamist. It was that it was possible rather than who had done it that mattered: before trains arrived most people were lucky if they went to London twice in their lives.

From a standing start in 1831, the annual number of passenger journeys in Britain jumped to a million in 1840; ten years later the figure was 67 million; by 1860, 154 million; and in 1870, 316 million. While many of these, by pre-rail standards, were made for whimsical reasons for such long journeys – a day at the races, a temperance outing, a once-in-a-lifetime reunion with a sibling – a large number were to get to and from work: commuting had begun.

Perhaps the first railway line to draw much of its business from commuters was the London and Greenwich, which opened in 1836, with a mere three and three-quarter miles of track. It was built to compete with steamboats on the River Thames, which had a huge volume of holiday and excursion traffic. Its locomotives were nicknamed 'boxers' as they seemed to duck and weave like prizefighters when in motion. They were also very fast, reaching 60 mph on trial runs. Its carriages were built for people rather than commodities, and by 1844 it was carrying more than two million passengers per annum: an analysis of passenger fares indicated that many were using the service to get to work rather than to escape from the capital and drink deep at Greenwich at Whitsun.

The LSWR, meanwhile, found that the nascent demand to commute was so great that it could shape the demographics of the land around its rails simply by building a station. When it was refused permission to site one beside its tracks at Kingston upon Thames, thanks to the opposition of local coaching companies and aesthetes, it created a new stop a mile and a half away in 1838.

Within three years, it was noted that 'upon the South-western line a new town, called Kingston-upon-Railway, is fast rising, 800 houses being built or in progress'. The station at Kingston-upon-Railway was subsequently shifted half a mile down the track to accommodate a branch line and re-christened Surbiton after a nearby farm. By 1855 Surbiton had become a borough in its own right and a favourite haunt of the Pre-Raphaelite painters, who sacrificed any philosophical objections they might have had to railways to the convenience of access to nature that they offered, and reverse-commuted from London.

By the middle of the nineteenth century, commuting was recognized as a growing trend: in 1849, the *Southport Visiter* reported that, thanks to the opening of the Liverpool Crosby & Southport Railway, the town had become a haven for 'gentlemen of business, who daily visit their offices in Liverpool, returning in the evening to their families located in healthy Southport'. The next year, Dionysius Lardner, an Anglo-Irish professor who specialized in explaining the wonders of science and progress to the masses, and who was horsewhipped by Captain Heaviside of the Dragoon Guards for philandering with Mrs Heaviside, noted in *The Railway Economy* that locomotivity was creating a new way of living:

> It is now not unusual for persons whose place of business is in the centre of [London] to reside with their families at a distance of from fifteen to twenty miles from that centre. Nevertheless they are able to arrive at their respective shops, counting houses or offices at an early hour of the morning, and to return

without inconvenience to their residence at the usual time in the evening. Hence in all directions around the metropolis in which railways are extended, habitations are multiplied.

The railway companies responded to demand by issuing 'season tickets', in imitation of the operators of steamboats on the coast who offered holiday-season-long discounts to advance purchasers. There was pull as well as push: in 1851, for instance, a clerk at Reading station was forced by passenger pressure to ask for a rate for an annual season ticket from his employers, which was set at £50 – equivalent to a year's income for the average worker. Although they were expensive, demand soared as soon as the season tickets became available. The North Eastern Railway, for instance, recorded an 800 per cent rise in sales between 1860 and 1875.

The high cost of season tickets tells us something about the social status of the first generation of commuters. As noted by both Dionysus Lardner and the *Southport Visiter*, these were generally businessmen or members of one of the professions. An Enumerator's Return from Bromley in Kent, ten miles outside London, which received its first railway station in 1858, provides further insight. The people who had settled in or near the town after the coming of the rails included a South African merchant, a stockbroker, an underwriter at Lloyd's, and an architect who sat on the Poor Law Board. This class of early commuter was educated and opinionated as well as affluent. They wrote letters to *The Times* when train services didn't match their expectations. The following example from 15 January 1864 shows how quickly their number was growing, and that delays without reason – so much for locomotivity! – were as infuriating then as they are now:

> *Sir – I live with thousands of others down the Mid Kent Railway… ten miles from London Bridge, all of us requiring to be in town more or less punctually every morning. The recent 'facilities of new lines', as the phrase goes,* have only woefully obstructed our business journeyings… I arrived at the London Bridge Station to go home… and found that our train had taken a trip to Charing Cross, leaving 200 or 300 of us on a very unsafe, cold, exposed, narrow platform, kicking our heels while engines and trains passed to and fro… in dangerous proximity.*

The references in the letter to danger and punctuality give us clues as to the matters that vexed or preoccupied early commuters. They needed to be brave, for a start: Victorian railways were truly dangerous. Ticket offices sold life insurance from the Railway Passengers' Assurance Company as well as tickets. The hazards that steam trains posed to life and limb were demonstrated in the most vivid fashion when William Huskisson, the eminent parliamentarian, had his legs mangled by George Stephenson's *Rocket* locomotive at the opening ceremony of the Liverpool and Manchester Railway on 15 September 1830. He died of his injuries a few hours later. The inaugural festivities of the Stockton and Darlington Railway were also marred by a serious injury to a

---

* The modern euphemism for such disruptions is 'engineering works'.

joyrider, who lost a foot. It seemed that whenever a train moved, people were mutilated or killed. The average derailment, collision or explosion, such as the Staplehurst rail disaster of 1865 (ten dead, forty injured), was a veritable bloodbath. Charles Dickens was involved in the Staplehurst crash, when a train from Folkestone to London travelling downhill at fifty miles an hour shot over a viaduct whose rails had been removed for repairs. The first six carriages fell into the riverbed below, and the seventh, where Dickens was sitting with his mistress, ended up hanging from the bridge. He rescued the passengers from his carriage, then climbed down to the others with a hip flask of brandy to tend the injured. He gave drams to a man with a fractured skull, and a woman whose face was caked with blood, both of whom died before his eyes.

Accounts of train crashes made compelling reading, and the press encouraged this morbid fascination with macabre reports of fresh disasters. It justified its sensationalism on the grounds that a train crash, unlike a ship sinking mid-Atlantic, or a cave-in down a Chilean mine, took place in the meadows of old England, and could have involved its readers. 'We are all railway travellers now,' the *Saturday Review* explained in 1868. 'These trains and collisions, these stations and engines, and all the rest of it, are not only household words, but part of our daily life.'

Punctuality was also an obsession of early commuters: They had to change the way they thought about time as well as close their minds to the risk of death. Before the railways appeared, only princes were expected to be precise. Most Britons divided their days into mornings and afternoons rather than hours and minutes. Moreover, time itself altered in British towns as you travelled to the east or west of Greenwich. Liverpool, for instance, was twelve minutes behind London, while Norwich was five minutes ahead. The official time even changed between villages, each of which followed its church clock, so that if you stood in the fields at a distance from several hamlets you could hear their bells chiming the same hour at different and apparently random instants. People might age seven minutes by stepping over the boundary of a neighbouring parish, and regain that portion of lost youth by hopping back. Such differences were unimportant when the greatest speed one could expect to travel at over any distance prior to the railways was 12.1 mph aboard the 'Wonder Coach'. If you had to catch a train, however, the provenance of the time on your watch was critical.

The railways needed to operate to a standard hour, if nothing else to prevent collisions. Following the example set by the London and Birmingham Railway in 1838, they printed 'Time Tables' that told their customers where and when to find their trains. After some initial differences as to what time to use as the reference hour for their timetables, most operators adopted 'railway time', i.e. Greenwich Mean Time (GMT), which had been introduced by the Great Western Railway in November 1840.* Many timetables also detailed the differences between GMT and local time at each station, and boards at the major stations also listed variations

---

* The tables were changed as often as every month, transforming the contents of prior versions from fact into fiction, and rendering them not only useless but also possibly dangerous. In order both to remove them from circulation and gain a reputation for benevolence, the LSWR donated its obsolete timetables to lunatic asylums, whose inmates separated their pages and threaded them on strings to use as toilet paper.

at destinations up and down the line. People nonetheless still missed trains either because they followed some idiosyncratic village hour, or because the idea that a minute could make a difference remained alien. To maximize revenues, and drag the country kicking and screaming into the nineteenth century, the companies pushed for railway time to be extended beyond their platforms to the whole of the rest of the nation. Henry Booth, secretary of the Liverpool and Manchester, invited his fellow Britons to conceive of an age when 'The great bell of St Paul's strikes ONE, and, simultaneously, every City clock and village chime, from John of Groat's to the Land's End, strikes ONE... The finger of every watch or timepiece... points to the same hour!' There was, he suggested, a 'sublimity in the idea of a whole nation stirred by one impulse; in every arrangement, one common signal regulating the movements of a mighty people!' While some resisted change – notably the dean of Exeter Cathedral, who kept its thirteenth-century clock fourteen minutes behind GMT until 1852 – the plain good sense of a common hour prevailed, and by the time the dean capitulated, 98 per cent of Britain had elected to conform to 'railway time'.

The need to know the right time led to a huge increase in demand for watches, and a revolution in watch-making. Whereas in the past only ships' captains and, perhaps, adulterers had had to carry watches, now millions of people worried about missing trains. Cheap pocket watches with standardized parts were produced to cater to their collective phobia. Watches became common sights, especially around railway stations. Like the White Rabbit in *Alice in Wonderland*, anxious travellers were forever fishing them out of their pockets, and muttering to themselves 'oh dear oh dear I shall be too late'. The new fixation was lamented in medical journals, where it was debated whether the fear of being late was more dangerous to a person's peace of mind than being involved in a train crash. Cases of sudden death from a terror of being behind schedule were reported, including one in the *Association Medical Journal* which described how a commuter to London 'fell down dead on the platform of a railway station; his life being the forfeit paid for the exertion which he had made to reach the starting train'.

Was such paranoia justified? What was it like to ride a steam train into work in the Victorian era? How different was it from catching the 07.01 from Botley to Waterloo in the twenty-first century? It was certainly far noisier then than now: one could hear the train approaching long before it reached the station, and the din was tremendous when it pulled up alongside. The brakes, which consisted of iron levers with wooden pads that the guard in each carriage screwed against the rims of its wheels, shrieked; the rails rang; the train's whistles and escape valves screeched; and its carriages rattled and clanked against each other as they came to a halt, while steam dissipated around them. The tank engine at the front, although smaller than a modern locomotive, made up with presence what it lacked in size, and resembled a demon or dragon, with a long snout that belched sparks and smoke from its nostrils, while the drive wheels and side rods ground like massive jaws underneath. The circular windows on the driver's cab served as its eyes, which sometimes flared red if the firebox door was open.

There was then, as now, a skill in choosing the right place on the train. The carriages in its centre were reckoned to be both the safest and most comfortable. Passengers in the leading ones usually perished first in a crash or if the boiler exploded, and those at the back received a constant rain of sparks and ashes, for while Parliament had decreed that steam trains should 'consume their own smoke', i.e. not spew fire and filth everywhere they went, the railway companies complied loosely at best. The rear carriages also tended to wag about in an alarming manner when the train cornered, and sometimes decoupled and were left in the middle of nowhere – a sitting target for the next service on the line.

Passengers entered their preferred carriages via ladders under their doors. There were three classes of accommodation – first, second and third, although from the 1870s onwards most commuter services offered only first and third. First-class carriages consisted of a line of three stagecoach bodies bolted onto a wood and iron bed, mounted on four iron-rimmed wheels. Each coach was an independent space with a door to each side, and no communication with its neighbours. Inside were two facing rows of three seats, divided by armrests. The seats were upholstered, and the interiors of the carriages had wooden panels and glass windows that could be opened outwards. There was a paraffin lamp in a well overhead for lighting, and passengers could call for foot-warmers if they felt cold. Each carriage had a seat at both ends of its roof for a guard or porter, and an iron railing between them to store luggage. The guards and porters scrambled between the carriages via their roofs and sides like spider-men. It was a dangerous occupation: they routinely lost fingers when trying to link carriages together or their heads or arms in tunnels. A few were burned to death trying to put out fires in the luggage. They seem to have had a morbid sense of humour. In 1853, for instance, Porter Bull was dismissed by the Great Western Railway for writing 'Coffin No. 2' in chalk on the inside of his hooded iron perch.

Once commuters had boarded their chosen carriages, they aimed to secure a seat with its back to the direction of travel as these were thought to make the motion of the train feel less unnatural. Meanwhile, the cold, dirty air that washed in through the windows went straight into the faces of those facing forwards. Novices were advised by *The Railway Traveller's Handy Book*, an 1862 guide to the practicalities and etiquette of train travel, to wear 'a species of green or black spectacles, known as eye-preservers', and caps with lappets (earflaps) that might be tied together under their chins.*

Departure was signalled by bells, whistles and flags, and the train left with a similar level of ceremony to a boat setting off on a voyage. The noise as the locomotive powered up and dragged the carriages away was terrific, like heavy breathing on a gigantic scale that accelerated into panting and grew ever more urgent as the train gathered speed. After the thrill of departure had subsided, the Victorian commuter was free to admire the view from the window, to read the advertising panels above the seats, or the officious notices –'modelled' (according to a critic of such

---

* Sherlock Holmes is described as wearing just such a traveller's cap in *The Adventure of Silver Blaze*, which was later transformed into a deerstalker by Sidney Paget in an illustrated edition of the story.

presumptuousness) 'on French or Russian police ordinances' (*plus ça change*) and stamped on brass plaques – warning him not to smoke or drink alcohol.

Then, as now, people avoided conversation. A code of silence quickly developed among commuters and indeed railway travellers in general that seemed as binding as the Mafia's *omertà*. It was lamented when it first appeared: 'Why should half a dozen persons, each with minds to think and tongues to express those thoughts, sit looking at each other mumchance, as though they were afraid of employing the faculty of speech? Why should an Englishman ever be like a ghost, in not speaking until he is spoken to?' It was also, however, understood to be unavoidable: the Victorians were acutely class-conscious, and trains were notoriously egalitarian. A peer who found himself sharing a carriage with a commoner who could afford first class wouldn't want to have to acknowledge the commoner's existence once they'd stepped off the train, which meant that even saying 'hello' was risky. The middle classes, meanwhile, were paranoid about making fools of themselves, and the workers didn't dare speak unless they were spoken to, unless it was among themselves.

Sometimes this convention broke down. Although most railway companies forbade drunkenness, on pain of unenforceable fines, Victorians often took alcohol with their breakfasts, which sometimes loosened their tongues on the way to work. On such occasions, a fail-safe protocol came into force: what's said on the rails stays on the rails. In the words of the *Handy Book*, 'the acquaintance begotten in the railway carriage ceases with the journey, and although you may have conversed as freely with a person as though you had known him twenty years, you would not be justified in accosting him in the street subsequently'. There was, moreover, a whole vocabulary of 'abrupt or tart replies', and 'a species of grunt expressive of dissent or dissatisfaction' that the experienced commuter might employ to silence the loquacious and save them from themselves.

The best defence against unwanted conversation was a book or newspaper. According to a proverb of the time, 'he who rails may read'. The railways were credited with causing a surge in literacy in the UK. There were boys on most platforms selling papers and travel guides such as *Bradshaw's Monthly Railway Guide*, and many stations had kiosks, run by crippled guards or their widows, that offered bodice-rippers and adventure yarns. Chain stores, notably W. H. Smith in England and John Menzies in Scotland, soon replaced these, and stocked their outlets with generally wholesome and highbrow fare. Indeed, William Henry Smith, grandson of the founder of the former, and the man responsible for introducing the practice of selling books and newspapers at railway stations, was treasurer of the Society for Promoting Christian Knowledge and acquired the nickname 'Old Morality'. Publishers supplied the chains with special railway editions, most of which cost less than 'two pots of ale', and included many of the classics and a number of contemporary works. Our commuter might well have read Darwin's *On the Origin of Species*, or Macaulay's *History of England* while rattling along into town.

The mania for reading on trains was criticized as well as praised. Its enemies feared that 'readers' emotions were being heightened by gripping narratives at the same time their bodies were being shaken and jostled in carriages packed with members of both sexes. This combination of mental and physical stimulation could lead to nervous collapse or the suspension of moral judgement'.

There were other diversions available to those in transit who didn't have anything to read, or didn't dare to. The *Handy Book* recommended that they could try humming, for the 'noise made by the train in its journey will accommodate itself to any tune, whether lively or sad, so that if a passenger choose to hum any of his favourite airs, he will find an accompaniment ready made'. Humming was especially recommended for any passenger needing the lavatory. British trains didn't start to have WCs until the 1890s, and passengers were expected to hold tight until they dismounted. Anyone wanting to answer the call of nature had either to cross their legs or buy a 'secret travelling lavatory', which consisted of a rubber tube and bag arrangement worn inside one's trousers.

While most of the first generation of commuters were wealthy and travelled first class, a number came from further down the social scale and went third, sometimes on third-only trains. The Railway Regulation Act of 1844 had obliged the railway companies to offer 'the poorer Class of Travellers the Means of travelling by Railway at moderate Fares, and in carriages in which they may be protected from "the Weather"'. In order to comply they had to run a service on all their lines each way every day that travelled at a minimum speed of twelve miles per hour and stopped at every station, for a fare of no more than a penny a mile. The Act resulted in so-called 'workmen's trains'. In general, these were organized so as not to interfere with the more lucrative parts of railway companies' schedules, and, if possible, to force the poor to pay more by travelling on other services. The outbound workmen's train on the LSWR's Richmond line, for example, started for London at 6 a.m., and the return left at 3 p.m. Specific companies were also required to offer more frequent services, as compensation to the slum dwellers that they had displaced when building their tracks and stations. Some, notably the Great Eastern, which had been granted permission to build Liverpool Street Station in 1861 on condition that it ran 'workmen's trains from Edmonton and Walthamstow for 2d return', made a virtue out of necessity, and by concentrating their lower-class passenger services on a single line, turned them into a profitable business.

In general, however, even the workmen's trains were beyond the purses of the labouring classes. A twelve-mile journey twice a day for five days a week cost half the average manual worker's weekly earnings. Tailors, cabinet-makers, and the lower orders of clerks were the usual occupants of third-class carriages rather than ditch-diggers and tanners, and they started to commute from the 1850s onwards.

Third-class carriages were modelled on cattle wagons rather than stagecoaches. They were open to the elements on all sides, although, in deference to the parliamentary requirement that they protect their passengers from 'the Weather', they were topped with rigid canopies that sported a perch for a guard and a luggage rail. Seating consisted of three pairs of facing wooden benches, with a division at chest height between each pair. Five or six people were expected to sit on each bench, which was the same width as three first-class seats. The benches were bare, and some commuters carried 'pneumatic caoutchouc' (inflatable rubber) cushions to spare their piles. The sides of the third-class carriages were required to be at least three feet high, after too many people had fallen to their death from them, but were still low enough to topple over when the train lurched. They were often very crowded: on some routes they carried several times their nominal load, plus a few boys in the luggage rack.

They were also places of riotous good humour, whose passengers yelled conversations between themselves or sang together at the tops of their voices. Often people who could afford to travel enclosed went open, if not for the company, then for the pleasure of being exposed to the elements as the train rocked along. It was like being on the deck of a ship rather than skulking in its cabins. In Glasgow, for instance, some of 'the most wealthy and influential merchants… arrived at the station in their own carriages then travelled to Greenock standing up'. However, such behaviour was criticized as class betrayal and it was even suggested by William Crawshay, a baron of industry and a millionaire, that his local railway company hire chimney sweeps to lurk in third and scare off any members of the upper class wanting to travel with the rabble. Going third, moreover, was thought to have social repercussions beyond the rails. The *Handy Book* provides a solemn little parable about a clerk who travels first class while his parsimonious employer is at the back of the train. When they meet by chance on the platform one day, the clerk explains that if he travelled third class word would get out to his butcher and greengrocer, who would treat him like a pauper and refuse him credit. The employer realizes that he is demeaning himself for the sake of a few pennies, travels first thereafter, and gives the clerk a handsome pay rise.

In truth, no one who valued their clothing would go third. Passengers were blasted with showers, hail, sleet and snow as the seasons changed, buffeted by the near gale-force winds generated by the speed of the train, and subjected to a constant rain of soot and drizzle of steam, so that they often resembled the survivors of the shipwreck of a steamer in some frigid northern waters when they unboxed at their destination.

Those Victorian commuters in first-class carriages, whose appetites had been stimulated by fear or their reading material, and their counterparts in third, made hungry by talking non-stop between lungfuls of freezing air, endured further tests of their characters on the way into work. While many stations had refreshment rooms, and cafés had multiplied near them, like coaching inns around staging posts, the food they offered seems to have been atrocious. According to Dickens, the best one could hope for were such horrors as 'stale sponge-cakes that turn to sand in the mouth' or 'a class of soup which enfeebles the mind, distends the stomach, forces itself into the complexion, and tries to ooze out at the eyes'. Dickens and other critics reserved their especial bile for the new-fangled sandwiches that were appearing under glass counters the length and breadth of the rail network. The infamous British Rail sandwich has deep roots. In 1869, Anthony Trollope wrote 'the real disgrace of England is the railway sandwich', and the reformer William Galt thought the same: the 'fossil sandwiches' on show at the average station were 'absolutely a national disgrace'. In consequence, many commuters took their own food and drink with them. The working-men cooked herrings in the waiting rooms, and first-class passengers (like Dickens) carried hip flasks of brandy to steady their nerves while in transit.

Anyone still hungry upon arrival in London might graze at will: costermongers in and around its major stations sold 'hot eels; pickled whelks; fried fish; sheeps trotters; ham-sandwiches; baked 'tatoes; hot green peas;... cat and dogs' meat; coffee and tea; ginger-beer... elderwine;' and 'peppermint-water' from their barrows, carts and baskets. They prided themselves in their peculiar cries, which added to the general cacophony that greeted Victorian commuters en route to work. Any neophytes hoping for some quiet time to reflect on the seminal journey they had just made were disappointed. The concourses were packed with passengers and people who had come to meet them or see them off; porters ran to and fro through the crowds with boxes and packages; and there were shoe-shine boys, pickpockets, beggars, and even missionaries in search of converts. Trains clanked and groaned, bells rang, and whistles shrieked above the hubbub of the crowds.

William Frith's giant painting *The Railway Station*, which shows a crowd scene at Paddington in 1861, provides a snapshot of the pandemonium. It was immensely popular: more than 21,000 people paid a shilling each just to look at it and try to decipher all the stories the hundred or so figures that it contains are acting out. These include commuters looking stony-faced inside the carriages of the train at the back of the composition, a party of army recruits saying their farewells to their sweethearts, and such identifiable figures as Detective Sergeants Michael Haydon and James Brett of Scotland Yard, one with a warrant, the other with a pair of handcuffs, and both wearing ginger beards and top hats, arresting a fugitive as he's stepping onto the commuters' train. The steam engine at its head is the Iron Duke Class 4-2-2 *Sultan*, which exploded twelve years later when it collided with a goods wagon in Ealing, killing six passengers.

Indeed, the best hope a first-time commuter in the Victorian era had of finding somewhere calm where they might reflect upon the giant step they had taken, was to join the platform missionaries in a rousing hymn. Evangelists considered the stations to be happy hunting grounds for sinners in need of redemption, and as the era progressed were to be found in ever-increasing numbers on the concourses. The Salvation Army, founded in 1865, handed out 'Hallelujah Tickets' that offered their holders a one-way trip to 'Glory Land' where they might 'praise the lamb forever'. Bibles were chained to station walls for the edification of travellers, much to the astonishment of a visiting Frenchman, who thought this displayed an unchristian lack of trust. In 1881 a special society, the Railway Mission, was established whose periodical *Railway Signal: or, Lights along the Line* exhorted its readers to 'become spiritual commuters'. It provided timetables for prayer meetings, including such unmissable events as the daily bible class at Liverpool Street for working men on the 05.57 train from Enfield.

The evangelists who stalked the railway termini took pains

to make their message sound contemporary. The vocabulary of the railways had crept into the vernacular. Phrases such as 'going off the rails', 'getting steamed up', and 'on the right lines' were used to express emotions and states of mind as well as the movements of locomotives. They were later incorporated into a hymn aimed at commuters, 'In Thy Service Faithful Keep Us' by Samuel Peach, whose verses once rang out during rush hour when rush hour itself was young:

Keep us watching and refiring
With full pressure on
For promotions still aspiring
'Til the prize is won.
Chorus:
In thy service faithful keep us
Guard us night and day
Fit us for the final signal
Ready, right away!

♦ ♦ ♦ ♦ ♦

CHAPTER II

Suburbanization

New forces, new cravings, new aims, which had been
silently gathering beneath the crust of re-action, burst
suddenly into view.

John Richard Green, *A Short History of the English People*, 1874

The average first-class commuter in the latter half of the
nineteenth century enjoyed a first-class way of life. Locomotivity, abundant cheap building land and the effective absence
of planning laws enabled commuters to build dream homes
in the countryside close to railway stations, while still keeping
office hours in town. This migration, though slow initially –
with 'only around 27,000 daily rail commuters entering London
in the mid 1850s' – was nonetheless the first step in a process
that transformed patterns of settlement in Britain. In effect,
commuting created the suburbs and the suburban way of life,
and travellers to and from such places as Surbiton, Bromley and
Ealing were its pioneers.

Once they had blazed a trail, there were many others on
their heels: reasons to commute multiplied as the nineteenth
century advanced. The temperance movement had revived the
idea of zombie-like drunks, as pictured by Hogarth during

the Gin Craze of the 1750s, as a real and present threat; there were more missionaries saving souls in the East End of London than all the rest of the British Empire; and filth, overcrowding and contagion were still endemic. In 1861, Lord Salisbury told Parliament that the state of the capital was 'a scandal to our civilisation'. Over 135,000 people left its centre for the suburbs during the next twenty years. In the opinion of the historian Roy Porter, 'rising real incomes, the expansion of white-collar occupations, reductions in hours of work, new opportunities to borrow money and a social competitiveness which expressed itself in the determination to buy the best property and most prestigious address possible', gave further impetus to the exodus.

People's hearts as well as their heads advocated taking up commuting. Although the Romantic Movement was fading into sentimentality, its glorification of the countryside and demon-ization of cities as being the wrong places either to contemplate the human condition or raise children struck a chord in would-be commuters. Finding the right place to settle down and breed – without compromising one's career – was especially important. Love, for perhaps the first time in history, was felt to be a necessary ingredient of marriage. It was elevated for practical reasons. Late nineteenth-century Romeos and Juliets had greater freedom of movement, and more choices, if they lived in a city, than their ancestors did. They weren't tied to the land anymore, became independent of their parents sooner, and met strangers every day instead of once a year at the village fair. Nor did they have to consider such minutiae as whether a prospective partner might own the adjacent field. Customs changed to accommodate these new freedoms. A man would propose to a woman rather than her father, and do so because he thought he loved her, rather than because of her acres. After wedlock, the couple would nest, and atomic rather than extended households became the norm.

Hence those who could afford it seized the chance to commute: one could be sanitary, sober, romantic and paternal* at the same time; one could have both the dash of the town mouse and the calm of the country mouse; and could enjoy the thrill of a train ride twice each day between one's alter egos. The rewards of commuting were summed up by a correspondent to the *Builder* magazine in 1856:

> *It is better, morally and physically, for the Londoner... when he has done his day's work, to go to the country or the suburbs where he escapes the noise and crowds and impure air of the town; and it is no small advantage to a man to have his family removed from the immediate neighbourhood of casinos, dancing saloons, and hells upon earth which I will not name.*

The first wave of railway commuters settled close to stations, and their arrival soon changed the characters of the places where they put down roots. In Ealing, for example, a little village surrounded by fields before the Great Western Railway arrived in 1838, large detached houses sprang up in the vicinity of the station, and by

---

* Almost all Victorian commuters were men.

1861 one-sixth of its householders were classified as 'professional and managerial'. In nearby Acton, in contrast, which didn't get a railway with a passenger service until 1871, only one-twentieth were so highly graded.

Landowners and builders spotted the trend and began speculative developments in areas outside cities that were suitable for commuting. In the hamlet of Surbiton, for example, shortly after the LSWR opened its station nearby, a local maltster named Thomas Pooley bought a farm and laid out the nucleus of a new town, composed of handsome neoclassical houses on ample plots of land, arranged along wide streets and crescents. His scheme, however, provoked the ire of the business community in nearby Kingston upon Thames, who had refused the LSWR permission to build a station in their town, and they colluded to ruin Pooley before his development was completed. The railways had already destroyed their coaching industry, and they were loath to see their wealthier clientele migrating to a rival location. Commuting, it seems, was redrawing the map, benefiting some locations at the expense of others.

The architecture of the new commuter homes was varied. Speculators took their designs from books 'such as *The Builder's Practical Director*, *The Gentleman's House*, and *Suburban and Rural Architecture*'. While many of the earlier examples were neoclassical, inspired by the villas of the Eyre estate in St John's Wood that have been held to be 'the origin, through mutation and debasement, of all suburban houses', they became more adventurous as the era progressed. The ideal commuter home of the 1840s, 'a villa miraculously transported from the Lago de

Como to Surrey' was supplanted by a mock '17th century Dutch farmhouse' in the 1870s, and by the 1890s, rustic Dutch had given way to 'what might be called the Picturesque Swiss style, with lavish balconies, verandas and timber-work'. While many of the commuter homes were undistinguished architecturally, there were some gems amidst the general mediocrity. Joldwynds in Holmbury St Mary, for instance, which was built in 1874 by Philip Webb, the leading architect of the Arts and Crafts Movement, for the surgeon Sir William Bowman, was centred around an octagonal hall that was three storeys tall, and featured a diagonal wing housing a laboratory and billiards room. Its owner commuted to his work at the Royal London Ophthalmic Hospital from the nearby station at Gomshall and Shere, near Guildford in Surrey. The site of this station had been decided by a competition: several places along the line were shortlisted as potential locations, and the one which had the most people waiting on a given day was to be chosen. The landlord of the Black Horse at Gomshall, whose trade had thrived on the custom of navvies while the tracks were being laid, offered free beer on the appointed day and the resulting crowd ensured that Gomshall won.

The homes of first-class railway commuters, whether Palladian, neo-Dutch, Venetian Gothic, Arts and Crafts, or an unsightly mixture of these and other styles, were usually set in their own grounds. Their owners wanted gardens, not neighbours. This desire for privacy, according to foreign observers, was innate and peculiar to the British, and extended to almost every aspect of their lives. In 1853, for instance, the *Kölnische Zeitung* described the average Englishman as 'a non-gregarious animal... even in his coffee house and eating room he boxes himself up between high partitions'.

In addition to performing the useful function of separating houses, gardens were a vital part of the commuter dream. Each was a piece of green space, whose owner might imagine it as a private park, or a microcosm of empire and plant with Indian shrubs and Australian eucalypti. Gardens were for leisure, or show, rather than growing food, and lawns and rockeries took precedence over potato patches. A good lawn was a prized asset. Victorian commuters were addicted to games and used their lawns for croquet, bowls, archery and Sphairistike.*

Many of the early commuters had picked up their taste for games at public school. These were booming, along with the railways and the middle class. By the 1860s there were nearly 3,000 of them in England, ranging from the King's School in Canterbury, founded by King Ethelbert in 598 to celebrate his baptism, to the new Woodard schools, the brainchildren of Canon Nathaniel Woodard whose heaven-sent mission was to establish Anglican boarding schools for the middle classes. These included Lancing, Hurstpierpoint, and Ardingly. Woodard schools drilled 'sound principle and sound knowledge, firmly grounded in the Christian faith' into their pupils. It was a muscular sort of Christianity. Like older public schools the

---

* From classical Greek, meaning 'ball game'. Major Walter Wingfield coined the name in 1874 when he patented a 'New and Improved Court for Playing the Ancient Game of Tennis'. It was later shortened to 'sticky', then abandoned for 'lawn tennis' and finally 'tennis'.

Woodard establishments encouraged their pupils to discover teamwork through sports such as rugby and football.

Public schoolboys kept their love of sport alive after they left their Alma maters. Those of them who took up commuting and bought houses in the new dormitory communities also established recreational facilities where they could indulge this passion. Indeed, commuters were responsible for changes in British leisure activities as well as patterns of settlement. They eschewed the old country sports involving animals – like dog fighting, badger drawing and bull baiting – for ball games. Instead of hunting, they took up golf and tennis. Whereas England had only one golf course (at Blackheath) in 1850, by 1900 it had nearly 1,000, most built as close as possible to suburban railway stations and settlements. Bromley, Surbiton and Ealing all acquired one or more courses during this period. By 1897 even Acton had one. Lawn tennis became popular equally quickly. The average villa had plenty of space for a court. Between 1877 and 1904, every Wimbledon champion was British, many of them the children of commuters.

The spaces in between the dormitory suburbs and workplaces of railway commuters were filled in with housing as well as golf courses. Cities expanded towards their satellites. Their growth was facilitated by omnibuses – horse-drawn public carriages that ran fixed routes and charged by the mile – which had appeared in Britain alongside its first railways and offered people who couldn't afford an Arts and Crafts mansion in Surrey and a season ticket the chance to commute.

The first British omnibus company was started by George Shillibeer, a fat, jovial coachbuilder who had spent time in Paris designing oversized coaches. When he returned to England in 1827 he was commissioned to build a special communal conveyance with twenty-five seats by the Newington Academy for Girls, which is thought to have been the first ever school bus. These projects were the inspiration behind the passenger services he introduced to London in 1829, which ran between Paddington and the Bank of England. Although his vehicles took an hour to travel only five miles, they were a breakthrough in coach design, being sturdy, spacious and comfortable. They were drawn by three horses and carried up to twenty-two passengers, every one of whom had a seat. The service was an instant success, and rivals appeared. Buses started to race each other for passengers and the competition bankrupted Shillibeer, although for a while the vehicles he had introduced to London were called Shillibeers rather than omnibuses.

The fare was a shilling – too much for the average worker, and Shillibeer's service and its imitators started at 8 a.m., 'long after the working classes were at work'. Their target market was the white-collar worker. *The Times* acknowledged that some of its readers took the omnibus to their offices, and in 1836 published a twelve-point list of dos and don'ts so that they knew how to comport themselves while in transit. These included:

> *Reserve bickerings and disputes for the open field. The sound of your own voice may be music to your own ears – not so, perhaps, to those of your companions.*

If you will broach politics or religion, speak with moderation: all have an equal right to their opinions, and all have an equal right to not have them wantonly shocked.

Do not spit on the straw. You are not in a hogsty but in an omnibus travelling in a country which boasts of its refinement.

Buses increased in size and speed over the following decades. In 1845 seating on the roof was added to some services, which were the forerunners of the double-decker. The passengers sat back to back against a 'knifeboard' that ran the length of the vehicle. Buses were pulled by four horses and averaged seven or eight miles an hour, thus extending the range of their passengers into a new ring of suburbs that was blooming between the cities and the first-class commuter belt. In 1862, the writer George Rose Emerson described the view from Primrose Hill in *London: How the Great City Grew* and noted that 'sixty years ago even the hill was as secluded and rural, as completely removed from the hum and bustle of a great city, as any Sussex or Devonshire hillock. Now, as we look Londonwards, we find that the metropolis has thrown out its arms and embraced us, not yet with a stifling clutch, but with ominous closeness'.

The suburbs rising to accommodate omnibus commuters had none of the space and grace of the homes of their counterparts on the rails. Most development was piecemeal, with a builder throwing up a terrace here, a crescent there, and often going bankrupt before the houses these contained were complete. In 1872, '80 per cent of building firms had six or fewer houses under construction'. The difference between the middle-class idyll of nesting in a detached residence with a garden where the children might chase butterflies and listen to birdsong and the more humdrum reality, was summed up by T. M. Thomas, a Manchester man who had started doing business with London by rail, and who wanted to move to the capital. In an 1851 essay in *Household Words*, Thomas explained how he'd liked the look of the pretty railside developments near London that slid by the windows of his train, so had bought maps and marked off all those that were within commuting range of his office, either by omnibus or train, yet suitably bucolic in appearance. His first viewing was at 'Salisbury Crescent' in 'Agar Town', both fictional names, but understood by his readers to be part of one of the new mini suburbs near St Pancras. The crescent turned out to be a cross between a wasteland and a battlefield, with, according to one of the poverty-stricken wretches who lived there, a stench that was 'enough fur to knock down a bullock'. Its houses had been built on shallow foundations, with square-sectioned drains without any fall so that sewage never left the premises and banked up under the floorboards, unless homeowners were 'lucky enough to have a ditch afore their doors' to carry it away. The crescent itself was unpaved, and when it rained its residents had to wade through black mud to reach their porches. The houses were a similar mess to the streets. Even though newly built, they already had rising damp, their decorative features were falling off the walls, and draughts blew freely through the gaps around their window frames.

Jerry-built homes, faulty sewers and roads that existed in

name alone were common problems in the new suburbs served by omnibuses, as indeed were ugly views and difficult neighbours. The views were often spoiled by the industrial operators who had followed commuters out of town, so that suburbanites had brickfields, coal yards, steam-powered mills and the ubiquitous 'dust heaps' to admire through their windows rather than hay-fields and apple orchards. Although the phrase sounds innocuous, 'dust heap' was a Victorianism for rubbish dump. Charles Dickens described a typical example as 'a large hill... in the vicinity of small suburb cottages, [rising] above them like a great black mountain'. They were composed of a mixture of building spoils, and industrial, commercial and domestic waste. The Victorians generated refuse in quantities that would have represented serious wealth in previous eras. Although, by present standards, they were a make-and-mend society, by those of their ancestors they were incredibly wasteful. City councils made good money by auctioning their obligations to collect rubbish. There were seven separate working-class trades dedicated to dealing with it, ranging from pure finders – usually old women or little girls who gathered dog faeces from the streets of London and sold them to its tanneries – through rag-and-bone men to merchants who made fortunes out of recycling. Indeed, dust heaps, and the wealth they held for anyone brave enough to comb them, were central to Dickens' novel *Our Mutual Friend* (1865) and emblematic of a new social mobility that commuting was facilitating.

Omnibus suburbs, moreover, could deteriorate quickly. The Victorian property market went up and down like a roller coaster. Rents in the periphery were cheaper than in town, and landlords were usually happy to subdivide unlet houses. Some developments built with businessmen or doctors in mind were occupied instead by the working class who crowded together to save money, and created mini-rookeries in some of the new Victoria Crescents and Albert Roads. Indeed, one could never be sure of one's neighbours. According to Jane Elizabeth Panton's *Suburban Residences and How to Circumvent Them* (1896), 'unless one has a really large place, one must be so close to one's neighbours owing to the way the ground is arranged for building, that one nearly dies of them'. Irritants included 'barking dogs, banging gates, neighbours who raise livestock' and 'servants who "hang out the clothes and themselves at the same time"'.

The rapid appearance and chaotic nature of the inner ring of suburbs alarmed many Victorian observers, who felt that the new way of life that commuting made possible not only despoiled the landscape but also damaged the characters of those who pursued it. Ruskin, for example, thought that suburbs were as bad as rail travel, and thundered against them in *The Seven Lamps of Architecture* (1849):

I look upon those pitiful concretions of lime and clay which spring up, in mildewed forwardness, out of the kneaded fields about our capital – upon those thin, tottering, foundationless shells of splintered wood and imitated stone – upon those gloomy rows of formalised minuteness, alike without difference and without fellowship, as solitary as similar – not merely with the careless disgust of an offended eye, not merely with sorrow for a desecrated landscape, but with a

> *painful foreboding that the roots of our national greatness*
> *must be deeply cankered when they are thus loosely struck in*
> *their native ground; that those comfortless and unhonoured*
> *dwellings are the signs of a great and spreading spirit of*
> *popular discontent; that they mark the time when every*
> *man's aim is to be in some more elevated sphere than his*
> *natural one.*

The suburbs also acquired an equivocal reputation in fiction. Their very novelty made them something of an enigma, and writers started to feature their crescents and closes as places where morality was suspended and deviants, atheists, evil sects and temptresses might lurk in anonymity. In addition to being represented as sanctuaries to vice, the suburbs were portrayed as ruinous vortexes that dragged in the unwary and destroyed them. Wilkie Collins highlighted the fictional excitement and the danger that they might contain in *Basil: A Story of Modern Life*, published in 1852 and an early example of the sensation genre of novels. The book's titular hero, a scion of one of the oldest and snobbiest families in England, gets on an omnibus one day and falls in love with Margaret, the teenaged daughter of a linen draper who lives in the suburbs. They marry in secret; her mother turns out to be deranged; another lover turns up and Basil blinds him in one eye; Basil's father disowns him; Margaret dies of typhus; and it all goes downhill thereafter until a terrific dénouement in Cornwall and a final reconciliation – by which time Basil himself is a broken man. The *Athenaeum* described the novel as 'a tale of criminality, almost revolting from its domestic horrors' and the *Westminster Review* thought it 'absolutely disgusting'. It established the suburbs as locations where anything might go in the popular imagination, and thereafter they popped up all over Victorian fiction.

Critics' fulminations and novelists' speculations upon the iniquities of suburban life generally went unheeded. As the nineteenth century progressed, commuting became affordable for more and more people. Real wages increased by 75 per cent between 1850 and 1900, and per capita income nearly doubled over the same period. London's immediate suburbs grew by 50 per cent *per decade* between 1861 and 1891, and this growth was spurred in part by the appearance of underground railways. The first underground line in the capital and indeed the world was the Metropolitan Railway's Paddington to Farringdon service, built between 1860 and 1862. William Gladstone, the chancellor of the exchequer, inspected it prior to its opening and a photograph of the event shows him and fellow grandees seated on hard wooden benches in the open carriages used to carry tunnel workers to the point to which they'd progressed. The Metropolitan's initial track was three and three-quarter miles long and had stops at Edgware Road, Baker Street, Portland Road, Gower Street and King's Cross. It was wildly popular, notwithstanding the negative associations – for a culture that buried its dead – with going underground,* and the railings of preachers who warned that it might lead to the gates of hell. Thirty-six thousand people rode it

---

* Cremation wasn't legal in Britain until 1885.

on its opening day, and the Metropolitan had to borrow carriages from the Great Western Railway to accommodate the crowds. It carried nine million passengers in its first year of operations.

The Metropolitan's trains were steam-powered and spewed the familiar cocktail of soot and sparks into the narrow tunnels and along the platforms. The carriages were either first, second, or third class, were all enclosed, and were modelled on the borrowed GWR eight-wheelers. Gas lamps, supplied from gas boxes on the carriage roofs, illuminated their interiors. Early versions had a tendency to derail, as the underground tracks had tighter curves than surface lines. This was because their operators had to pay for permission to build them from the owners of the land above, and whenever possible followed roads or other existing rights of way. The Metropolitan Railway was followed by the Metropolitan and District, which opened a line between Westminster and South Kensington in 1868, and the Inner Circle line, which was completed as a joint venture by the first two operators in 1871.

The initial underground lines were built to connect the mainline railway stations to each other and the centre of the city and so enable rail commuters to get a little closer to their workplaces. However, as the networks grew, they began to reach out of London and to compete with the surface operators. They also started to electrify their rails, which made travel far more comfortable, as passengers were no longer exposed to the smut generated by steam trains. The first electric railway, co-incidentally the first deep-level underground line, was the City and South London Railway, which ran from King William Street through a tunnel under the Thames to Stockwell, and opened in 1890. The tunnel was both a feat of engineering and a graveyard for navvies. The soil through which it was dug was waterlogged, and so the engineers pumped compressed air into each new section as it was excavated to stop the walls caving in. This had the unintended consequences of killing many of the labourers from caisson disease,* and capsizing boats in the river overhead, where the escaping air boiled several feet above the surface. When the line was complete, the Prince of Wales was given a tour of Stockwell station. An engraving of the event shows him admiring one of the new carriages, which had been built to be the last word in comfort for short-distance commuting. They were small and totally enclosed, with facing rows of upholstered seats inside. However, the line was so popular that there was scarcely room to move inside them during rush hour, and the City and South London was nicknamed the 'sardine box railway' by *Punch* magazine. Its carriages meanwhile were dubbed 'padded cells'.

The underground lines and their overground extensions gave ever more people the chance to commute, and hastened the suburbanization of the countryside around London. In some areas, tube commuters displaced the original rail commuters. In Willesden, for instance, which had been colonized by a few wealthy city merchants after its train station opened in 1844, the arrival of the Metropolitan's Extension Line in 1880 resulted in an influx of 'clerks and artisans', who 'stampeded in at the rate of 100 per week'. The merchants' villas were sold off and

---

* Decompression sickness, caused by the pressure of the water overhead.

torn down and their gardens were filled with terraced housing. Within fifteen years Willesden and neighbouring Kilburn had 80,000 inhabitants. Ealing, the 'Queen of the Suburbs', was also dragged downmarket when the Metropolitan District opened a branch line to it off its Richmond line in 1879. The clerks rushed in and the villas of the first generation of commuters were soon marooned in a sea of terraces.

A similar pattern was evident in the outer railway suburbs. As real incomes rose and season tickets became more affordable, they too were inundated with commuters. The population of the once pretty market town of Croydon, for example, grew from 5,743 to 133,895 over the course of the nineteenth century. By 1876, 'monotonous streets and lines of villas' were 'fast encircling' it. The commuters who had moved there in the 1840s after its first railway station opened, to enjoy the 'pleasant and picturesque' countryside nearby and the easy journey into London, had their views obstructed by new builds and their seats on the trains taken by newcomers.

By 1900 the ability to commute, whether by train, omnibus or underground, had transformed London and its environs within a radius of thirty miles. First the wealthy then the middle classes had decamped to the suburbs, creating vast settlements in what had once been open fields. The separation of work and home had become the new norm for the middle strata of British society, as had the commuting that connected them. The speed of the change seems to have taken even its participants by surprise, and its consequences were lamented. They were summed up in a turn-of-the-century editorial in *Building News*:

Go where we will – north, south, east or west of this huge, over-grown Metropolis, the fungus-like growth of houses manifests itself stretching from town to suburb and village…

In every direction we see the same outward growth of dwelling house of a small and unpretending class – generally a repetition of a type of house that has been found to meet the requirements of the middle class and artisan. The larger and more commodious residence of fifty years ago is being pulled down, or swamped by this tide of small houses: where a large house existed ten, or a hundred more have been built, absorbing the acres of gardens and private park lands. This is one of the social revolutions of the age.

The individuals who inhabited the 'fungus-like growth' of houses around London seem to have been happy with their lot, and as they grew in number, they found champions ready both to speak up for their happiness and to celebrate the ironic sense of humour that they were believed to have developed. The life of the average suburban commuter may not have been perfect, but at least it was pleasant. Although their critics continued to rain scorn on the suburbs – to the novelist and historian Sir Walter Besant, 'the life of the suburb without any society; no social gatherings or institutions' was 'as dull a life as mankind ever tolerated', and in the opinion of the author G. K. Chesterton, 'atheism was the religion of the suburbs' and they 'ought to be either glorified by romance or religion, or else destroyed by fire from heaven, or even by firebrands from earth' – such views were balanced by more positive opinions.

The Semi-Detached House by Emily Eden, a novel published in 1859, was the first popular comedy of manners set in the suburbs, and marked a departure from contemporaneous writing on the subject (such as Collins' *Basil*), which had focused on the wounds the suburbs had inflicted on the landscape and their threat to the established order, rather than their potential for pleasure. In retrospect this change in treatment is no surprise: the suburbs had arisen in response to demand, and their inhabitants had money to spend, salubrious homes and time for leisure. These were energetic people who loved games and even DIY, and these positive characteristics were catered to by a number of publications, *Punch* in particular. While *Punch* poked fun at the suburbs and the foibles of their inhabitants by, for example, lampooning the pretentious names they gave their houses and gardens, it also celebrated their existence. Even aesthetes started to smile on them: Max Beerbohm suggested – tongue in cheek – in the short story *Diminuendo* (1896) that a suburban villa might be the perfect retreat for someone wishing to devote themselves to beauty and truth.

The best comic account of the new commuter lifestyle appeared in George and Weedon Grossmith's *Diary of a Nobody* (1892), the fictional journal of Charles Pooter, a clerk who lives with his wife Carrie in 'The Laurels', a semi-detached house in Brickfield Terrace, Upper Holloway, and takes the train to work. Pooter has all the petty faults of his class. He's a snob through and through, and much of the humour in the book stems from his attempts to prove the superiority of his tastes and behaviour to his fellow suburbanites. But Pooter also has great strengths: he's a loving husband, faithful to his friends and employer, and anxious to set his ne'er-do-well son Lupin on the right path. This combination of pretentiousness and fidelity made the *Diary of a Nobody* a minor classic. Evelyn Waugh, later a vitriolic critic of the suburban way, labelled it the 'funniest book in the world'.

The suburbanites' pleasure in smiling also influenced the drama of the Victorian era. Commuters used their mobility for entertainment as well as getting to and from work, and London theatres flourished on their custom. The most popular shows of the late nineteenth century were comic operas or farces, reflecting the tastes of the new audiences. Gilbert and Sullivan's shows at the Savoy Theatre were often preceded by 'improvised concerts' of favourite arias performed by 'suburban amateur societies' to whom the tunes were 'as familiar as the national anthem, "Rule Britannia", or "Hymns, Ancient and Modern"'.

In addition to shaping tastes in entertainment, commuters were entering the mainstream as representing if not the voice of reason then that of the middle class. Walter Bagehot, the influential writer on politics and economics, believed that 'the opinion of the bald-headed man at the back of the omnibus' was the purest expression of the beliefs 'of the ordinary mass of educated, but still commonplace mankind'.

By 1900, commuting and the suburbs it engendered had changed Britain's landscape and the culture and behaviour of its inhabitants forever. It was a silent revolution, supported by desire and opposed only by perfectionists and nostalgics. Our grandparents' grandparents dreamed of being able to travel to lucrative employment from homes they owned and loved. Although the reality didn't quite match the dream, it was close enough, and better than remaining poor, backward and isolated in the country, or malformed and destitute in the rookeries of a new Babylon.

However, the social revolution that commuting sparked was slow to reach most of the working class, who constituted nearly 85 per cent of the population. Although the railway companies had run workmen's trains in obedience to Parliament since 1844, most did the bare minimum to comply. In 1882, there were fewer than 25,000 workmen's tickets being sold each day for travel to London, which was less than 10 per cent of total sales. The figures for other cities were worse: in Liverpool, only 1,700 workmen commuted by train. Indeed, the situation of the working class had improved little since the advent of commuting. Most were still crowded together in insanitary lodgings in city centres, or in tenements within walking distance of their places of work. There were fresh cholera epidemics in London in 1854 and 1866. Its sewer system failed entirely during the 'Great Stink' of 1858, when the outfall from tanneries, slaughterhouses and flushing toilets* in the suburbs upstream flooded the Thames with effluvia during a dry summer. The smell was so vile that Parliament rose and the Royal Courts of Justice made plans to evacuate to St Albans. While Joseph Bazalgette overhauled London's sewers during the 1860s, and most of its 220,000 cesspits were filled in, living conditions for the average worker – who couldn't afford to commute – were still abominable. Even the air around their accommodation was

---

* Later nicknamed 'Crappers' after the firm of Thomas Crapper & Co., who specialized in lavatorial equipment.

thought to be noxious. The eminent surgeon Sir James Cantlie, who pioneered first aid and research into tropical medicine, claimed in a lecture given in 1885 that to breathe London's air too often led to '*urbomorbus*'. This form of degeneration, peculiar to Londoners, was caused in his opinion by lack of ozone. Ozone was only to be found in 'fresh air' and none of this ever reached the centre of town, because 'the outer circlet of, say, half-a-mile of human beings, absorbs the fresh air, and not only so, but adds various pollutions to it, so that the air breathed within a given area, centred around, for instance Charing Cross, or the Bank, has not had fresh air supplied to it for, say, 50 or 100 years.'

Matters came to a head in the 1880s when politicians at both the national and local levels decided that resettlement as well as sanitation was key to tackling the housing problem. There had been a revolution in transportation; it was time that the workers benefited from it. The first step was the 1883 Cheap Trains Act, which aimed to force an increase in the number of workmen's trains. It was a qualified success. Some railway companies ran more cheap trains that they were compelled to. The Great Eastern Railway (GER), for instance, had forty-nine workmen's services each day, even though it was only obliged to provide five. It turned these into a profitable business by concentrating them on its East London line. They were out-and-out workers' services: William Birt, the General Manager of the company, thought them quite unsuitable for the better-off classes and indeed women of any class: 'I should be very sorry indeed to allow any respectable female connected with my household to travel third class upon the GER during those hours of the day in which the workers are travelling.'

The services nonetheless enabled the creation of suburbs for working-class commuters in Tottenham. Developers built terraces of identical houses to accommodate them, which were laid out in rows, forty or fifty to the acre, like 'soldiers at a military review'. Tottenham's population shot up from 9,100 in 1851 to 97,000 in 1891. Its commuters didn't play much golf or tennis in their free time. There wasn't, after all, any space for courses or courts. Popular recreation consisted of spectating rather than participating. The local Hotspur Football Club, which began life on a common in the Tottenham Marshes in 1882, had moved to its own ground in White Hart Lane by 1899 and was charging admission money at its fixtures.

While no other railway company went as far as the GER in running trains for working-class commuters, some also offered more services than the law required them to. Both the LSWR and the City and South London Railway sold workmen's tickets for any train before 7.30 a.m. By 1893, the LSWR was issuing nearly two million such tickets per annum. The Metropolitan Railway, meanwhile, ran two early trains for workers with a fare of three pence rather than the usual nine pence, and allowed them to return on any service they liked. Some companies, however, resented the Cheap Trains legislation and painted themselves as martyrs to the whims of politicians. The *Railway News* spoke for this class of operator in an 1890 editorial: the 'railway companies have on the whole done more than was required of them by Act of Parliament, and have provided, at great inconvenience to the working of their system and a minimum of profit, services of trains which have enabled the working classes to live at a distance from their work, which would otherwise be impossible'. Some of the railway companies went further by branding the poor they were forced to carry as vandals and fare-dodgers. The Metropolitan, for instance, claimed that passengers on its workmen's trains stole the leather hanging straps from its carriages.

Political pressure on transport operators to provide commuter services for the workers increased during the 1890s, especially at the local level. The Local Government Act of 1888 had placed county government in the hands of elected councils, which were to have, among other matters, responsibility for housing and sanitation in their districts. The first council elections were held in 1889 and the Progressive Party, which comprised Liberals, leaders of the labour movement and members of the Fabian Society, won a majority in the London County Council (LCC). The Progressives felt the needs of the workers outranked those of the railway companies. In 1893, the LCC's Public Health and Housing Committee resolved that, 'having regard to the urgent necessity which exists of further encouraging the migration of the working classes to the suburbs', it would ask the Board of Trade 'to use its power to obtain an increase in the number of trains, a prolongation of the hours during which the trains run, increased uniformity of fares, and a more convenient and uniform system of tickets'. Some Progressives, however, thought this approach too meek. James Hole, a 'celebrated writer on working-class housing problems', announced that 'he saw no reason why all trains should not be workmen's trains'.

The LCC took direct action as well as making resolutions. It was empowered to make compulsory purchase orders for land for housing by the Housing of the Working Class Act of 1890, and an amendment to this Act allowed it to buy land beyond its borders to build 'working-class tenements'. It was also permitted to buy tram services by the Tramways Act 1870 if the services had been operating for over twenty-one years. London's trams had had a chequered history as a form of public transport. Horse-drawn services that pulled carriages along fixed rails had been running since the 1860s, but most had been banned from the central district because their rails interfered with other forms of transport, and they were felt to have a negative effect on property prices. A few had nonetheless established themselves in the suburbs, and some, notably the Metropolitan, which ran from Brixton to Kennington, and the North Metropolitan, which connected Bow to Whitechapel, carried significant numbers of working-class commuters. In 1895 the LCC began to purchase tram operators, buying the London Streetways Company in 1895, and the North Metropolitan in 1896. The same year it was authorized by the London County Council Act to operate as well as own tramlines. Using its powers of compulsory purchase, it then created a new estate of cottages for workers in Totterdown Fields in Tooting, which was connected to the Embankment in central London by its own tramline. The cottages were built in the Arts and Crafts style and, when the estate was completed in 1911, it consisted of 1,229 of them, housing 8,788 people.

The LCC's decision to run commuter services as well as build housing represented a momentous change in public policy. It was both an early experiment in nationalization and an acknowledgement that commuting had become indispensable to progress. In an industrial nation, the separation of work and resting places was now as important as the division of labour: mass transport could – perhaps even should – be public transport, and was a matter too important to be left to market forces. Other local authorities pursued the same course of action. The Glasgow Corporation started running its own trams in 1894 and these dominated its transportation system for the next sixty years. In 1900 over 50 per cent of its commuters used the corporation trams, against 10 per cent on its privately operated trains.

This sea change was recognized at the national level. In May 1900 the Conservative cabinet member A. J. Balfour told the House of Commons during a debate on how and where to house the working classes that:

I am quite sure that the remedy for the great disease of overcrowding is not be found in dealings, however drastic, with insanitary areas. If you can accommodate by raising the height of your buildings, a larger population on a given area, well and good. But if you cannot do that, then you must go outside the narrow area at the centre of your congested district, and you must trust to modern inventions and modern improvements in locomotion for abolishing time.

Commuting was a necessary ingredient of modern life, and should be available to all classes.

◆ ◆ ◆ ◆ ◆

CHAPTER III

Snakeheads and Gourmands

> In the United States nature and domestic life are better than society and the manners of towns. Hence all sensible men gladly escape, earlier or later and partially or wholly, from the turmoil of cities.
>
> Andrew Jackson Downing, 1848

> Space is killed by the railways and we are left with time alone.
>
> Heinrich Heine, 1843

Commuting spread around the world with the railways. It took root in America at the same time as in Britain. Its first rail commuters travelled on the New York and Harlem Railroad, which by 1837 was carrying passengers on so-called 'accommodation' trains from the metropolis to Harlem, a seventeenth-century Dutch village, and soon after as far as Croton Falls. It was, by contemporary accounts, a scenic journey, with views from the windows of a 'charmingly rural region' decorated with 'green, grassy lawns, forest trees, rugged rocks and the beautifully clear Bronx River'. Other tracks were laid towards New York from all points of the compass, including New Jersey to the south and west. The term 'commute' originates from the Paterson and Hudson River Railroad where passengers who wanted to 'commute' their fares, i.e. buy a season ticket in return for a discount, were invited in 1843 to 'enter into such an agreement by calling on an agent of the company'.

The reasons for taking up commuting in America were much the same as they had been in Britain. Its major cities were likewise overcrowded and insanitary. In New York, for instance, the city's Association for Improving the Condition of the Poor noted that its subjects lived in 'dark, contracted, ill-constructed, badly ventilated and disgustingly filthy' accommodation. Their number included 18,000 cellar dwellers, whose lodgings were often flooded with putrid mud. Cholera arrived in New York in 1832, and struck again in 1849, 1854 and 1866. There were typhoid epidemics in 1847, 1848, 1851 and 1864. Nineteen per cent of children born in the city in the mid-nineteenth century died before their first birthday.

Nesting was also an incentive. 'Home! Sweet Home!' (1823) was one of the best-loved songs of the era and the sentiments that it expressed made many yearn for houses of their own. The subsequent obsession with home building was reckoned by the Reverend William G. Eliot Jnr to be central to the health of America: 'The foundation of our free institutions is in our love, as a people, for our homes. The strength of our country is found, not in the declaration that all men are free and equal, but in the quiet influence of the fireside, the bonds which unite together in the family circle. The corner stone of our republic is the hearthstone.' The poet Walt Whitman concurred and thought property ownership an essential part of manhood: 'A man is not a whole and complete man unless he owns a house and the ground it stands on.'

Americans also took up commuting to evade excessive taxation. Residential taxes were high in the cities but fell considerably outside them. By crossing the East River to 'Beautiful Brooklyn', a New York City-dweller could cut their bills by 90 per cent. They responded by commuting via ferry in vast numbers. By 1854 the principal operator, the Union Ferry Company, ran '1,250 crossings daily'. Whitman had watched them from his office at the *Brooklyn Eagle* a few years earlier and found them entertaining, especially during rush hour: 'in the morning there is one incessant stream of people – employed in New York on business – tending towards the ferry. The rush commences soon after six o'clock… it is highly edifying to see the phrenzy exhibited by certain portions of the younger gentlemen… they rush forward as if for dear life, and woe to the fat woman or unwieldy person of any kind who stands in the way.'

The ferries were fed by the railways, which were snaking deeper and deeper into the countryside. Commuters were soon so numerous that the loss of revenue in New York City became a major concern. A leader in the *New York Tribune* in 1847 highlighted the problem:

> *Property is continually tending from our city to escape the oppressiveness of our taxation, many who have made fortunes here carrying them away to be expended and enjoyed, while thousands who continue to do business here, reside, and are taxed elsewhere… Thus, while every suburb of New York is*

growing rapidly, and villages twenty and thirty miles distant
are sustained by incomes earned here and expended there,
our City has no equivalent rapidity of growth.

As had been the case in Britain, most first-generation American commuters were middle class or outright rich. Even after commutation, the daily fare into New York and Boston was around twenty-five cents, which, when set against the average wage of a dollar a day, didn't leave much over to feed the average family of seven, and there were no such things as workmen's trains. The typical commuter was a white-collar professional – a lawyer, a trader, a land speculator or an industrialist. Cartoons from the period show smartly dressed, heavily whiskered, confident young men lounging in their seats, as if they were in a private club rather than a train carriage.

The pioneers of the American rush hour had to overcome the same fears as their British counterparts before they climbed aboard. Trains crashed or blew up all the time, following the example set by the first American-built locomotive, the *Best Friend of Charleston*, which exploded in 1831 and killed the stoker who was trying to tie down its safety valve with his scarf. There were similarly newsworthy catastrophes at least every month – on average – for the rest of the nineteenth century, and the American press always had space for them.*

---

* Its obsession with the dangers of railway travel was later lampooned by Mark Twain in his essay 'The Danger of Lying in Bed' (1871), in which he pointed out that since most people passed away between the sheets rather than in train crashes and other accidents, they should buy themselves bed rather than travel insurance.

American trains were also more dangerous than the Iron Duke 4-2-2 *Sultan* and its ilk. Most burned wood instead of coal, and spewed fireballs as well as whirlwinds of blazing embers from their curious, bonnet-shaped exhaust stacks. At night they resembled Roman candles and frightened even foreigners who thought themselves seasoned and fearless railroaders. When Charles Dickens visited America in 1842, he was awestruck by his first ride: 'on, on, on – tears the mad dragon of an engine with its train of cars; scattering in all directions a shower of burning sparks from its wood fire; screeching, hissing, yelling, panting; until at last the thirsty monster stops beneath a covered way to drink, the people cluster round, and you have time to breathe again.'

There were also peculiar local hazards, including the much-feared 'snakeheads'. Some of the first American tracks were laid with strap rails (wooden rails with a strip of iron nailed on top) that were used for horse-drawn trolleys in mines and quarries, but which weren't strong enough for eighty-ton locomotives. The wood snapped, and the wheels of the locomotive curled up the iron straps and speared their heads into the bellies of its carriages, and sometimes their passengers. In 1843, for instance, a certain Isaac Staats climbed aboard a New Jersey service 'and the train had gone but a few miles when a "snakehead" passed up through the car, striking Staats under the chin and killing him instantly'.

Early American commuters were required to brave spiritual as well as physical dangers. The Transcendentalists, whose mixture of romanticism and metaphysics became fashionable in the glory decades of railroad building, reckoned train travel was bad for the soul. Their opposition to it was all the more bitter because they'd celebrated it in its infancy. When Ralph Waldo Emerson tried to pin down the zeitgeist in his seminal 1844 lecture on the 'Young American', he declared that the railroads had given his subjects an 'increased acquaintance… with the boundless resources of their own soil'; had annihilated time and converted the country into a wonderland, for railroad iron was 'a magician's rod, in its power to evoke the sleeping energies of land and water'. When, however, he returned to the same theme a decade later, he now felt that too many Americans were spending too much time on trains, and the passivity of the activity was bad for them: 'Things are in the saddle / And ride mankind'. Henry David Thoreau had a similar change of heart. While he was fascinated at first by the potential of rail travel – 'five times a day, I can be whirled to Boston within an hour' – he opposed it subsequently: 'We do not ride upon the railroad; it rides upon us.'

Anyone bold enough to disregard both railroad casualty registers and the admonitions of the Transcendentalists and take to the rails was amply rewarded. American trains, by the standards of the rest of the world, were luxury on wheels. There were no such things as first or third class – carriages were designated as either gentlemen's or ladies' cars, 'the main distinction between which', according to Dickens, was 'that in the first, everybody smokes; and in the second, nobody does'. The accommodation in both types of carriage was sumptuous. When a reporter from the *Illustrated London News* got his first taste of American rail travel in 1852, he dedicated much of his report to eulogizing the interior of his carriage, whose seats were 'well stuffed, and covered with a fine plush', with arms 'made of polished black walnut or mahogany'.

American passenger carriages were much longer than British ones, with a corridor running end to end, and two-person bench seats either side of the aisle. In contrast to their counterparts in Britain, Americans had a phobia of travelling facing backwards, and the seats usually had 'walkover' backs that allowed commuters always to face the direction of travel. Walkovers also let people sit in groups of four if they were feeling sociable – and could overcome their prejudice against facing the wrong way. In winter the carriages had charcoal-burning stoves, kept red-hot by the guard, who also controlled the windows, so that whereas British trains were freezing in winter, American ones could be hot, stuffy and airless. In summer, meanwhile, they were supplied with a water cooler and a public cup on a chain – though these were famously filthy and were removed later in the century, when a mania for sanitation took hold. 'Water boys', who carried gooseneck kettles filled with iced water and poured out tumblers for the passengers, also provided cold drinks gratis on some services. On the Boston and Worcester line the water boy had a silver urn and goblet. Last but not least on the list of the relative splendours of American railroad carriages were their toilets. These were little enclosures in one corner of the carriage, about the size of a cupboard, which concealed a wooden thunderbox that opened directly onto the rails.

Such physical differences between rolling stock, however, were thought to be small in comparison to the contrasting etiquettes of British and American commuters. Whereas the

British had chosen silence, Americans had opted to talk. Stranger accosted stranger and debated politics and religion, both taboo subjects to the British traveller. Some visitors found such familiarity intolerable. According to Sir William Mitchell Acworth, the doyen of nineteenth-century railway writers, the English way was the only way: 'We maintain in England our "lonesome stuffy compartments" simply because we like them… I would rather be boxed up in a Midland third class than have "the privilege of enjoying the conversation of the general public" in the most luxurious car that Pullman ever fashioned.'

In addition to talking while in transit, American commuters indulged in all sorts of fun and games. A cartoon from the era in *The Truth*, a New York satirical magazine, shows them dressing up, reading books, smoking pipes and 'stogies', lifting weights and playing cards. It was common practice for commuters to form fours at whist, and play every day on the way home from work. They 'walked over' the backs of their seats, balanced a baize-covered board between themselves on their knees, and were renowned for missing their stops in order to finish a crucial hand.

Some American commuters took the concept that a carriage might be a club on wheels further by banding together to buy or rent private subscription passenger cars. These were built by the Pullman Palace Car Company, founded in 1862, which specialized in luxurious carriages for long-distance travel, and were fitted out with leather armchairs, card tables, libraries, bars, and smoking and non-smoking sections. The subscription cars were hitched to specific morning and evening services, and gave their passengers the chance to carry out a little land speculation and a spot of insider dealing in between being pillars of the community both at work and at home.

In theory, such opulence was available to anyone who could afford it. In practice, however, if you were black the only chance you'd get to see the interior of a private subscription car was as a guard or servant. American trains were racially segregated. In the South, before the Civil War (1861–5), there were special slave cars, 'great, blundering, clumsy' chests, according to Dickens, that resembled cattle wagons. In the rest of the country, both before and after the war, there were 'negro' cars for anyone black wishing to travel by rail. Such discrimination sickened visitors. In 1857, the *Illustrated London News* published a cartoon entitled 'Negro expulsion from a railway car, Philadelphia' that showed an angry white man in crumpled clothing berating a far better-dressed black man, prior, presumably, to ejecting him from the carriage.

As in Britain, the boom in commuting in the United States led to a boom in suburb building. America's new dormitory settlements, however, enjoyed a sunnier reputation. They were the new social idyll – low-tax Arcadias within kissing distance of the cities – and they were thrown up and cherished everywhere the railways reached. Americans took pride in their suburbs. They were founding communities not clusters of isolation cells, and most built churches and libraries as a matter of course, rather than waiting for a critical mass of inhabitants to sustain them.

These new places often had Old World names. The millions of immigrants flooding into the country wanted familiarity as well as freedom. When Welsh squires and Quakers settled some of the prime commutable land near Philadelphia in the seventeenth century, they named their farms and towns after places in Wales, so that the Pennsylvania Main Line, which runs through some of the richest commuter settlements in the world, makes a somewhat more random tour through the mother country: Berwyn to Merion via Bryn Mawr.

Schools and clubs were built close to the railroads as well as neocolonial homes. Being near a good school, or the chance to found a new school, were reasons often given by Victorian-era American commuters for taking up commuting. Meanwhile, they were as fond of ball games as their British counterparts: the Merion Cricket Club (founded 1855, the oldest country club in the USA) ensured it was within 600 feet of a Pennsylvania Main Line station when it chose its present site. The Merion played as much tennis as cricket and laid out the first of two golf courses in 1896.

The commuter influx wasn't always welcomed. In Long Island, farmers threw stones at the first steam trains that passed through their fields; and the Flushing Railroad abolished season tickets in 1862 in an attempt to keep commuter numbers down. It was felt that they were hindering the company from developing its excursion and freight businesses. The editor of the *Flushing Journal* lamented their extinction: 'Their pleasantries, their growlings, their exclusive privileges of finding fault with everything that ran counter to their feelings for the time being – and all their agreeable and disagreeable peculiarities have been swept away at a jerk by the broom of reform.' The obituary was premature: commuting fares were restored within two years, and soon new lines were snaking into Long Island to lure commuters out of New York. In 1869 Alexander T. Stewart, the Sam Walton of the nineteenth century and one of the richest men in America, bought 8,600 acres in Hempstead Plains for a Garden City for the middle class and built the Central Railroad of Long Island to carry its inhabitants to and from New York City. Custom was slow at first – Garden City had a complicated code about who could live there and didn't offer incomers outright ownership of their homes. But after Stewart died, his widow commissioned a Catholic Cathedral of the Incarnation to cover his tomb, ownership restrictions were lifted, and commuters flocked to nest in Hempstead Plains.

While Garden City had been picky, initially, as to the sort of commuter it wanted, the rest of Long Island simply wanted anyone who could pay local taxes and build new communities, as did most of the rest of the countryside near New York. Both the railroad companies and places with railway lines running through them commissioned celebrities to laud their virtues in print. The boom in promoting suburbia converted some unlikely people into hacks. Gustav Kobbé, for instance, who spent most of his time writing about opera and trying to persuade Americans that Wagner was a genius, was paid by the New Jersey Railroad to wax lyrical about the lands around its tracks. He gave them page after page of purple prose, intended to lure New Yorkers onto the rails and into the suburbs. He began by assuring would-be commuters that they were about to join the elite:

Thousands of the best citizens of New York are not citizens of that city at all. In the morning they flood the business districts of the metropolis; in the evening they ebb away... Among the most intelligent and progressive of these non-citizen citizens are those who reach the city by the Central Railroad of New Jersey – doubtless because of the charming and healthful surroundings amid which they have chosen their homes, and also because they are conveyed to and from their places of business by a railroad which combines the greatest speed consistent with safety with the greatest comfort.

Kobbé painted the suburbs he was paid to promote as a cross between a Christian paradise and a giant amusement park. He listed their churches, racecourses and country clubs and pointed out that living outside the city didn't mean leaving it entirely. Wives of commuters could still go shopping in town, enjoy lunch together, and catch matinée shows on Broadway. His hyperbole was standard fare across America, where overstating the virtues of a town in order to attract newcomers was sufficiently common to have a name of its own: 'boosterism'. Boosterism was most rampant in the western states of Ohio, Illinois, Wisconsin and Minnesota, where everyone wanted the railroad to run past their front doors, so that they could turn their farms into townships, and make a fortune from selling off their fields in the process. Nowheresvilles with minuscule populations lobbied the railroad companies to build and the federal government to sell them land on which to lay their tracks. They competed in hyperbole when describing their charms and prospects, so that even hamlets in the midst of fever-ridden swamps became, after a bit of boosterization, New Yorks-to-be in blissful surroundings.

Boosterism was epitomized by the efforts of Duluth, Minnesota, a straggling settlement of fourteen people in 1869, which wanted a new railroad to St Paul built right through its centre. When a bill to grant the necessary federal land for its construction came before Congress, J. Proctor Knott of Kentucky made a speech about it that contained all the funny things he ever said in nearly fifty years of public life, and skewered the hype that had been submitted as evidence in support of the bill. Knott pretended to have been taken in by the claims of Duluth and its handful of occupants. The name itself was a chance to make dullness shine:

> *Who, after listening to the evidence of these intelligent, competent and able bodied witnesses [laughter], who that is not as incredulous as St Thomas himself, will doubt for a moment that the Goshen* of America is to be found in the sandy valleys and upon the pine-clad hills of the St Croix [laughter]? Who would have the hardihood to rise in his seat on this floor and assert that, excepting the pine bushes, the entire region would not produce vegetation enough in ten years to fatten a single grasshopper [Great Laughter].*

The speech from a hitherto placid congressman took his fellow representatives by surprise: 'they mistook the alligator for a log,

---

* That part of Egypt gifted to Joseph and the Israelites by its Pharaoh.

until they sat on him'. Knott had a reputation for wit ever after, Duluth thrived from the association, and the Duluthians had the last laugh. It is now a port city with a population (including its extensive suburbs) of more than 280,000.

There was also a kind of reverse boosterism, where instead of talking up their own virtues, suburbs-in-waiting played up the vices of life in the big city. This tactic was particularly successful around Chicago after the Great Fire of 1871, which destroyed more than three square miles of the city's centre and left 100,000 people homeless. The fire took place in the middle of the evangelical revival movement known as the Second Great Awakening, and during the first flowering of the temperance movement, both of whose participants believed that cities were places where sinners and drunks congregated. The drunks put on quite a show. Americans were in love as never before with spirits, drinking as much of them – mainly domestic rum and whiskey – as the British had during their celebrated Gin Craze a hundred years before, when the scene in London's streets resembled a medieval *danse macabre*, and the body count matched that of a plague epidemic. Many of Chicago's new satellites were built by specific sects of Christians, mostly of the muscular Protestant variety, and were dry. As had been the case in the Eastern States, many of these sects founded universities and schools and became centres of academic excellence. Some even acquired a Bohemian veneer. Oak Park, for instance, which grew rapidly after the Great Fire, was known as the 'favourite resort for literary and religious people'. The architect Frank Lloyd Wright built his own first home there in 1889 while commuting to Chicago. He designed a number of other houses in Oak Park and continued to work on suburban homes throughout his career.

While a Chicago trader might commute home to Geneva every night after work, a Milwaukee brewer return to Berlin, and a New York attorney rest his head in Bayonne, their counterparts in the European places of the same names had to wait several decades before they too could commute. Although the railways had spread from Britain to the continent very quickly – both France and Germany opened their first lines in the 1830s – progress thereafter was slow. The principal obstruction to commuting was the absence of free enterprise. In most European countries the railways were owned or controlled to a greater or lesser extent by the state. Such public ownership must be distinguished from the London County Council's decision to operate trams. Whereas the LCC wished to secure freedom of movement for the workers, European governments wanted to control such movement. Hence they had different priorities for the railways than enabling their subjects and citizens to separate their domestic and professional lives. These were summed up by Friedrich List, the 'father of the German Railways', author of the *National System of Political Economy,* advocate of German unification and staunch opponent of free trade, as: (a) national defence; (b) 'the improvement of the culture of the nation'; (c) the distribution of food; and (d) to create national coherence: 'The iron rails become a nerve system, which, on the one hand, strengthens public opinion, and, on the other hand, strengthens the power of the state for police and governmental purposes.'

The position was similar in France, where defence and other strategic considerations took priority over giving freedom of movement to the bourgeoisie. The railways were also opposed by the country's canal operators who feared that they'd lose all their freight business to them, as had happened in Britain. In consequence they developed slowly, and took the form of a series of regional monopolies run on a part-private, part-public basis. The growth of commuting in Europe was hindered not just by government ownership of the rails, but also by the layout and planning regulations of its cities. Most built upwards rather than outwards, and their inhabitants lived in apartment blocks. It was illegal to knock up a few villas or rows of semi-detached houses just outside a city's limits, and boosterism was out of the question. Finally, continental Europeans worked longer hours for less pay than their counterparts in both Britain and America and since 'travelling cost money and took time' there simply wasn't the demand for commuting.

However, as the era progressed the practice began to appear. While the European version of commuting shared some characteristics with the British and American, there were also local differences. Continental commuters were as anxious as their English-speaking counterparts over safety. In France, for example, the Versailles train crash of 1842 – 'one of the most famous and horrible railroad slaughters ever recorded' – had made a deep impression on the minds of would-be rail users. An excursion train carrying revellers back to Paris from King Louis-Philippe's birthday celebrations at Versailles derailed when the axle of its locomotive snapped. The carriages piled up on each other and caught fire, and – since the doors of the carriages were locked – 'a veritable holocaust of the most hideous description' ensued. At least fifty, and possibly as many as two hundred, people died. An accurate count was impossible, as many of the bodies had been 'calcined and fused into an indistinguishable mass'. The practice of locking passengers into carriages was terminated after the accident, but its memory sent a frisson of fear into travellers for decades afterwards.

The French, like the British, also welcomed the egalitarianism of rail travel. Even the lowest sans-culotte, if she scrimped and saved, could travel on the same train as the highest in the land. The railways provided 'a continuous lesson in equality and fraternity', albeit in four different classes of carriage. The French did not, however, imitate their fellow republicans in America and converse freely while in transit. Passengers in the first two classes adopted the English vice of silence. As in Britain, many resorted to reading to keep loquacious strangers at bay. Their preference for print over conversation inspired Louis Hachette, a rising Parisian publisher, to approach all the main railway companies in France in 1852 with the plan of selling books at their stations. He claimed that passengers with nothing to do became bored by the monotony of their journeys, and this boredom could easily flare into resentment against being 'pulled along by a machine like a piece of baggage' that would be directed against the railway companies. As a solution, he proposed that he create 'a railway library that will provide only interesting volumes in a handy format and at a moderate price', and that such choice reading material would keep their passengers quiescent. The railway operators approved his plan and within a few years Hachette had over sixty branches on station concourses. He was credited with having 'spread the taste for books throughout France' and supporting 'the cause so dear to all serious minds – the diffusion of instruction and enlightenment'. His *Railway Library* was colour-coded by genre – tan for French literature, green for history and travel, and so on. Not a single volume of it contained 'morally questionable' material or 'anything that might excite or harbour political passions'. No one wanted the spirit of 1789 to flare up on passenger trains. The *Railway Library* was also the original publisher of a number of foreign authors. Many French readers got their first taste of writers such as Edgar Allan Poe and Nikolai Gogol while rattling along the rails into town.

Hachette's books were expensive and cost anything from a third of to twice the average day labourer's wage. As had been the case elsewhere, French commuting started as a rich man's game. Like America, France didn't force its railway operators to run workmen's trains or carriages. There were few berets on the platforms alongside the top hats during rush hour. Instead, the third and fourth classes of daily services were filled with an ever-changing mixture of France's poorer citizens, such as farmers' wives on their way to market, or servicemen home on leave, providing inspiration to artists and novelists alike. Honoré Daumier, for instance, celebrated them in his painting *The Third-Class Carriage* (1864), which shows a buxom country girl with the face of a Madonna breastfeeding a baby in the foreground while a crowd of heads look this way and that on the banquette behind her. The novelist Alphonse Daudet, meanwhile, travelled third class in search of authenticity. In his opinion, a novel should be 'the history of people who never have any history' – and where better place to meet them than on a train? 'I'll never forget my trip to Paris in a third-class carriage,' he wrote, 'in the midst of drunken sailors singing, big fat peasants sleeping with their mouths open like those of dead fish, little old ladies with their baskets, children, fleas, wet nurses, the whole paraphernalia of the carriage of the poor with its odours of pipe smoke, brandy, garlic sausage and wet straw. I think I'm still there.'

Any similarities between French and British rail travel ended with food. Gourmands had been the first class of French men to welcome the rails. They enabled the grand restaurants of Paris to procure fresh ingredients from the provinces and beyond: 'all that sea, land and air provide for human sustenance'. A connoisseur might dine off oysters harvested that morning on the Île de Ré, or partridges so fresh that they had reached Paris with their blood still warm and with a light dusting of soot from the train journey on their feathers. A sommelier, meanwhile, could take day trips to his favourite chateaux in Bordeaux and taste the wine in its birthplace, rather than having to wait for it to be boated to him along the canals at walking pace. This spirit of perfectionism was apparent in the food served at railway stations. When Britons went to France, they were amazed by its quality, and ashamed of their own country's efforts. The difference between the two was satirized by Dickens in *Mugby Junction*, a series of stories set around a station of the same name. The ladies who serve its refreshments, Mrs Sniff, Mrs Whiff and Mrs Piff, travel to France to see what their counterparts in the 'land of the frog-eaters' offered to their customers, and feign horror on their return when describing the plenty available: 'There was roast fowls, hot and cold; there was smoking roast veal surrounded with browned potatoes; there was hot soup with (again I ask shall I be credited?) nothing bitter in it, and no flour to choke off the consumer; there was a variety of cold dishes set off with jelly; there was salad; there was – mark me! – *fresh* pastry, and that of a light construction.' Piff, Whiff and Sniff reserved their especial scorn for the frog-eaters' railway sandwiches, which were not just edible, but also works of art, and therefore monstrosities when compared to the sawdust-filled variety they served at home: 'Take a fresh crisp long crusty penny loaf made of the whitest and best flour. Cut it longwise through the middle. Insert a fair and nicely fitting slice of ham. Tie a smart piece of ribbon round the middle of the whole to bind it together. Add at one end a neat wrapper of clean white paper by which to hold it. And the universal French Refreshment sangwich busts on your disgusted vision!'

The French also had a different attitude to railway time, which they saw as a metaphysical issue as much as a practical matter of adopting a universal standard and then synchronizing watches. The problem of local time vs railway time was far more acute in continental Europe than in Britain. Some countries followed different calendars* and were a dozen or so days behind or in front of each other, and the hours, meanwhile, skipped around like lunatics over very small distances when people crossed arbitrary cartographic boundaries. The problem was compounded by the

---

* Russia, for example, did not exchange the Julian calendar for the Gregorian one until 1918.

perception that as well as changing time, railways had annihilated space, or at the very least forced people to think again about the concept. If you could cover as much distance in twenty minutes by rail as you could in a day on foot, then perhaps maps should be redrawn to reflect the change. The economist Constantin Pecqueur imagined one such with 'the new France fitting into the space of the old Ile-de-France, or its equivalent'. So should one change the clocks, or the maps – or both?

In the event, only the clocks were changed and time was standardized across France and several other European countries. Not all of their inhabitants surrendered to the new convention at once. Honoré Daumier contrasted the converts and the traditionalists in a pair of prints. *The New Paris* features a self-important bourgeois staring at his watch against a background of vehicles and crowds dashing to and fro, whereas *Landscapists at Work* shows two artists lying on their backs on a beach, smoking their pipes, with only their shadows to measure the hour.

Once the principle of railway time had been accepted, thoughts turned to its implementation. Electronic distribution systems were invented to bind all the public clocks in towns to a single principal clock. In France each was called the *horloge mère*, or 'mother clock', in Germany it was the *primäre Normaluhr* ('primary reference clock'). Leipzig was the first town to have an electronically distributed system, followed by Frankfurt and Bern in Switzerland 'where a hundred clock faces began marching together in 1890'. European governments, meanwhile, encouraged research into perfect time and competed with each other, as a matter of national pride, as to whose was the most precise. Henri

Poincaré put France in the lead with *The Measure of Time* (1898), a masterpiece of theoretical physics, which gave anyone curious about the matter both barrels. Time was a memory, but did we form memories at the speed of light, or faster?

Albert Einstein also linked railway time to physics. He was inspired to wonder whether time might be constant – or not – when commuting to work as a patent clerk in Bern. The clock on the town hall tower showed eight as his tram drew level with it, but its hands scarcely seemed to move when it passed on towards the next stop. What if the tram went faster? What if it moved at the speed of light so that the clock always read eight? Einstein decided that if you went fast enough, time *would* stand still, and maybe even go backwards. According to his theory of relativity, you need never – theoretically – be late for work again.

◆ ◆ ◆ ◆ ◆

CHAPTER IV

Automobility

> There is something uncanny about these newfangled vehicles. They are unutterably ugly and never a one of them has been provided with a good or even an endurable name. The French, who are usually orthodox in their etymology, if in nothing else, have evolved 'automobile', which being half Greek and half Latin is so near indecent we print it with hesitation.
>
> *The New York Times*, 3 January 1899

I n 1901, fresh from his success with *The War of the Worlds*, the first English novel to feature encounters with aliens, H. G. Wells took a break from science fiction and wrote some predictions as to what he thought the future held for mankind. His *Anticipations of the Reaction of Mechanical and Scientific Progress upon Human Life and Thought* imagined what the world would be like in the year 2000. It had some spectacular misses – for instance Wells didn't think flying would ever take off – and some equally impressive hits. Transport was the key to the future, and the railways were going to be sidelined. Wells knew how much they meant to his fellow Victorians and wanted to warn them that while a steam train might be the symbol of the nineteenth century, new modes of travelling, and indeed commuting, were on the way. He predicted that instead of taking the train to work, the average twentieth-century commuter would use a 'highly mobile conveyance capable of travelling easily and swiftly to any desired point, traversing, at a reasonably controlled pace, the ordinary roads and streets'. These 'motorized carriages' would add 'a fine sense of personal independence to all the small conveniences of first-class railway travel'. The commuter of the future, moreover, would be free to hurry when they chose, to 'stop and pick flowers, turn over in bed of a morning and tell the carriage to wait' and still get to his or her desk on time for work.

Motorcars spread all over the West within twenty years of the publication of *Anticipations*. While the speed at which Wells's prophecy had come true surprised many, in retrospect the signs had been only too apparent. Inventors had been building self-propelled wheeled vehicles since 1769 and their designs had evolved from slow, cumbersome steam carriages to small, nimble machines powered by internal combustion engines. At times progress was fitful. In Britain it was retarded by the 1865 Locomotives on Highways Act, which decreed that any mechanical vehicle travelling on the public roads had to be preceded by a man walking sixty paces ahead waving a red flag and blowing a horn, and could travel no faster than 4 mph in the country and 2 mph in town. The Act further stipulated that 'at least three persons shall be employed to drive or conduct such locomotive' and that if it was hauling carriages or waggons, further personnel were required. While the legislation was clearly aimed at steam tractors, it had the unintended side effect of keeping cars off Britain's roads at a crucial stage in their development.

In the United States, in contrast, motorcars were encouraged at state level as having the potential to perform useful service on farms. In 1871, for instance, the state of Wisconsin offered a $10,000 reward to anyone who could make a machine capable of maintaining an average speed of 5 mph over a 200-mile course, which would be a 'cheap and practical substitute for the horse and other animals on the highways and farm'. The Oshkosh machine, built by Anson Ferrard and named after its town of origin, took the prize,* averaging 6 mph.

In continental Europe, meanwhile, real headway was being made towards the creation of the 'motorized carriages' that Wells had envisaged, and which might one day compete with the railways in carrying people from place to place. The Germans Karl Benz and Gottlieb Daimler both built vehicles powered by internal combustion engines in the 1880s, and in 1891 the Frenchman Emile Constant Levassor designed the 'prototype of the modern automobile' – a 'horseless carriage' with four wheels and a front-mounted engine. By 1900 automobiles were in commercial production in France, Germany and Britain,† albeit as toys for the rich rather than practical working vehicles. Their transformation from 'a luxury for the few to a conveyance for the many' took place in America over the next eight years.

Although the USA, in terms of technological progress, had

---

* This sum was reduced to $5,000 by the state legislature, which wasn't convinced the Oshkosh was more useful than a horse.

† The Red Flag Act was repealed and the speed limit raised to 14 mph in 1898. Motorists celebrated with a London-to-Brighton rally.

followed rather than led since the glory days of the Oshkosh, between 1900 and 1908 its annual automobile production climbed from 4,192 vehicles to 65,000 – and kept on climbing. By 1912 it had a million of them on its roads. This explosive growth was caused by a combination of latent demand and the invention of mass production. The demand may be gauged from a 1900 press release issued by Colonel Albert A. Pope, then chairman of the American Bicycle Co., which had started building cars as well as bikes. The colonel noted that his sales agents were 'fairly howling' for automobiles and predicted that they would become 'the universal means of transportation' and that 'inside of ten years there will be more automobiles in use in the large cities of America than there are now horses in those cities'. Their potential, moreover, as a commuter vehicle had also been recognized. Automobiles might complete what railways, trams and omnibuses had only partially achieved, and extend the benefits of the separation of work and home even to manual workers: 'Imagine a healthier race of workingmen, toiling in cheerful and sanitary factories... who, in the late afternoon, glide away in their own comfortable vehicles to their little farms or houses in the country or by the sea twenty or thirty miles distant! They will be healthier, happier, more intelligent and self-respecting citizens because of the chance to live among the meadows and the flowers of the country instead of in crowded city streets.'

The only problem was the expense. Enter Henry Ford and his Model T. Ford wanted to build a car that was technically advanced, reliable, and which could be sold at so low a price 'that no man making a good salary will be unable to own one, and enjoy with his family the blessing of hours of pleasure in God's great open spaces'.

He pioneered production-line assembly and standardized parts, and the first Model T was completed in August 1908. Although only eleven cars were finished in the first month, production grew at a meteoric rate: by 1915 there were a million of them, and by 1922 the Ford Motor Company was building that number of cars a year.

Some Model Ts were put to work on farms. They were designed so that one of their rear wheels could be removed and its axle used as a drive shaft for a bucksaw or a water pump. They were also customized by their owners, who repainted them in bright colours (for the Model T only came in black) and converted them to tractors and cultivators. Many more were used for the function that Ford had envisaged: enjoying God's great open spaces, and for visiting. Most, however, were employed to get to work and back: auto-commuting had begun. A 1920 survey of car owners revealed that 90 per cent of them used their vehicles 'more or less for business', and that 60 per cent of mileage was 'for business purposes'. While their number included such early users as doctors, lawyers and land speculators, all of whom had to cover a lot of ground if they worked outside towns, most people who drove 'for business' did so from one fixed point to another.

The decision to commute by car was driven principally by the sense of freedom that it gave. Model Ts were slower and less comfortable than trains. They could only manage 40 mph downhill on an open road (about half the speed of the average American express train), didn't have a fixed roof, and were nicknamed 'flivvers' on account of the noisy, rattling ride that they provided. They did, however, liberate their drivers from the temporary surrender of control that a passenger made when climbing onto a form of public transport which both Ruskin and Hachette had considered odious. Instead of being imprisoned on a train and subject to the whims of its operators, each was now the captain of their own little ship and could, in theory, escape from routine whenever they wished by turning off at the next junction.

Auto-commuting was encouraged in its early years by America's cities, which hoped that cars would displace the horse-drawn transport that still formed the majority of their internal traffic and had become a significant sanitary problem. At an international urban planning conference held in New York in 1898, horse pollution was top of the agenda. It was estimated that the host city's horses deposited '2.5 million pounds of manure and 60,000 gallons of urine' on its streets every day. The problem was especially acute in summer when farmers were occupied with the harvest and couldn't spare the time to collect the dung for fertilizer, which was piled up in vacant lots and sometimes reached sixty feet in height. It was calculated at the conference that if the horse population kept growing at its current rate manure would fill the city's streets up to the level of its third-storey windows by 1930.* Horses also died in service at a rate of 15,000 per annum, and their bodies clogged up the traffic. Although New York had special teams to remove them, these 'often waited for the corpses to putrefy so they could more easily be sawed into pieces and carted off'. Automobiles were therefore seen as deliverance. *Scientific American* summed up their perceived advantages over horse-

---

* *The Times* made a similar calculation for London in 1894, and predicted that by 1950 it would be nine feet deep in manure.

drawn transport in 1899: 'The improvement in city conditions by the general adoption of the motorcar can hardly be overestimated. Streets clean, dustless and odorless, with light rubber tired vehicles moving swiftly and noiselessly over their smooth expanse, would eliminate a greater part of the nervousness, distraction and strain of modern metropolitan life.'

Would-be auto-commuters who wished to drive to work in the cities that were waiting to welcome them had to master new skills. The first challenge was learning to drive. There were no such things as driving schools in 1900s America. While a modern driver of a car with manual transmission might with a little practice master the controls of a Model T (three foot pedals for the gears and transmission brake, no clutch and a lever throttle on the steering wheel), they demanded what was then an alien kind of coordination between hands and feet, while still keeping one's eyes on the road. As John Steinbeck observed in *East of Eden,*

> *It is hard now to imagine the difficulty of learning to start, drive, and maintain an automobile. Not only was the whole process complicated, but you had to start from scratch. Today's children breathe in the theory, habits and idiosyncrasies of the internal combustion engine in their cradles, but then you started with the blank belief that it would not run at all, and sometimes you were right... so that a man about to turn the crank of a Model T might be seen to spit on the ground and whisper a spell.*

Many solved the problem by employing chauffeurs. When New York State pioneered driving tests in America in 1910, only chauffeurs were required to sit them. All those who had driven for less than a year had to pass a practical assessment and a written examination. Over 20,000 were granted licences in the first sixty days after the Callan Automobile Law came into effect, testament to the number of cars – and number of chauffeurs – already on New York State roads.

Once the debutant auto-commuter had learned to drive, or hired someone else to do it for them, a series of further obstacles had to be overcome en route to the office. Fuelling, for a start, required careful planning.* When cars were few, petrol was sold from livery shops by the bucket. As demand grew, the livery shops converted old boilers into fuel dispensers by turning them upside down and fitting them with sight glasses and spigots. In 1905, Sylvanus Freelove Bowser patented a 'self-measuring gasoline storage pump' which was fitted with a flexible hose. His 'bowsers' soon became the new standard across America and gas stations a feature of the American landscape. Their owners wanted to attract passing trade, and so used giant signs and bizarre architectural styles, including 'colonial houses, Greek temples, Chinese pagodas, and Art Deco palaces' to tempt automobilists into their forecourts. These dispensaries were so elaborate in comparison to their function that many rural examples became 'local landmarks and a source of community pride'. While fuel was uneven in quality in the first decade of auto-commuting, and the risk of filling up with a contaminated batch another uncertainty to be faced on the journey to and from work, it became standardized

---

* The Model T, for instance, could only go up hills in reverse gear if it was low on gas, so it was essential to keep it topped up.

as chemical engineers at the oil companies dedicated their careers to optimizing its performance. They advanced not only via more refined refining, but also by experimenting with additives that evened or retarded combustion. Their poster child was tetraethyl lead, also known as 'loony gas' after seventeen workers died from inhaling it neat at two New Jersey refineries, which was added to gasoline from the 1920s onwards as an anti-knock agent to ensure that engines ran smoothly.

Once the first wave of auto-commuters had mastered their vehicles, located a reliable source of fuel, dodged farm vehicles and speed traps* and made it to the city, they were faced with the problem of finding somewhere to park. Although *Scientific American* had predicted in 1896 that cars would cause far less urban congestion than horse-drawn transport, this turned out to be wishful thinking. While the number of horses fell precipitously as auto-commuting grew, the number of vehicles on the streets rose and the cities soon ran out of parking spaces.

In their early days, cars were stabled in custom-built premises, as if they were the most finicky of thoroughbreds, which would lose their mettle if left out in the rain. In 1905, for instance, the Chicago Automobile Club built a six-storey home for its members with Beaux Arts-era motifs on its façade, where they might house their chariots on working days and drink cocktails before driving home. Twelve years later, it had grown so much it built new premises – a seventeen-storey 'Raymond Hood-esque phallus in miniature adorned with machine age flora',

---

* These had, according to the *New York Times*, proliferated in villages on the outskirts of the city, where they were a lucrative source of income.

with six floors of parking that was intended to embody the values of so 'virile and fearless an organization of motorists'. Chicago automobilists who couldn't get into the club used the commercial lots that were appearing all over town.

Providing parking to commuters was a profitable business. Instead of building housing, developers turned vacant city lots into car parks or tore down existing structures to make space for them. The money that might be made from stabling autos at ten cents each a day inspired inventors to patent a range of contraptions that aimed to store as many vehicles as possible in the smallest of spaces. They drew scissor movements, elevators and carousels – these last like mini-Ferris wheels with parking cradles instead of gondolas – that might one day grace city streets. Few such brainchildren ever materialized. The 'cage deck garage', which first appeared in Boston in 1933, satisfied the needs of parking lot entrepreneurs so perfectly that it was copied everywhere and tiers of concrete slabs linked by ramps on a skeleton of iron girders sprang up all over America. As cage garages had no walls they weren't subject to burdensome fire regulations, and so were cheaper to build and more profitable to run than any other urban structure of a similar size. Cities as well as entrepreneurs cashed in on the parking bonanza by installing meters along their kerbs. The first such, a coin-operated model called the 'Black Maria', designed by two professors at Oklahoma State University, went into service in Oklahoma City in 1935. It charged 5 cents per hour, or about $1.50 in today's money.

In addition to solving the horse problem in cities and enriching parking-lot operators, surging car ownership was becoming an important source of revenue at the state level, through licence fees and gasoline taxes. Oregon introduced a tax of a cent a gallon in 1919; and by 1929 every other state had followed suit. The money raised was spent on roads and, since most people wanted an automobile and those who already possessed one wanted better roads, the new imposition passed almost unprotested in a country founded on its opposition to taxation. Even gasoline excise collectors were surprised at the public's acquiescence: 'Who ever heard, before, of a popular tax?' asked the chief collector in Tennessee.

Dreams of freedom at the wheel, civic invitations to end the horse age and tolerable taxation – all contributed to the ascent of auto-commuting at the expense of public transport. In 1929, a committee appointed by President Herbert Hoover worried over the 'the steady decline in railway passenger traffic since 1920', and the 'curtailment of train services or abandonment of branch lines' due to 'severe' competition from cars. It left the question hanging over whether to take action. In his election campaign Hoover had promised voters 'a car in every garage'. The auto industry had become 'the bellwether of the American economy' and produced 5.3 million cars a year.* It was the principal customer of the steel, oil and rubber industries, and a host of middle- and small-sized businesses also depended on it. Why place stumbling blocks in the path of a giant?

The giant was not just powerful but also paranoid. Even though both the zeitgeist and Washington favoured them,

---

* Or about the same as Germany in 2012.

American auto manufacturers weren't prepared to take their success for granted. While cars had driven horses off the road very quickly, and eaten some of the railways' share of commuting, they still faced competition, at least for short-hop journeys, from America's tramway operators. What if people tired of driving and switched back to public transport? General Motors, in concert with Firestone Tyres, Standard Oil, Phillips Petroleum, Mack Trucks, and various other companies with direct or vested interests in the triumph of auto-commuting and the death of public transport, decided to head off such an eventuality by buying up the opposition and closing it down. Together they set up National City Lines, ostensibly a tramway operator, which spent most of its time and money on acquiring electric tramlines and terminating them. If there were no trams left to worry about, then the government might absolve itself of the responsibility of saving them. Whereas Americans made nearly 15.7 billion journeys by streetcar in 1923, by 1940 the number had fallen to 8.3 billion, and thereafter most of the remaining lines withered away.

The Great Streetcar Scandal, as it was known, is still shrouded in mystery. Some claim it is a conspiracy theory, on a par with the belief that the moon landings were faked; others that it is true in every detail. When it was investigated by the Senate in 1974 at the height of the first oil crisis, General Motors issued a public denial, the opening section of which ('General Motors Did Not Assist the Nazis in World War II') was dedicated to countering allegations that it had collaborated with Hitler via Opel, its wholly-owned German subsidiary, whose Blitz trucks had been built with slave labour. Buying out and closing down the competition seemed small beer in comparison to such grave accusations, and besides, the war had taught them to build better, cheaper and faster cars. In the words of GM's president, Charles Erwin Wilson, 'I thought that what was good for the country was good for General Motors and vice versa.'

The public concurred. Automobiles had ridden deep into the American psyche. At first their allure had derived in part from their danger. Novelists played on both their ability to whisk people away to new lives and their tendency to crash. The plot of F. Scott Fitzgerald's *The Great Gatsby* – one of the defining novels of the Roaring Twenties – revolves around auto-commuting and careless driving. The car, however, soon changed from being a deus ex machina to a symbol of hope. The Joad family jalopy in John Steinbeck's *The Grapes of Wrath* is the four-wheeled ark that carries its owners across America on their exodus to the promised land, and the book shows the affection and reverence that Americans had developed for their motors.

Indeed, at the height of the Depression, people still hung onto their cars. According to a long-term sociological study of 'Middletown' (the City of Muncie, in Indiana), car ownership was found to stand for 'a large share of the "American Dream"'. People clung to it 'as they cling to self-respect'. Families would drive up to a relief commissary in 1935 to stand in line for food handouts rather than sell their car and feed themselves properly. America's attachment to the car was even blessed by some of its leading Christians. According to one such evangelist, the church aside, there was 'no factor in American life that does so much for the morals of the public as does the automobile… Any device that brings the family together as a unit in their pursuit of pleasure is a promoter of good morals and yields a beneficient influence that makes for the good of American civilization… The automobile is one of the country's best ministers and best preachers.'

By 1939, motorcars were the principal form of commuter transport in America. No other country in the world took to driving to work so quickly. In Britain, which at the time was second to America in car ownership, with 2 million vehicles on the road (there were 25 million in the States), just 9.1 per cent of commuters used cars, against 22.5 per cent who walked and 19.1 per cent who cycled, while the remainder travelled on public transport. Indeed, commuting by bicycle was the most significant upward trend in British commuting in the first twenty years of the twentieth century. It had begun in the 1880s, after the invention of the 'safety bicycle', the first mass-produced example of which was John Kemp Starley's Rover. The Rover had wheels of almost equal size, springs under its seat, and, from 1890, pneumatic tyres. Its pedals drove the rear wheel via a chain. It looked just like a modern sit-up-and-beg bike and represented a giant leap in technology. Hitherto the last word in bicycles had been the penny-farthing (named after the disproportion in size between its front and rear wheels), whose riders sat four or five feet off the ground above the front wheel, which they drove by pedals attached to its hub. The diminutive rear wheel trailed behind and acted as a stabilizer. High-wheelers, as they were also known, were unstable, hard to mount and dismount, and dangerous to ride. Indeed, before the appearance of the safety bicycle, cycling was considered an adventure sport rather than a practical form of personal transportation, and the daring young men who practised it borrowed slang from the hunting world – including such phrases as 'taking a header'* – to glamorize their pastime. Although surprisingly fast – in 1891 Fred Osmond covered 23.72 miles in a single hour† – penny-farthings were useless for commuting. Rovers and their imitators, in contrast, were easier and more comfortable to ride, and perfect – if the condition of the roads allowed – for the average four- to five-mile journey to work of the 1890s and 1900s. They were especially popular with factory workers, including those at Starley's works in Coventry. Starley himself, however, like Colonel Albert Pope in America, believed that the future of transportation lay in motorized vehicles, and before his death in 1901 he had experimented with electric cars and motorbikes. In 1904, his successor gave up on bicycles and started building automobiles under the Rover brand.

Although car commuters in Britain were fewer overall, they were growing more quickly in number, rising ninefold between 1909 and 1939, against a doubling in the number of cyclists. Relations between the two were tense. It was suggested in motoring circles that cyclists should be kept out of the way on their own roads. The cyclists, however, would have none of it. G. H. Stancer, the secretary of the Cyclists' Touring Club, wrote an angry letter to *The Times* on the matter in April 1934. In his opinion, it was motorists, not cyclists, who needed special roads. Cycle tracks were an evil dreamed up by duplicitous speed freaks in order to have the highways all to themselves:

---

* That is, flying over the handlebars when their bike hit a bump.
† His record still stands.

The demand for separate tracks for cyclists is part of the campaign of motorists to appropriate public highways for their exclusive use. Have we yet got to accept a condition of affairs when cyclists have to renounce their use of the roads to escape annihilation? If motorists do not wish to conform to a standard of conduct on public highways compatible with the safety of all other users, then it is they and not cyclists who should abandon the use of the highway... There is nothing to prevent motorists from building at their own expense private roads where they can indulge their craze for speed without let or hindrance.

The debate continued throughout the 1930s. The Cyclists' Touring Club even sent a delegate on a fact-finding mission to Germany to see what inspiration the Nazi's autobahn-building programme might offer to British cyclists in their war against cars.

Notwithstanding the decade-by-decade doubling in the number of Britons who commuted by car, those manufacturers who hoped for automobility in the UK along the lines of the American precedent were disappointed. Ford had opened its first overseas factory in Trafford Park in 1911 to assemble Model Ts, and although it had nearly one-third of the British car market by 1913, it was building a mere 6,000 vehicles a year. While the number shot up in subsequent decades, growth did not approach that achieved by similar plants in the United States. Ford and other motorcar builders found that there were physical, financial and cultural obstacles to British car ownership. The principal physical impediment was inadequate infrastructure. Although the railways had cleared routes for themselves into the centres of British cities, many still had convoluted, sometimes medieval, roadways, which were clogged with pedestrians and horse-drawn transport, and filthier than farm tracks. Access was also hindered by the electric trams, many council-owned, that had about the same number of riders as bicycles and whose rails, stops and sheer bulk were serious hindrances to the flow of traffic.

The roads outside town were equally inadequate. Those wishing to drive to work from their villas in Surrey rather than travel first class on the train had to contend with meandering lanes that wandered around landholdings, natural obstacles and parish boundaries, whose twists and curves were held to be an essential part of the British landscape. William Blake had praised them in The *Marriage of Heaven and Hell*: 'crooked roads without improvement are works of genius'; the Romantics, true to form, loved them for their lack of self-control. Their cherished convolutions were praised by G. K. Chesterton in 1913 in an anti-temperance poem that celebrated both winding roads and staggering Englishmen:

Before the Roman came to Rye or out to Severn strode,
The rolling English drunkard made the rolling English road.
A reeling road, a rolling road, that rambles round the shire...

There were even lamentations when the roads were straightened in the 1920s to facilitate motorized transport. In 1927, *The Times* complained that they were becoming 'bare, open, shadeless and shameless, as shiny as steel and as hard as the rigour of commerce'.

The financial obstacles to automobility consisted of the purchase and running costs of motorcars. Although they were becoming more and more affordable – the price of a car halved in real terms between 1924 and 1935 – they were a third more expensive in Britain than in America, and beyond the reach of all but the middle class. In 1938 the Society of Motor Manufacturers and Traders (SMMT) reckoned that no one earning less than £250 per annum could afford a car. This figure 'was commonly viewed as marking an economic dividing line between the middle classes and the rest of society', and 75 per cent of households fell beneath it. Cars were also much more expensive to run in Britain. In addition to road tax and fuel duty, car owners had to pay a horsepower tax from 1920 onwards, and buy compulsory third-party insurance from 1930. According to one calculation, 'in the late 1930s total standing charges on an average eight horsepower car were £32.35 while total annual running costs would amount to £24.75: a grand total of £57.10, or over a third of the car's original cost price'. Finally, would-be car commuters had to own or rent a garage, as they were required by law to park their cars off the roads at night, or alternatively to leave them lighted – which was impractical.

Cultural obstacles to automobility in Britain were also significant. The middle classes who constituted the target market for car manufacturers were acutely conscious of social status. They didn't want to appear pushy or be seen to have aspirations above their station, but equally they dreaded demeaning themselves. Indeed, 'status anxieties' were a significant influence on middle-class behaviour when it came to buying a car, and were acknowledged by those in the motor trade. In 1920, for instance, a writer for *Autocar* magazine, alert to such sensitivities, advised aspiring motorists to follow the guidance Polonius gives to Laertes in *Hamlet*:

> *Costly thy habit as thy purse can buy,*
> *But not expressed in fancy; rich, not gaudy,*
> *For the apparel oft proclaims the man...*

Selling to the middle class was fraught with complications. Manufacturers had to 'cultivate technical, aesthetic or snobbish appeal' with their products, which gave buyers 'the opportunity to display real or fancied discrimination'. The middle classes were sensitive to the way a car was marketed as well as its appearance and performance. When Morris introduced its Minor SV model in 1931 and made much in its adverts of the fact that it cost only £100, orders poured in for its other models, while the Minor sold very badly. According to Miles Thomas, sales manager at Morris at the time, 'it was an interesting exercise in consumer preference that although attention was undoubtedly attracted to the Morris Minor by the fact that one *could* be purchased for as little as £100, the actual buyers wanted something that showed that they had *not* bought the cheapest product. And so everybody was happy. No one wants to keep down with the Joneses!'

Although it seemed to some, in what has since been labelled Britain's 'Golden Age of Motoring', that buying a car was like crossing a minefield, especially if they wanted to use it to drive to work in town, a car culture was nonetheless developing in Britain. The present-day fascination with *Top Gear* was born in the early decades of the twentieth century. The SMMT staged its first British

Motor Show at the Crystal Palace in 1903, and thereafter every year at Olympia. By the 1930s the shows were drawing a million or more visitors per annum. They received extensive coverage in the press. Most papers had motoring correspondents, including such unlikely publications as the *British Medical Journal*, which carried two pages on the 1931 event. Its correspondent was impressed by the Morris Minor SV he saw at the show, and several other small cars, including Rover's new 7 h.p. four-seater Scarab. His report included a section on Cars for Medical Men, and advised that doctors who commuted to practices in towns would find that 'one of the "baby" cars' would 'amply meet their needs'.

Other classes of professional were switching to automobiles for personal transportation. A survey carried out in the mid-1930s found that the car had become an 'important occupational tool' and that 40 per cent were bought to get to work. It noted that car commuters came from a wide range of white-collar occupations, including 'accountancy and actuarial practice; architecture; consultant engineering and surveying; consultant practice in chemistry and other science; dentistry; education; industrial and trade associations; law; art; literature and music; medicine; political associations; religion; social welfare associations; and veterinary surgery'. To these must be added the managers who worked for the car-makers and their associated industries such as tyres, and indeed some of the workers at the factories themselves. In 1939, during a House of Commons debate on the horsepower tax, Herbert Parker, the Labour MP for Romford, noted that 'among the 12,000 workers in the Ford works at Dagenham there are 1,500 to 2,000 who possess motor cars of their own'.

The infrastructure, meanwhile, was improving. Grand plans formulated by the Greater London Arterial Roads Conference between 1913 and 1916 were slowly being put into motion. The Southend Arterial Road,* 'England's longest new road since Roman times', which ran for thirty-eight miles between Gallows Corner in Havering and Southend-on-Sea, was opened in March 1925 by Prince Henry, later Duke of Gloucester. Work on London's North Circular, its first orbital road, commenced in 1922, and was completed eleven years later. Although in its present incarnation, as the A406, it is one of London's most hated roads among commuters, traffic flowed freely along it during the 1930s. When Sir Charles Bressey and the architect Edwin Lutyens timed its traffic in 1935 they recorded an average speed of 23.6 mph.†

Commuters began to settle along the new roads, much as they had done beside the railway lines in the 1840s. The population of the Essex village of Laindon, for instance, whose thirteenth-century church of St Nicholas was one of the landmarks along the Southend Arterial Road, grew from 401 in 1901 to 4,552 by 1931. Like the omnibus suburbs before them, Britain's new auto suburbs were thought to be typified by unnecessarily ugly houses and were christened by Sir Osbert Lancaster in his *Pillar to Post* as 'By-pass Variegated'. Crazy combinations of ugly materials, ridiculous ornaments and shoddy workmanship distinguished this class of architectural gem, which were equipped with red-brick garages for their owners' cars that were 'vaguely Romanesque in feeling'. In Lancaster's opinion, the houses were not only eyesores in their

---

* Now the A127.

† The average speed in 2011 was 18 mph.

own right, but also destructive of their surroundings, and even offensive to each other: 'Notice the skill with which [the houses] are disposed, that insures that the largest possible area of countryside is ruined with the minimum of expense; see how carefully each house-holder is provided with a clear view into the most private offices of his next door neighbour.' Echoing Chesterton, who had hoped that God might one day rain fire on the railway suburbs of his day, Lancaster suggested that their premature obliteration was a prospect cheerful enough to 'reconcile one to the prospect of aerial bombardment'. The poet John Betjeman felt the same way about the consequences of automobility, writing in a poem of 1937: 'Come, friendly bombs, and fall on Slough! / It isn't fit for humans now.'

In the event, Lancaster's and Betjeman's wishes were granted. Just as commuting by car was becoming a significant practice in Britain, the Second World War paralyzed it for the next decade. The same autobahns in Germany that the Cycle Club had inspected as part of a German Roads Delegation during its fight against bicycle lanes were used by the Nazis to annex Austria in 1938, and to launch blitzkrieg against Poland the following year. By 1945, over 200,000 British homes had been destroyed by German bombers and a further 3,500,000 damaged. Slough received its share of this destruction, as did the new roads, and a number of the 'By-pass Variegated' houses along their verges.

✦ ✦ ✦ ✦ ✦

CHAPTER V

The Spaces
in Between

> Modern suburbia is a creature of the automobile and
> could not exist without it.
>
> John B. Rae, *The American Automobile*, 1965

America's commitment to automobility continued more or less unhindered during the Second World War, and had profound consequences for its patterns of human settlement. The suburbs that the railroads had created had tended to radiate outwards like the spokes of an umbrella from city centres into the surrounding countryside, and had left vast tracts of land untouched in between their lines. These were filled in as commuters built themselves dream homes that could only be reached by car. They struck off left and right from highways, and settled in places that had remained rural throughout the railway boom. Henry Ford, who had done so much to make this relocation possible, led the way by creating a 2,000-acre estate ten miles outside Detroit. 'The city is doomed,' he declared. 'We shall solve the city problem by leaving the city.' By 1939, millions had followed his example and Stewart H. Mott, a Federal Housing Association official, was able to advise the American Association of Planners that 'decentralization is taking place. It is not a policy, it is a reality – and it is as impossible for us to change this trend as it is to change the desire of birds to migrate to a more suitable location.'

This four-wheeled flight to virgin lands around the cities accelerated after the Second World War. It was encouraged by federal home-owning programmes for veterans, and tax breaks for suburb builders. Nearly four million new homes were constructed between 1946 and 1951, most of them on the assumption that their owners would drive to work. A full 97 per cent of all new single-family dwellings were detached, and as a rule were provided with garages, emblematic of the assumption of automobility. Garages had been creeping into American domestic architecture since the 1920s. At first they were separate structures constructed behind homes, like stables. The *Home Builders*' pattern book of 1928 offered designs for several dozen types of garage in a variety of styles for automobilists who wished to build stalls for their steeds. The architect Norman Bel Geddes was perhaps the first to integrate the garage with the home in his plans for *The House of Tomorrow* for the 1931 World's Fair. Frank Lloyd Wright also included carports in the 'Usonian'* style of houses he designed in the 1930s. Integral garages and carports soon became the norm, so that by 1937 the *Architectural Record* could report that 'the garage has become a very essential part of the residence'. It was as if the

---

* Lloyd Wright thought that the United States of America should be renamed Usonia, to reflect the fact that Canada and Mexico were also 'American'. He designed cities and suburban houses to suit his vision of a distinctive American style of urban planning. The name survives in Esperanto as Usono.

car was one of the family, and needed accommodation alongside its other members. Garages continued to grow in importance and prominence after the Second World War, and by the 1960s they often took up a third of the house itself.

Detached homes with ample parking were the building blocks of what was perhaps the archetype of the auto-commuter suburbs: Levittown, New York. Levittown was designed by William Jaird Levitt, who applied Fordian principles of mass production to housing to create a 17,000-home community on former potato fields between 1947 and 1951. Levittown began with only one type of house, the 'Cape Cod', which was, in effect, the Model T of the auto suburb. *Time* magazine celebrated the town with various features, and made Levitt its man of the year for 1950. *The Weekly Magazine*, meanwhile, sensing that a giant shift in demographics was underway, described Levittown as a 'revolution in epitome' and predicted that it would be copied from coast to coast. Such was its success that Levitt founded two more settlements in Pennsylvania and New Jersey (both also called Levittown) in the next decade.

The third Levittown, which was planned to contain 12,000 houses, 'organized into neighborhoods of about 1,200 homes, each serviced by an elementary school, playground and swimming pool' was infiltrated by Herbert Gans, a pioneering sociologist, who was determined to find out what life was like for the average auto-commuter on the new frontier. He bought a four-bedroom Cape Cod for a down payment of $100, moved in with his family, and set about analyzing the new settlement. If this were to be a 'Mayflower moment', then posterity would be grateful for a better and less partial record than the diaries of zealots and witch-hunters.

Gans discovered that most of the community depended on male auto-commuting breadwinners. These spent an average of 37 minutes driving to or from work, which, for the ex-city dwellers who had moved to Levittown, was less than they had in their urban pasts. Most said they actually liked their commutes – only those who spent significantly more time on the road found the experience 'wearing'. People who car-pooled also shared this general joy of commuting. In contrast, the majority of Levittowners who had to rely on the buses to get to work said that their journeys were tedious or painful. The wives of Levittown working men were on the pessimists' side of the fence when it came to commuting, and this difference was a cause of friction in marriages. As Gans details, 'commuting seems to influence the marital relationship, particularly for wives; both joint couple activity and marital happiness are affected negatively when the wives consider their husband's commuting wearing. The men do not agree however, [and claim to get] … along with their wives as well when the trip is wearing as when it is not.'

Levittowners were into community as well as commuting. They were 'hyperactive joiners' and signed up for a plethora of activities. Their enthusiasm was shared with auto suburbanites elsewhere. The Chicago suburb of Park Forest, for instance, which was immortalized by William H. Whyte, an early guru of management theory, in *The Organization Man*, was 'a hotbed of participation', and 'probably swallows up more civic energy per hundred people than any other community in the country'. Indeed, the growth of auto suburbs coincided with the golden age of civic participation in America. Voter turnout, and involvement in bowling leagues, little leagues* and so on all grew steadily in the 1940s, 1950s and 1960s. The demographic was in favour. The Levittowners and their counterparts in similar developments were 'young people (in a society which values youth) who hold the new technical and service jobs that are transforming our economy'. Even after taking commuting time into account (which many seem to have counted as leisure), they had plenty of free time and used it to turn their settlements into communities. Auto-commuters wanted to connect at home, if only for neighbourhood cocktail parties.

The new suburbanites were first-class consumers. They had steady work, cash to spend, and access to credit that their grandparents could only have dreamed of. They filled their houses with televisions, vacuum cleaners, refrigerators, toasters, trouser presses, curling tongs and washing machines, often bought on tick. The shops left the cities to meet them. Sears were the pioneers of out-of-town retail. In 1925, Robert E. Wood, the company's vice president, noted that 'motor vehicle registrations had outstripped the parking space available in metropolitan cores' and advanced the policy of locating new stores in low-density areas that people could reach by car – and where rents were cheaper. Destination malls, likewise only accessible on four wheels, also sprouted around or within the suburbs. The first was Kansas's Country Club Plaza, founded 1923 and still going strong. The Country Club featured a half-size model of the Giralda tower

---

* The Levittown team won the Little League World Series in 1960.

in Seville, a huge range of shops and restaurants, and parking for thousands of cars. It inspired numerous imitators, and drive-in malls became another good reason to live in the suburbs – and another reason to avoid visiting an old-fashioned city where there wasn't anywhere to park. Why go to Macy's if it came to or near to you? The malls drew attention to the difference in the experience by highlighting their hygiene and safety. One didn't have to dodge drunks and beggars on the sidewalks, and instead of having to wait for delivery or carry armfuls of packages home on public transport, you could load up your car boot right then and there.

The Levittowns all had retail centres, starting with the Shop-O-Rama at the first settlement, which was 'the largest pedestrian shopping mall east of the Mississippi'. The Shop-O-Rama was built on the northern corner of the community, right next door to its baseball diamond. It was bordered on two sides by six-lane highways and by an arrangement of Cape Cods in cul de sacs, and rows of Ranches* on its remaining edges. It featured branches of Pomeroys, Woolworths and Sears, and had parking for 6,000 cars. It served as a community as well as retail centre and hosted beauty pageants, Easter Day parades and political rallies. In 1960, John F. Kennedy delivered a campaign speech in its car park, and the votes of Levittowners, who were generally Democrats, helped him win that year's presidential election.

Employers also followed auto-commuters out of town. They could use trucks to transport goods from their suburban factories to market, and rely on their workforces to have their own wheels.

---

* A second model of Levittown house introduced in 1949.

General Foods established the trend when it moved from Manhattan to White Plains, just north of New York City, in 1954. Many other corporate behemoths followed suit, including IBM, PepsiCo and Texaco. Interestingly, it seems that once a decision had been made to move out of town, a company's executives were sufficiently confident of the automobility of their employees that 'the most important variable in determining the direction of a corporate shift was the location of the home and country club' of its CEO.

Many American baby boomers grew up in auto suburbs. Daddy went to work in an Ambassador, Cadillac or Ford, depending on his status at his destination. On weekends he and Mom drove the family to the shops, or to a drive-in movie via a takeaway hamburger chain. All classes of Americans benefited from the trend: wages were rising, prices were falling, and even assembly-line workers could afford to drive. Bit by bit the cities leaked into the countryside. By 1963, a full third of America's population lived or worked in suburbs. To judge by the TV sitcoms of the period – many of which required suburbs and commuters for both their situations and their audiences – it was a happy, wholesome existence. Such classics as *Bewitched* and *Leave It to Beaver* pictured the 'revolution in epitome' promised by Levittown as a new idyll, and added magical or innocent perspectives to it.

Family cartoons of the era also represented auto suburbs and their nuclear households as the new norm, and equipped them with both a history and a future. *The Flintstones* and *The Jetsons* series both starred commuter breadwinners. Fred Flintstone shouts 'yabba dabba doo!' as he jumps into an arrangement of stone rollers and wooden beams and pushes it along by the steering wheel to his work at a quarry; George Jetson smiles as he flies around the sky in his space-car, and literally drops off his son and daughter at their respective schools and his wife Jane at the shopping mall, enveloped in translucent domes and released from the vehicle as if they were bombs, before reaching his office at Spacely Space Sprockets. When George steps out of his vehicle he flicks a switch and it folds itself up into an attaché case, thus neatly – apparently – avoiding the issue of whether there would be problems parking in 2062.

The Jetsons touches on many aspects of auto-commuting, including buying a new car. In Episode Four, George and Jane visit the local Molecular Motors dealership, where they're ferried about in levitating egg chairs and treated to a promotional video, then a test drive. Canned laughter follows everything the dealer says to them – lest viewers should miss the parallels between cartoon 2062 and real-life 1962, when the programme first aired. The test drive is in that year's model, the 'out of this world Supersonic Suburbanite', which has a top speed of several thousand mph, and the acceleration of a ballistic missile. 'How's that for a getaway?' asks the car dealer, as g-forces whirl the Jetsons around in the cabin behind him, before he aims the Supersonic Suburbanite at an asteroid in order to demonstrate its brakes.

The real-life commuter who wished to buy a new car was faced with a dizzying variety of choices. Car design and advertising became increasingly splendid during the 1950s and 1960s. Styling favoured form over function and adverts focused on novelty in support of a general strategy within the industry of 'planned obsolescence'. Although the phrase is taken to mean that manufacturers built their products with limited lifespans, it actually referred to cars made to fall out of fashion rather than to fall apart. It first appeared in the 1920s, when all the principal automakers started producing new models every calendar year. According to Alfred P. Sloan of General Motors, the 'styling changes' in the 'annual model' were intended 'to create a certain amount of dissatisfaction with past models as compared with the new one'. The concept had come to rule the car market by the mid-1950s. A TV advert for the 1955 Motoramic Chevrolet, for instance, whose 'jet smooth look of luxury attracts attention', declared that it was 'more than a new car – a new concept! See it soon!' Not content with being merely new, Plymouth introduced its Plymouth '62 in 1957 as 'the car that breaks the time barrier!' The 1958 Ford release, meanwhile, was supported by a TV commercial entitled 'What Makes a New Car New' that said 'new' once every three seconds, apart from the first six, when it appeared almost every other word: 'Ford for '58, new in every way, new styling, new power, new performance, new handling, new comfort, new ride. There's nothing newer in the world!' The newest thing about the Ford '58 range was 'magic circle steering' that made 'turning as easy as pointing', but which was in fact merely a rehash of an earlier system. It was praised as a thing of awe in adverts, the product of America's best brains. Competing masterminds at other manufacturers came up with similar non-innovations, each touted as the greatest advance in transportation since the wheel. No one blushed – they were, after all, feeding dreams.

As well as vying in exterior styling, the auto manufacturers fought for market share through interior innovations. In 1954, Nash Motors introduced air conditioning to its flagship Ambassador model; by 1960, 20 per cent of cars had air conditioning, a figure that had risen to 54 per cent by 1969, and included convertibles. Drivers could chill out as well as cool down by listening to the radio. The first commercial car radio was the Motorola, introduced by the Galvin Corporation in 1930, which later took the brand name for its own. The Motorola was followed in Europe by Blaupunkt's AS5, which was the size of a small suitcase and cost a third of the price of a new car. By the 1950s, however, radios had shrunk sufficiently to fit on the dashboard and came as standard in top-of-the-range autos. Car radios, like the vehicles themselves, had new features every year. Ford's 1956 Concord, for example, had a 'Signal Seek' sound system, which tuned itself after it had been set to 'Town' or 'Country' mode. The Signal Seek, according to its hype, featured '9 tubes, a printed circuit board, and self-cleaning speaker' and relied on 'military technology developed during the Korean war'. Drivers who didn't want to hear endless car adverts on the radio could buy a Chrysler '56, which boasted a Highway Hi-Fi, a 16 2/3 RPM record player that took up half the dashboard and played 7" discs without skipping when the car went round corners or over bumps. It was, however, too fiddly for a lone commuter, and offered a choice of only ten discs, including such exotica as Borodin's *Polovtsian Dances*, Ippolitov-Ivanov's *Procession of the Sardar*, and dramatic readings from Bernard Shaw's *Don Juan in Hell*.

Since the cars had to be built to match the dreams, rather than to be practical or efficient, they grew in size and weight throughout the 1950s. By 1958, 'intermediate sized cars, like the Ford Fairlane and Oldsmobile F-85 [were] larger than the full-sized Ford of 1949'. They were also unnecessarily powerful. Even though more than 75 per cent of all car journeys were made for the purposes of work, and 90 per cent of them were shorter than 25 miles, the average commuter's chariot boasted a four- or five-litre V8 engine, which drank gas like an alcoholic on a bender. Performance, in terms of miles per gallon, was going backwards.

Although building wasteful products would have been seen as commercial suicide in most other industries, only one insider – George Romney of American Motors – campaigned against the 'Dinosaur in the Driveway'. His attitude was sufficiently curious to merit an interview with *Life* magazine, headlined 'Long Shot Gambler on Short Cars'. 'Why', Romney asked the bemused reporter, 'does a 105-pound woman have to drive 4,000 pounds of car to the drugstore to pick up a package of hairpins?' Romney fought an uphill battle to persuade Americans that big wasn't always better in their autos.* He wasn't accepted as a prophet until the Arab oil embargo of 1973, when oil prices quadrupled almost overnight, and the fuel efficiency of the average American auto had fallen to 13.5 miles to the gallon.

---

* George Romney's opposition to oversized gas guzzlers didn't rub off on his son Mitt, the Republican presidential candidate in 2012, who has fought measures to raise the standards for fuel economy in American autos on the grounds that this would 'limit the choice available to American families' by forcing them to buy expensive, if more efficient, foreign cars.

The auto-commuting way of life, with its overpowered and extravagantly styled cars and mass-produced homes, was viewed with horror in some quarters. John Keats, a splenetic journalist turned social critic, author of *The Insolent Chariots*, a splendid diatribe against the auto manufacturers in the 1950s, and *The Crack in the Picture Window*, a long moan about the state of America, treated its practitioners with contempt. In the first instance they were suckers to buy cars whose tyres were too small for their engines, which meant that they slid out at corners or when they braked; and whose cabins were too cramped for their bodies so that however streamlined they might appear, they were fundamentally unsafe. His pet hate was the Ford Edsel,* which was so ridiculously overpowered that it was uncontrollable. When a reporter from *Mechanix Illustrated* tried to give it a 'full jump start', i.e. open up the throttle and roar away from a stationary position, he found the 'wheels spun like a gone-wild Waring Blender' while the tyres smoked and the Edsel stayed still. The standard model, moreover, was about as safe in traffic 'as opening a Christmas basket of King Cobras in a small room with the lights out'. In Keats's opinion, the Edsel represented another missed opportunity to make the average American auto safer. Although more Americans were killed on the roads each year than had died in the Korean War, Detroit still saw itself 'as selling dreams of speed, luxury, sex and horsepower' and 'it would no more occur to Detroit to try and sell safety at the same time than it would occur to a fashionable restaurant to provide sodium

---

* Named after the only son of Henry Ford.

bicarbonate and a stomach pump with every place setting'.

Keats was equally scathing about the auto suburbs for which the Edsel had been built: 'For literally nothing down... you too can find a box of your own in one of the fresh-air slums we're building round the edges of American cities... inhabited by people whose age, income, number of children, problems, habits, conversation, dress, possessions, and perhaps even blood type are also precisely like yours.' The historian and sociologist Lewis Mumford had similarly harsh words: the home suburbs of auto-commuters were 'a multitude of uniform, unidentifiable houses, lined up inflexibly, at uniform distances, on uniform roads, in a treeless, communal waste, inhabited by people of the same caste, the same income, [who eat] the same tasteless prefabricated foods, from the same freezers, conforming in every outward and inward respect to a common mold'. Mumford predicted that 'the ultimate effect of the suburban escape' would be, ironically, 'a low-grade uniform environment from which escape is impossible'.

A further complaint against the new settlements was that they were displacing the smallholdings that had made America great. If its citizens lost touch with their rustic roots, it was presumed they would become effete, like the stereotypical English as portrayed in patriotic US histories of the struggle for independence. The fear that the auto-commuting way of life might be emasculating men was widespread in the 1950s and 1960s. There were books and articles galore on how the freeborn male was losing his mojo. Rugged self-reliance seemed to be melting away in the suburbs. Herbert Gans remarked on its scarcity in his Levittown, where husbands had even tried to get their wives to mow the lawn until 'block social pressure' sent them scurrying back to their yards. Emasculation was also blamed on corporate employers, who were demanding conformity and obedience in a country founded on rebellion. IBM, for instance, had a company dress guide that advised its workers how to pair ties with shirts, and how to style their hair.*

There were, however, some rather more serious charges against the auto suburbs. Rather than homogenizing America demographically as well as architecturally, they had fathered a renaissance in segregation: 'in 1960 not a single one of the Long Island Levittown's residents was black'. Discrimination was often active as well as accidental; many developments had covenants restricting who could buy or rent there by religion or colour – some took no Jews, others no 'coloureds'. Moreover, it was harder to get a mortgage on a house in a mixed neighbourhood than one adjudged to be all white. While the Supreme Court had outlawed restrictive covenants based on race in 1948 in *Shelley* v. *Kraemer*, they persisted *de facto* if not *de jure*, and segregation was also maintained through sharp practices such as 'blockbusting'. An unprincipled real estate agent would sell a house to a black family, then tell the other homeowners in the neighbourhood that it was about to become a ghetto. The panicked whites would sell at a loss and move to the suburbs, and the agent made a handsome profit from reselling their houses.

The problem was particularly acute in Detroit, home of the auto industry, which was an equal opportunities employer and

---

* These accusations of unmanliness were at their height during the baby boom, when American men were fathering children left, right and centre.

drew many African Americans into town from the countryside. However, once a certain number had moved into a neigh-bourhood, assisted perhaps by unscrupulous blockbusters, the whites fled to the suburbs, the city lost tax revenue and so on in a vicious circle. Moreover, new highways built to facilitate com-muting had broken the unity of the city. Over 2,800 buildings in the old core were removed to make room for the Edsel Ford Expressway, and the road became a barrier between previously interdependent districts. Indeed, problems created in the heyday of auto-commuting are still with us: in July 2013 Detroit filed for bankruptcy. By that point the city's population had declined from a peak of 1,850,000 in 1950 to 701,000, and it had insufficient tax revenues to meet its liabilities. Both employers and workers had used their automobility to move elsewhere.

From the driver's point of view, the principal problem created by burgeoning car ownership in mid twentieth-century America was congestion. Although the average commuter had a head-turning vehicle that gave him or her more horsepower than most Texan ranchers, for many the thrill of ownership was diminished by the often static nature of the experience. The roads were choking up and radio stations broadcasted traffic reports during their rush-hour programmes to warn their listeners of frustration ahead. Commuters began to ask themselves: what pleasure was there in gunning an overpowered, underbraked, chrome-plated behemoth into work of a morning if other vehicles boxed you in and forced you to crawl?

Congestion in cities had been a problem since the era

of ancient Rome, when edicts had been issued regulating the movement of chariots and pedestrians. Julius Caesar, for example, had banned horse-drawn conveyances from the city during the hours of daylight. It persisted through the Dark and Middle Ages and became a matter for science during the Age of Enlightenment, when the movement of people and traffic was compared to the circulation of the blood. A rational city should be 'a city of flowing arteries and veins through which people streamed like healthy blood corpuscles'. However, as the blood clotted in the nineteenth century, and the arteries and veins became clogged up with manure, practical as well as theoretical methods of traffic control became imperative. The first concrete measure to manage flow was John Peake Knight's 'traffic light', which was installed in London at the junction of Great George Street and Bridge Street in 1868. It had red and green gas lamps to indicate stop and go, but exploded after a month in service, fatally injuring the policeman who was operating it. The next innovation in traffic planning was the stop sign, which William Phelps Eno, a wealthy New York dilettante, suggested might help tame the city's streets in a 1900 article, 'Reform in Our Street Traffic Urgently Needed'. Stop signs could be placed at busy intersections, forcing tram, cab and omnibus drivers to pause and reflect before plunging forwards. The article was a sensation and Eno built a career out of making plans to manage traffic, which were adopted in New York, London and Paris. He was an advocate of one-way systems, and these, together with traffic signs and traffic lights, helped control, if not reduce, congestion in cities. By the 1950s, however, it was clear that more radical solutions were required, and not just in cities, but also in the auto suburbs that fed vehicles into them, and indeed in the hinterland beyond.

The answer to congestion, in the collective opinion of the car manufacturers, wasn't traffic management but a new generation of superhighways that ran straight into city centres. From the 1930s onwards they lobbied the government and the public for support for their vision. The star exhibit at the 1939 New York World's Fair was 'Futurama', designed by Norman Bel Geddes and sponsored by General Motors, which imagined the America of 1960. It consisted of a giant automated scale model of a chunk of the country that covered an acre, had 500,000 miniature buildings, a million similarly diminished trees, and 50,000 automobiles. Visitors took an eighteen-minute ride over the exhibit on a conveyor system and marvelled at the teardrop-shaped cars, kept at regular distances apart as they would be in the future by 'automatic radio control', buzzing around fourteen-lane highways that bisected wilderness, suburbia and cities alike.

New Horizons, the propaganda film that accompanied Futurama, claimed it was self-evident that 'Americans need 'new roads to go places' and proposed them on a scale that looks unfeasible even with the hindsight of real superhighways. The lanes on the Futurama exhibit were so tightly packed they resembled uncooked spaghetti strands, some of which peeled off around vertiginous curves into cloverleaf junctions, fell away at improbable angles into the countryside, or regrouped and dissected cities. 'Here is an American City, replanned around a highly developed modern traffic system,' announces *New Horizons*, as the camera tracks bubble cars and buses over a suspension bridge into a grid of city blocks. The 'outworn areas of an older day' had been replaced with parkways, skyscrapers and futuristic General Motors factories – or, as the film describes it, 'rights of way have been so routed as to displace outmoded business sections and undesirable slum areas. Whenever possible man continuously strives to replace the old with the new.' Its message, in short, was that the only way to accommodate new roads was to blow holes right through the hearts of cities and start again from scratch.

This theme was revisited in the 1950s, when a new Highways Act was under consideration in America. The automakers took up propaganda with the same enthusiasm they were applying to selling vehicles, and beleaguered the government with all their might. GM established the American Road Builders Association, 'a lobbying front second only to that of the munitions industry'. Ford, meanwhile, made half-hour-long advertorial films that were shown at drive-ins and on television to sway people to vote for bigger and better roads, at local, state and national levels. *The Freedom of the American Road* (1955), for instance, presented case studies that highlighted why such freedom could only be preserved by building more roads. The Pittsburgh Spur, with its maze of nineteenth-century streets, was offered as an example of a needless cause of congestion that had been eradicated by bold planning. 'You can't use halfway measures,' enthuses the film's presenter, over images of bulldozers flattening part of the old town centre. 'A big problem needs a big answer. You tear down the old and put in the new, with modern muscles, modern tools.' An aerial view of the rejuvenated Pittsburgh Spur, a complicated if geometrically pleasing series of interchanges, followed while the presenter explained that thanks to such scorched-earth measures 'the American road is being made free'.

In addition to offering visions of an America revitalized by a new circulatory system, the automakers enlisted safety to their cause: more and bigger roads would not only eradicate congestion, but also reduce the number of traffic accidents. *The Freedom of the American Road* featured San Francisco's Bayshore Freeway as an example of how new roads could save lives, in a mock crime documentary interlude. Whereas people were killed all the time on the old narrow freeway, the new wider version had become an accident-free zone.

Safety swung the balance in favour of a new highways programme, and in 1956 President Eisenhower signed the Federal Interstate Highway Act into law, which provided for a 41,000-mile system, with the federal government paying 90 per cent of the cost. This partial nationalization of the country's major roads acknowledged the changes that automobility in general, and commuting by car in particular, had wrought on both the culture and landscape of America. As well as establishing automobiles as the principal form of personal transport, it had committed the country, for better or worse, to a way of life 'organized predominantly on the basis of the universal availability of motor transportation'.

◆ ◆ ◆ ◆ ◆

CHAPTER VI

Bowler Hats and Mini Coopers

I have always liked the process of commuting; every phase of the little journey is a pleasure to me. There is a regularity about it that is agreeable and comforting to a person of habit, and in addition, it serves as a sort of slipway along which I am gently but firmly launched into the waters of daily business routine.

Roald Dahl, 'Galloping Foxley', 1953

While auto-commuting reshaped the landscape in America during the 1940s and 1950s, it was slower to advance in Britain. Its progress was retarded by the Second World War, at the outbreak of which petrol rationing was introduced, putting an end to travelling to work by car. Commuting on public transport was also affected by the war. The four principal railway companies and London Transport were taken under government control. Commuter rail services were altered to allow the evacuation of families from the cities and, after the Blitz commenced, to take account of damage caused in bombing raids. Although the engineers usually managed to piece the system back together quickly, tracks could be out of action for weeks at a time. When Waterloo was bombed in May 1941, for instance, it was a month before all services were restored. On the trains themselves, first-class travel was abolished, and passenger carriages were blacked out, which made it impossible for commuters to enjoy their favourite pastime of reading. Railway station signs on the platforms and elsewhere were taken down, lest the Germans used them to orientate themselves in the anticipated invasion. The blackout, erratic services and the absence of signs confused even seasoned commuters. According to a City secretary, who travelled into work from Potters Bar, 'we were absolutely snookered... we became strangers in our own beloved London'. The fact that most suburban stations along her line looked identical without their nameplates was 'even more confusing than the dim lighting. Many a time we went on too far or hopped off too soon'.

The government did, however, recognize that commuting was essential for certain occupations, and started a poster campaign with the slogan 'IS YOUR JOURNEY REALLY NECESSARY?' to deter casual rail users. One of the posters featured an opulently dressed couple with a dog, hesitating beside a ticket booth. Even the idle rich had to make way for essential workers. The campaign was altered in 1943, when housewives had started using trains to go shopping for food, as the vagaries of distribution during rationing meant that if some areas ran out of basic supplies, they might still be available elsewhere along the lines. A new slogan, 'If your journey is REALLY necessary and you can choose your times travel between 10 & 4', targeted this kind of transgressor. A short film shown in news cinemas that accompanied the poster campaign featured shots of women with parcels obstructing commuters. It advised that 'Before ten in the morning and four at night transport is wanted for essential workers, so do your shopping between ten and four. Please, don't travel in the rush hour.' The reliance on cooperation rather than compulsion was a success. A later poster in the series, 'If your train is late or crowded – do you mind?', which appealed to the 'Blitz spirit' of putting up with personal inconvenience for the common good, was received as positive rather than intrusive.

The government also tried to spell out to passengers the reasons why operating conditions were so difficult, notably via a BBC Radio documentary, *Junction 'X'*, a 'dramatization of events that occurred at a vital [railway] crossroads on the path to victory on a certain day in 1944 between the hours of 10 a.m. and 10 p.m.', which showed 'how British Railways are successfully carrying out their vital and gigantic war task in conditions of unparalleled difficulty'. *Junction 'X'* was popular with both the public and critics, and the script was published in June 1944. According to Desmond Shawe-Taylor, then radio critic of the *Sunday Times*, it was 'a beautiful piece of radio… grand entertainment and first-rate propaganda for the man on the platform'. Its opening scene, set at the eponymous junction* during the morning rush hour, features a dialogue – overheard by its Narrator – between two commuters, the Listener (Mr Smith), and his friend, a Mr Brown, who complain that their train is late, that delays are getting worse, and that the authorities care 'not a damn' for their plight.

---

* Named 'X' lest Nazi listeners tried to identify it with a real junction and bomb it.

The Narrator then leads the Listener up a dingy staircase to a set of offices over the station, where train movements are being coordinated along the lines and a Divisional Superintendent is trying to balance the need to move coal, troops, goods and commuters with a shortage of trains and personnel:

DIV. SUP.: *The position, in fact, is rather desperate all round. All the yards are heavy. We're waiting for engines at five depots. There's bound to be some late starts – likely to lead to more bunching on certain lines. I'm short of 15 drivers and firemen and 12 guards from one depot alone – reported sick. The labour problem's acute, sir.*

NARRATOR [close, quietly]: *Acute's the word. One hundred thousand railway men in the Forces, Mr. Listener.*

BOYLE: *What about cutting out some of those upline trains?*

DIV. SUP. [smiling ruefully]: *Which do you suggest, sir?*

BOYLE: *The 3.30.*

DIV. SUP.: *Impossible, sir. It's carrying locomotive coal. If we start cutting those, we'll have depots closing down.*

BOYLE: *Well, we've got to do something, Fairbank. What about the 4.40 – the 6.15 – and the 6.35?*

DIV. SUP.: *I'll try. But if I cancel many more, I'll need a load stop.*

NARRATOR [quietly]: *D'ye see his problem? Loaded waggons pouring out of docks and factories and goods yards onto lines already stiff with trains. If he could get a stop put on firms loading waggons…*

DIV. SUP.: *Is there any hope of that, sir? A three days'*
   stop and I could get that 12,000 down by half – and
   we'd be easy.

BOYLE: *We might. But we've got to try everything else*
   first. Any passenger trains we can cut?

DIV. SUP.: *And raise a howl, sir?*

BOYLE [losing his temper somewhat]: *Listen, Fairbank,*
   we've got to get those waggons moving. And if a few
   more passengers are left standing about – well, we just
   can't help it, that's all.

NARRATOR [rather maliciously]: *That's you,*
   Mr. Listener, see?

In the event, the railways had a good war. By 1944, they were
carrying 'about a million passengers per week more than in
1938'. They were rewarded, in 1947, with nationalization. The
new Labour administration had proclaimed its commitment
to creating 'socialized industries' in its 1945 manifesto *Let Us
Face the Future*. Its industrial programme included the 'Public
ownership of inland transport' on the grounds that 'Coordination of transport services by rail, road, air and canal cannot
be achieved without unification. And unification without public
ownership means a steady struggle with sectional interests or the
enthronement of a private monopoly, which would be a menace
to the rest of industry'. The terms on which the public acquired
ownership of the railways were claimed by the government to be
extravagant – £927 million for war-damaged tracks, dilapidated
rolling stock, and a collection of 'dingy railway stations' and

'miserable, unprepossessing restaurants' – and by the railway companies to be little better than outright confiscation. According to Sir Robert Matthews, the chairman of the London and North Eastern Railway (LNER), the terms of purchase imposed on them 'would bring a blush of shame to the leathery cheek of a Barbary pirate'.

There were few immediate changes to commuter services post-nationalization. Timetables were more or less unaltered and rebranding was gradual: trains carried their old corporate emblems until 1950 when the figure of a lion rampant astride a train wheel appeared on locomotives, which was nicknamed the 'lion on a unicycle'. It was replaced in 1956 by the 'ferret and dartboard' crest (a wyvern perched on a crown holding up a train wheel). While some suburban tracks were electrified, most locomotives remained steam-powered until the 1960s. The condition of the infrastructure, however, suffered. There was a permanent backlog of repairs that lengthened travel times. The railway stations were 'sorely neglected'. They were way down the list of priorities of a cash-strapped Labour government hoping to build a New Jerusalem. And the relationship between railway staff and passengers altered. When British Railways was created on 1 January 1948, its 632,000 employees became both public servants and the equals of the people that they served. Although the narrow pre-war class consciousness that had existed between commuters and those who sold them tickets and sandwiches or drove their trains was presumed to have been extinguished, it persisted. The passengers still expected deference, and were offended if staff failed to leap to attention. A new indifference was perceived in

the attitudes of railway staff post-nationalization, later satirized in
verse by John Betjeman:

I'm paid by the buffet at Didcot
For insulting the passengers there.
The way they keeps rattlin' the doorknob
Disturbs me in doin' my hair.

Prejudice was also alive and well between the commuters
themselves. Passengers in first and third classes stayed aloof from
each other, and looked down on anyone who appeared to be
out of place. When Paul Vaughan, the BBC science broadcaster,
travelled on the 08.32 from Wimbledon to Holborn Viaduct
en route to work at a pharmaceutical company in the 1950s, it
seemed a step backwards in time: 'In one carriage there would be
four men, always in exactly the same seats in their sober business
suits, and they would spread a cloth over their knees for a daily
game of whist, which I suppose they played all the way to the City'.
When Vaughan had to get out at Holborn, 'they would frown and
sigh and raise their eyes to heaven as they lifted their improvised
card table to let you pass'.

The persistence of a class consciousness is also apparent in
Roald Dahl's short story 'Galloping Foxley' (1953), in which the
life of William Perkins, a self-confessed 'contented commuter', is
thrown out of joint by the appearance on his regular 08.12 service
of a man he thinks he recognizes as the prefect, Foxley, who used to
abuse him at public school. The story begins with a little homily by
Perkins on the pleasures of his commute and his general love of an

orderly life. However, when Foxley appears in his carriage, Perkins can't break with convention and slay his demon by confronting him. He has surrendered his courage to routine.

The general image of the rail commuter in the 1950s and 1960s was of a staid, respectable figure rather than a snob. It was during this period that the enduring image of the commuter emerged: a man in a bowler hat,* black jacket and striped trousers, with a briefcase in one hand and a neatly furled umbrella in the other. This was the unofficial uniform of civil servants (who were nicknamed the 'bowler-hat brigade') and white-collar workers in the City of London, and while it was only really common for a period of about thirty years, it came to stand for strict adherence to convention. It was also taken to be emblematic of the ordinary, of the sacrifice of imagination to social correctness. Arthur Seymour John Tessimond's poem 'The Man in the Bowler Hat' (1947), for instance, casts his subject as a figure of pity:

> *I am the unnoticed, the unnoticeable man:*
> *The man who sat on your right in the morning train...*
> *I am the man too busy with a living to live,*
> *Too hurried and worried to see and smell and touch:*
> *The man who is patient too long and obeys too much*
> *And wishes too softly and seldom.*

---

* The bowler was designed in 1849 by a London hatmaker to protect the heads of the gamekeepers of Edward Coke from low-hanging branches. It was later adopted by tradesmen and cab drivers. It wasn't until the 1940s that it became the headgear of choice for season-ticket holders. The bowler had a different reputation in America, where it was worn by cowboys and outlaws.

The model commuter also became a figure of fun. In the 1961 film *The Rebel*, for instance, a bowler-hatted Tony Hancock boards a train full of commuters in identical garb, has an identity crisis, and gives up his work as a clerk to become an artist. Indeed, by the 1970s the bowler-hat brigade had become stock-in-trade for comedians and cartoonists. It was parodied by *Monty Python's Flying Circus* in its Ministry of Silly Walks sketch, which commences with a civil servant in the commuter uniform prancing into work at the eponymous ministry; and the *Mr Benn* cartoon series of 1971 featured a similarly dressed hero who changes into a caveman, a knight in shining armour and an astronaut, and has adventures instead of going into work. Perhaps the most famous comic representation of the commuter of the 1970s was Reginald Perrin, played by Leonard Rossiter in *The Fall and Rise of Reginald Perrin*, a TV series adapted by David Nobbs from his novel and first aired in 1976. Each episode began with Perrin, a middle-aged middle manager, arriving at his office 'eleven minutes late' after being delayed on the train for improbable reasons – 'Badger ate a junction box at New Malden'. In later series the delay was extended to seventeen minutes, and finally 'Twenty-two minutes late, escaped puma, Chessington North'.

However, by the time that Reginald Perrin appeared on television, commuting by rail had been in steady decline for twenty years. Passenger rail journeys fell from a peak of over 1.1 billion in 1959 to around 650 million in 1980. A proportion of the fall was caused by the so-called 'Beeching cuts', named after Dr Richard Beeching, who produced two reports, in 1963 and 1965, which recommended that British Railways' network should be pruned back to trunk lines and major branches. Several thousand miles of tracks were closed, including some commuter lines, although the Beeching axe fell mainly on rural stations, many of which had never been popular or profitable. The cuts were resented by the public, some of whom looked beyond the present inconvenience of losing their local station.* In April 1964, for instance, Barbara Preston had a letter published in the *Guardian* protesting about the planned closure of some of Manchester's commuter routes: 'is this what is really necessary here and now?' she asked, 'or shall we, in a few years, when traffic in Manchester has inevitably become denser, be bitterly regretting these closures and at great expense be rebuilding commuter lines?'

The cuts, however, were only a contributory factor to decline, which was part of a general trend towards travelling by motorcar. Whereas in 1949 only 6 per cent of people drove to work,† versus 53 per cent who took public transport and nearly 20 per cent who bicycled, by 1979 just over half the population commuted by car. The modes of transport that saw the steepest declines were those used by the blue-collar workforce: cycling, trams and buses. According to Peter Bailey, writing about coming of age in the early 1950s, 'bikes and buses provide the memorable images of town traffic... dense surging columns of pedalling workers released from the factories at the end of the day; long snaking queues of workers, shoppers and schoolchildren waiting to board the bus

---

* Beeching had no regrets. When an interviewer asked him in 1981 if he minded being remembered as a mad axeman, he replied 'most people aren't remembered at all'.

† Compared to nearly 10 per cent before the war.

home'. Bicycles were cheap and enabled commuters to live in places beyond the fixed routes of public transport. They were particularly popular with shift workers who had to get to and from work at hours when public transport wasn't running. Factories usually provided bike racks for their employees. The title sequence of the film *Saturday Night and Sunday Morning* (1960), based on the 1958 novel by Alan Sillitoe, who worked at the Raleigh factory* in Nottingham, shows a scene most of its audiences would have found familiar – a mad scramble for the bikes, followed by a mass exodus from the factory gates. In the 1960s, however, the number of cycle commuters in Britain fell by two-thirds. The bicycle manufacturing industry collapsed. By 1962, sales at Raleigh, which had peaked at over a million a year in the 1950s, had halved and the company had to accept a number of shotgun mergers with other manufacturers in order to survive. The decline occurred in part because the roads were becoming choked with motor vehicles, which made them unpleasant and unsafe for cyclists. Although the idea of providing dedicated 'cycleways' had been considered by the government when it introduced the Special Roads Bill in 1948, it was decided that such facilities should be the responsibility of local authorities, which in the event had different priorities for public transport.

Trams, in contrast, were abandoned by their operators rather than commuters. LCC's London network, once in the vanguard of public ownership, was nationalized after the Second World

---

* Unlike its competitors at Rover, Raleigh rejected motorized transport and sold the plans and parts of its innovative three-wheeler motorcar to its designer, who set up shop in Tamworth in the 1930s. The Reliant Motor Company would later create the iconic Reliant Robin.

War. It lost its access to cheap electricity after the nationalization of the power-generation industry, and, since there was no money for maintenance or new rolling stock, its lines were closed and replaced with bus services. This pattern was repeated throughout the country. In Manchester, which, like many other councils, had started to substitute buses for trams before the war, the number of the city's commuters who used trams fell from 60 per cent in 1936 to 21 per cent in 1946, and by 1950 the city had abandoned its tram system in favour of buses.* Corporation trams hung on a little longer in Glasgow. In 1957 the city still had 1,027 trams in operation, which carried 'over 300 million passengers a year over 256 route miles'. They were, however, phased out over the next five years. The last service, on 4 September 1962, was marked by a procession of twenty trams from Dalmarnock to Coplawhill. A quarter of Glasgow's population turned out to pay their last respects. Many placed pennies on the tracks for the trams to flatten as souvenirs of the event. Although the trams were crowded and squalid, Glaswegians had a sentimental attachment to them. They had been cheap, and services were so frequent that passengers could hang back in order to ride on their favourite model. These included the Coronations, introduced in King George VI's coronation year of 1937, Cunarders, named after the liners built in Glasgow's shipyards, and Green Goddesses, which had been bought from Liverpool in 1954 when it shut down its own corporation services.

The buses that replaced trams were the most widely used

---

* Trams returned to Manchester with the opening of the light-rail Manchester Metrolink in 1992.

form of commuter transport in Britain during the 1950s. Journeys were generally short in distance, but of a relatively long duration. In Manchester, for instance, the mean distance covered was 4.7 miles and the average commute time just over half an hour. In contrast to the London omnibuses of the nineteenth century, which were patronized by *Times*-reading members of the middle class, manual workers were the principal users of post-war buses.

In the opinion of the social historian David Kynaston, 'The Inner Circle', Birmingham's number 8 service, was 'arguably the most emblematic bus route' of the period. It was nicknamed the '"Workmen's Special" because of the large number of factories and workshops it served'. The industrial facilities it passed included the Saltley gas works, Ansells Brewery and the HP Sauce factory, and 'you could tell where you were on the No. 8 route by the perfumery'. Its buses were so crowded that extra conductors were deployed on foot at choke points such as Aston Cross to sell tickets to the queues of rush-hour passengers before they boarded. Conditions inside were uncomfortable. According to Bob Johnson, a former commuter: 'The buses were always full of workmen, the sweat would run down the inside of the windows, the cigarette smoke was like a London smog and the bus was always bloomin' freezin.'

The buses, like the trams before them, also fell from grace. Whereas Glasgow's buses carried 419 million passengers in 1965, by 1970 numbers had dropped to 264 million. Nationwide, passenger journeys on local buses declined from 15.5 billion in 1955 to 7.5 billion in 1975. They were deserted, in the main, for motorcars.

At the end of the Second World War, few would have bet on cars becoming the principal mode of commuter transport in Britain within the next twenty years. The likelihood that the average Briton would drive to work did not increase greatly in the 1940s. Although the country was manufacturing plenty of vehicles, most were reserved for export. At home, the waiting list for a new car was anything from one to two and a half years. The *Daily Express* labelled the Society of Motor Manufacturers and Traders' first post-war motor show, staged at Earls Court in 1948, as 'the biggest "Please-do-not-touch" exhibition of all time'. More than half a million people nonetheless went to look, an indication, presumably, of the level of pent-up demand. Even though Britain was the second largest exporter of cars in the world after the United States, the number of vehicles on its own roads remained below pre-war levels until 1950, and 'well into the 1950s a horse and cart… was as likely to be seen as a car on a northern working-class street'.

Even the lucky ones who owned cars couldn't use them to commute. Petrol rationing persisted until 1950, and the ration was insufficient to get to work and back five times a week. When rationing ended on 26 May of that year, there were scenes of jubilation as motorists tore their ration books into shreds and made for the nearest petrol station. A joint spokesman for the RAC, AA and Royal Scottish Automobile Club declared it VP (Victory for Petrol) Day and predicted that the 'effect on the industrial, commercial and community life will be electric. Ration books will now become as obsolete as the man with the red flag.' He was right: the number of cars on British roads multiplied four-fold in the next eight years and the number of car commuters nearly trebled.

The principal cause of surging car ownership was a rise in incomes. When the prime minister, Harold Macmillan, told a Conservative rally in Bedford in 1957 that 'most of our people have never had it so good', he spoke the truth. Real incomes grew by nearly 30 per cent during the 1950s and by a further 20 per cent during the 1960s. Access to credit likewise boomed. Not only did cars become more affordable for more people, they were also cheaper in real terms, as were their running costs. Apart from a spike in late 1956 and early 1957 during the Suez crisis, the price of petrol declined between 1953 and 1973. The next factor was convenience. Cars provided a flexibility that public transport couldn't match. A Glaswegian commuter of the 1950s summed up this aspect of their appeal: 'I got a car... because to travel to [work] was quite awkward. To do it by public transport would mean... a bus journey, an underground journey, and another bus journey... so it really wasn't terribly convenient, so I'd managed to accrue a little capital and I bought a car.'

The decision to commute by car was also influenced by a change in attitudes within British culture. The anxiety of the middle classes over appearing neither too cheap nor too showy in their choice of vehicle vanished in the 1950s.* The new attitudes that emerged were different from those that had developed in America, where the automobile had become a cultural icon far earlier, and where size, styling and novelty ruled. The 1956 Jaguar

---

* Only to be revived in the 1970s and 1980s as a result of tax breaks for company cars, which enabled executives to judge their relative status by the make and model of their respective vehicles.

Mark VII M saloon, for instance, which a company director might drive to work, was twenty inches shorter and 700 pounds lighter than the Ford Edsel Corsair. An average British car such as the Morris Oxford was two feet shorter than the Jaguar, and the Mini, which first appeared in 1959, nearly three and half feet shorter again. 'You don't need a big one to be happy,' ran one of the Mini's advertising slogans, and the British car-buying public agreed. If they had an obsession, it was with speed. Jaguar's design mantra was 'Grace, Space, Pace'. A Jaguar Mark VII M won the Monte Carlo rally in 1956 and Jaguar cars won at Le Mans in 1951, 1953, 1955, 1956 and 1957. Even the first model of Mini could manage 70 mph, and a sports model, the Mini Cooper (developed by John Cooper, who built Formula One racing cars), had a top speed of 83 mph. Its S variant won at Monte Carlo in 1964, 1965 and 1967.* Racing drivers such as Stirling Moss and Mike Hawthorn were national heroes, especially Moss, who, as a champion of British cars, declared that it was 'better to lose honourably in a British car than win in a foreign one'.

While Britain's car commuters might have dreamed of speed when they took up the practice, their ever-increasing numbers meant that they had to travel ever more slowly into work. In 1935 the Road Traffic Census Report recorded that the average number of 'mechanically propelled' vehicles at 467 different measuring points in Britain was 11 per hour, but by 1954 the figure had risen to 159 per hour. The roads themselves, meanwhile, had seen little improvement since the arterial roads programme of

---

* Mini Coopers took first, second and third places in the 1966 rally, but were disqualified in a controversial decision by a French judge.

the 1920s and 1930s. Although both Conservative and Labour governments had appointed commissions and debated legislation for new infrastructure in the intervening decades, there was little progress until 1956, when the powers granted under the Special Roads Act of 1949 were evoked to start work on motorways. The first to be completed was the Preston Bypass, later to become part of the M6. It was followed by the M1, whose initial stretch between Watford and Rugby was opened in November 1959 to feverish excitement in the media, stoked by bombastic government press releases claiming that 'the size of the road itself so far transcends the accustomed scale as to dwarf nature itself'. Journalists celebrated its opening with high-speed runs – the *News Chronicle*'s reporter managing 157 mph in an Aston Martin DB4, while 'the *Daily Herald*'s man clocked up 130 mph in an Austin-Healey'.

Although it was eulogized in the press, the M1 did little to ease the congestion faced by the average commuter on his or her daily journey to work. In London, plans formulated in 1944 to augment and improve the capital's orbital roads – so that rush hours weren't clogged by goods lorries en route from, say, Ipswich to Chichester, and commuters might have a route that resembled the Circle Line on the Tube and performed the same function – gathered dust for twenty years. It was as if car commuters were the elephant in the room.

Their existence was acknowledged and provided for after the publication of Professor Sir Colin Buchanan's *Traffic in Towns* report in 1963. The report had been commissioned by Ernest Marples, minister of transport between 1959 and 1964, the *éminence grise* behind the railway cuts, who had both employed Dr Beeching and handed him his axe. Marples, who resembled a second-hand car dealer, had made a fortune from property development and civil engineering, and stood to gain more from new roads than old railways. *Traffic in Towns* supported him. 'For the first time, the fact of unrestrained growth in car ownership was factored into town planning and urban design.'

Traffic in Towns predicted an apocalypse if Britain failed to adapt to the reality of car commuting: 'Unless steps are taken, the motor vehicle will defeat its own utility and bring about a disastrous degradation of the surroundings for living'. Both drivers and city-centre pedestrians would suffer as a result of congestion, and the aspirations of the entire population, of whom it was expected that they would take car ownership 'as much for granted as an overcoat', would be frustrated. The answer, in Professor Buchanan's opinion, was to create ring roads around cities, and car-free zones within them: 'Distasteful though we find the whole idea, we think that some deliberate limitation of the volume of motor traffic is quite unavoidable.' He had visited California and Texas as part of his research, and concluded that: 'The American policy of providing motorways for commuters can succeed, even in American conditions, only if there is a disregard for all considerations other than the free flow of traffic which seems sometimes to be almost ruthless. Our British cities are not only packed with buildings, they are also packed with history, and to drive motorways through them on the American scale would inevitably destroy much that ought to be preserved.' Rather than flattening city centres (as Ford had advocated in *The Freedom of the American Road*), they might be pedestrianized and served by orbital highways and park and ride schemes.

The plans made by Bressey and Lutyens for the North and South Circulars were dusted off, as was Sir Patrick Abercrombie's *Greater London Plan 1944*, which had proposed a total of five orbital roads, and combined with the findings of the 1964 and 1966 London Traffic Surveys, which had projected how travel patterns would develop by 1971 and 1981, to produce a total of ten new plans for London ringways. These were whittled down and work started on ringway 3 – the 'M16 motorway' – to the north, and ringway 4 to the south in 1973. The decision to combine them into a single circle around London, to be designated the M25, was taken by the Labour environment minister Anthony Crosland in 1974. In his opinion, roads were good for social mobility and the 'middle classes should not "pull up the ladder" of car ownership behind them'. It was a further twelve years before the M25 was opened by the then prime minister, Margaret Thatcher, who labelled it 'a great engineering achievement'. House prices soared in the towns around its perimeter as they all became commutable. The road itself, meanwhile, soon became a byword for congestion.

◆ ◆ ◆ ◆ ◆

CHAPTER VII

Two Wheels Good

In waking a tiger, use a long stick.

Mao Zedong

In Western Europe, as in Britain, a general trend towards driving – at the expense of other types of transport – prevailed after the Second World War, although it advanced at different rates from country to country. In Italy, whose infrastructure had been devastated by the war, bicycles were the principal form of commuter transport until the roads and railways were rebuilt with aid under the US Marshall Plan.* Their importance to workers is poignantly demonstrated in the film *Ladri di biciclette* (*Bicycle Thieves*, 1948), in which Antonio, the father of a young family and a man desperate for work, lets his wife pawn the bedsheets in order to redeem his bicycle from the pawnbrokers so he can take up a new job as a bill-poster. When the bike is stolen, his quest to recover it is a moral journey through changing times as much as an odyssey around Rome. Buses as well as bicycles feature in the film – appearing in the traffic like whales in a school of fish.

Bicycle Thieves became history as well as fiction within a few years of its release, as Rome's commuters switched from

---

* Officially the European Recovery Program, the Marshall Plan, named after US Secretary of State George C. Marshall, provided economic support to rebuild Europe.

pedal power to motor scooters. These had been introduced to the city's streets by Enrico Piaggio in 1946. Piaggio foresaw the demand for low-cost personal transport in the aftermath of the Second World War, and together with the aeronautical engineer Corradino D'Ascanio came up with a design (in the words of his patent application) for 'a motor cycle with a rational complex of organs and elements with body combined with the mudguards and bonnet covering all the mechanical parts'. His first production model, the Vespa, or wasp,* was received with curiosity when it was unveiled at the Rome Golf Club, but it performed well in road tests, and by 1948 Piaggio was producing 20,000 Vespas per annum. Vespas were ideal for urban commuting as their fairings offered riders some protection against the elements, and from dirt and oil from the engine itself. Their first market was among white-collar workers, to whom they offered salvation from the exertion of riding a bike, or the uncertainties of travelling on the buses. Annual sales soared to 60,000 in 1950 and 171,000 in 1953, and by 1956 there were a million Vespas on the roads worldwide. They were produced in Germany from 1950 onwards, and in several other European countries thereafter under licence, including Britain, where *The Times* declared that the Vespa was 'a completely Italian product, such as we have not seen since the Roman chariot'. In America, meanwhile, they became as Roman as the Colosseum after the release in 1953 of *Roman Holiday*, in which Gregory Peck and Audrey Hepburn fall in love astride a Piaggio Vespa 125. Although the movie is reckoned to have

---

* Named after its narrow waist rather than the buzz from its engine.

boosted sales of the scooter by 100,000, most were bought as tools rather than toys. Mobility equalled opportunity, and owning a Vespa might mean the difference between a good job and none at all. As had been the case with bicycles, Italians saved, borrowed and pawned in order to buy a scooter. Vespa's success inspired imitation, and by 1952 Lambretta, based in Milan, was selling as many scooters as its Roman rival.

Italy's economy, meanwhile, was growing at a stellar rate – GDP doubled between 1950 and 1960. Motorcars, albeit small ones, became affordable, and their manufacturers focused on building vehicles for the commuter market. The Fiat 500, which was even more diminutive than the British Mini, and which also progressed from workhorse to cultural icon, typified the average Italian worker's car of the late 1950s. Like the Mini it could be 'parked like a pram' and was ideal for navigating the narrow roads in the older quarters of Italian towns. Half a million had been produced by 1956. Thereafter, notwithstanding a renaissance in the Italian railways, cars became the preferred form of transport to and from work, replacing bicycles, scooters and buses. By 1975, 66 per cent of Italy's households had cars and the figure was even higher in the 'industrial triangle' between the northern cities of Turin, Milan and Genoa.

Car commuting developed even more quickly in Germany after the Second World War. It was fed at first with imported Italian vehicles and designs. In 1954 BMW* bought the rights to manufacture the Iso Isetta, a bubble car smaller still than the Fiat

---

* The company had built motorcycles for the Wehrmacht and aeroplane engines for high-speed bombers during the war.

500. By the end of the 1950s, Germany had surged ahead of Italy. Nazi plans to build a network of autobahns and mass-produce cars 'for the purpose of improving German trade and making Germany a great motoring country' were resurrected. Existing roads were repaired, those left unfinished in 1943 were completed, and new routes were added. The car-manufacturing industry, meanwhile, progressed from building copies of diminutive Italian vehicles to full-sized cars. Whereas the British manufacturers Morris had turned down the chance to buy the war-damaged Volkswagen works for a song in 1945, by 1950 the 'ill-repaired bomb site manned by semi-starved workers' had become a multi-million-square-foot facility with an annual output of nearly 100,000 vehicles, more than double that of Morris's best-selling car.

There was pull as well as push: Frankfurt, for instance, was rebuilt after the Second World War with the aim of being as car-friendly as possible. Autobahns led all the way into its centre, and space was cleared for multi-storey car parks. Segments of the old tram system were rooted up to help Frankfurt's planners realize their ambition of creating a 'rail-free inner city'. They were supported by the might of the German motor industry, and – before the Greens gained a voice in German politics – the freedom to car-commute and drive one's Mercedes or Volkswagen at high speed right into the heart of a metropolis became cherished throughout the nation.

In contrast to the West, where commuting was considered to be vital to progress and encouraged in all its forms, communist countries viewed the practice with suspicion and did little to facilitate it, either before the Second World War, or in subsequent decades. In the Soviet Union very few people ever got to travel in a car, let alone own one, after the Iron Curtain had descended. Indeed, the prospect for automobility had been sunnier in the early years of communist rule. The Bolsheviks thought motorcars should be a part of any socialist republic worthy of the name. They sent delegates to America to investigate its love affair with cars, and also asked them to check the state of its roads. This was because they were stuck on the horns of a dilemma: what should come first – the motorcar or the road? According to a pre-Soviet proverb, 'in Russia there are no roads, only directions'. Could automobility flourish in such an environment? Valerian Osinskii, an eminent Bolshevik who had travelled the length and breadth of America, thought so, and in a 1927 series in *Pravda* entitled 'The American Automobile or the Russian Cart?' argued that the Soviet state should imitate America, and both mass-produce cars *and* build a new road network. America was awash with motorcars, yet many of its highways would have challenged a Russian cart. In Alabama, according to Osinskii, 'the picture was absolutely Russian and even Russian squared, worse than in remote parts of Tambov province', yet all the farmers, and even some of their wives, had cars.

In the event, much of the responsibility for improving the roads was devolved to compulsory labour at the local level, and the issue of car ownership was addressed with propaganda and a factory-building programme. The Avtodor Society, a government sock-puppet set up to advance automobility, managed the publicity. It supervised driving lessons, ran lotteries with cars as prizes, and organized 'agitational' rallies – so called because they aimed to excite the hearts of every comrade with a love for motorcars. Peasants were given demonstration rides, villagers were shown propaganda films (though viewings were often cancelled because of the state of the roads), and in 1928 Avtodor launched its own journal – *Za rulem* ('Behind the Wheel'). Its first issue focused on how far Russia had fallen behind capitalist countries in the manufacture of cars: whereas the UK had around a million passenger vehicles at the time and America 22 million, the USSR had a mere 20,000. Mother Russia and her satellites were also lagging behind in the road stakes: America had 450 kilometres of roads for every 10,000 people, against their 1.7 kilometres. The workers deserved better.

The deficit in vehicles was addressed by setting up a joint venture with the Ford Motor Company. Many Marxist theoreticians were open admirers of Henry Ford's methods, which they called 'Fordizatsiia' or 'Fordizm' and interpreted as being the art of streamlining production in order to provide workers with fulfilling labour and plenty of leisure. In 1929, the USSR struck an agreement with Ford to supply it with know-how and help it to build a mammoth factory just outside Nizhny Novgorod, an industrial city east of Moscow on the banks of the River Volga, which was to be the communist Detroit. The Nizhegorodsky Avtomobilny Zavod (NAZ) factory started production in January 1932, building Ford Model As rebadged as NAZ-As. According to one of the Americans who worked on site, there were no such things as formal roads in 'Detroit by the Volga' when they started work on the project. The first to be built, coincidentally the 'first concrete road in the USSR located outside a city', was attached to the end of the factory's production line. The Constructivist poet Boris Agapov celebrated its texture and potency: 'it is smooth like the enamel of an automobile and straight like the ray of a searchlight. One hundred and forty thousand machines are moving along it, four in a row.' In the case of the machines, this was poetic licence: the factory only managed 100,000 vehicles in its first five years. In Fordian terms it was still in the 1910s.

Ford also helped the Soviets erect the KIM plant in Moscow, whose initials stood for 'Factory named after Communist Youth International'. Like NAZ, KIM started by building rebadged Model As. In 1940, it introduced its own design of car – the KIM 10-50 – modelled on the British Ford Prefect, but only 500 were completed before the Soviets joined the Second World War, by which time very little had been achieved in the name of automobility, or indeed auto-commuting, in the USSR. It didn't have the cars, it didn't have the roads, and it also lacked the commuters. Marx hadn't dedicated much thought to them, and they tended to be overlooked by his disciples too, who were obsessed with nineteenth-century theoretical models, which took insufficient account of the value of mobility of labour.

In the post-war period, production of passenger cars restarted in Russia. The NAZ (now GAZ) factory's new flagship model was the GAZ-M20 'Pobeda' (Victory), a four-door sedan with an underwhelming performance: its 50 h.p. engine gave it a top speed of just 65 mph. When a prototype was shown to Stalin, he was unimpressed. 'That is definitely not our best victory,' he said, and his criticism was borne out by events. The first two years of production had to be recalled to the factory because of faulty front axles. The M20 was followed by the Volga or GAZ-21, which was to become something of an icon in the USSR. While not particularly fast, it worked well in the cold and on bad roads, and would have made a fine commuter vehicle, were it not for its scarcity and price. Although, in theory, every comrade over the age of eighteen was entitled to order a new car, a Volga cost six times the average worker's annual salary, and there was a waiting list of eight to ten years. Indeed, the only types of people likely to be able to drive to work in Russia in the 1950s and 1960s were members of the elite – artists with international reputations, Olympic champions, military and party officials and Stakhanovites* who could jump the queues and get a car straight away.

Second-hand cars were equally hard to come by for the average worker. Once people had a Volga, they were reluctant to sell them and they also had to go through official centres to do so, where 'a commission of specialists evaluated the car and set a price'. People who wanted to purchase a used vehicle then registered with the centre, whose cadres chose the lucky individual who would be allowed to buy. As was the case with new cars, certain classes of people were given preference, which in effect closed the market to the majority. In reality, the likeliest way for the average worker to get his hands on a vehicle was by winning one in the lottery, which offered cars as well as cash as prizes.

---

* Named after Aleksei Grigorievich Stakhanov, a coal miner who mined 227 tons in a six-hour shift. He was honoured with the title of Hero of Socialist Labour for this feat, and held up as a model to Soviet workers.

Those few comrades fortunate enough to own a car, and who wanted to commute in it, faced additional challenges. Petrol stations were few and far between, and rather than proclaiming their presence with flamboyant architecture like their American counterparts in order to draw customers, they turned away more people than they served as they often had no fuel to sell. In 1963, when Moscow had 70,000 cars, or about the same number as New York in 1913, it had only eight official service stations, not all of which were in service at any one time. One could cover a greater distance finding petrol to get to work than on the commute itself. Pilfering was another problem faced by car owners. Spare parts were rare, and the temptation to take what one could not buy was great. Commuters had to remove their cars' windscreen wipers and take them into work if they wanted to be sure that they would still be there when it was time to go home. The climate was also against them: streets beyond the roads used by public transport were blocked by snow and ice for several months each winter, rendering commuting seasonal at best, and, between December and March, its practitioners had to find somewhere to park where they could raise their cars on blocks and take their wheels home for safekeeping.

The consequence of all these impediments to commuting was that Soviet traffic jams were so rare that tourist guides would 'point them out as a source of pride', especially if they occurred on cloverleaf interchanges, which were also few and far between in the workers' paradise. Although Moscow got its first ring road in 1960, it was still almost empty ten years later. Photographs show the odd cavalcade of officials, or a regiment in its trucks, but little in the way of private vehicles. In 1970 only one Soviet household in fifty owned a car, which put the USSR on a par with the Ivory Coast in Equatorial Africa and the Cook Islands in the South Pacific.

Soviet commuters had better luck trying to get to work via public transport than on four wheels. The Soviets loved flagship projects, and the Moscow Metro was one of its first, intended to prove – with its broad platforms and palatial stations – that they could beat the capitalists hands down when it came to moving workers en masse. Opened in 1935, the star turn of Stalin's second five-year plan, the Metro was built by *Udarnik Metrostroia* ('Metro shock workers') who died in droves during its construction, and whose efforts were commemorated in the 'Songs of the Joyous Metro Conquerors' that were issued to schools across the nation upon its opening, and included such classics as 'The Tunnel is Ready'. Although the Moscow Metro was slower than the London Underground at the time and had less than seven miles of tracks, its concourses lived up to the propaganda. The ideologues behind it wanted the Metro to be 'a majestic school in the formation of the new man', and the average shock-working commuter was treated to vaulted platforms with marble floors, giant mirrors surmounted by gilded rococo plasterwork, and chandeliers that a tsar might have coveted for his ballroom.

The Moscow Metro expanded during and after the Second World War, and had fifty kilometres of track in place by 1952 and over a hundred, with seventy-two stations, by 1964. Metros were built in other Soviet cities – according to official policy, any metropolis with more than a million inhabitants qualified for one – albeit slowly. Construction started in Lenigrad in 1941, and the first line, a mere 9.4 kilometres long, opened in 1955. Kiev, meanwhile, took eleven years between 1949 and 1960 to build a 5.2-kilometre system. Trams, trolleybuses and railways augmented these subway systems. The first two were for short-hop journeys; the latter, in theory, enabled every citizen to expand his or her range to the horizon and beyond. The Soviet rail system was growing while its counterparts in the West were contracting. In the 1960s, when the Beeching cuts removed several thousand miles of track from service in Britain, the USSR added nearly 500 kilometres every year. However, these were mostly for moving freight rather than people. Indeed, the freedom of movement that commuting implied was discouraged by the Soviets. Factories were built in wildernesses and tower-block suburbs were built around them, with dedicated transit systems to carry workers between the two. The usual symbiosis between commuting and home ownership was also denied: there were no speculative developments en route or beyond – no Surbitons or Levittowns. Why, in the perfect republic, should anyone want to live any-where other than where the state decreed?

Although the Soviets lagged behind the West in the practice of commuting, they were ahead of their time in its theory. Soviet transport planners decided that the comrades needed space to breathe on public transport and mandated that they received at least a seventh of a square metre each. They also investigated how long the average worker might spend commuting, before his or her shock-power diminished. They decided that as 'a fundamental norm' the desirable time for trips to work should not exceed 30–40 minutes for medium-sized cities, or an hour for larger ones. Beyond these limits productivity seemed to fall by 2.5 to 3 per cent for each extra ten minutes spent in transit.

Official disapproval and the general absence of facilities notwithstanding, commuting crept into the Soviet Union in the last decade of its 'great stagnation' (1964–85). The Stakhanovites of freedom of movement appeared in the main in small cities. They were categorized as 'young, low-skilled workers, occupying positions requiring low qualifications and yielding low wages', and served as cannon fodder during the USSR's last, futile attempt to win the Cold War through communist economics. Their mobility was permitted by the state because it was cheaper than having to build new tower blocks in the cities, and 'substituting migration with commuting' became official policy. It was also a partial solution to food shortages. As the Soviet system juddered to a halt and these became rampant, picking turnips made more sense than making cars slowly and badly in a state-owned factory for a culture that had been denied them. By the early 1980s, agricultural collectives offered higher salaries to manual workers than did car factories, and Soviet commuting took on a style of its own – a type of reverse commuting – where workers lived in the cities and laboured in the countryside. The descendants of the peasants who had been lured into the cities by the promises of socialism ended up moonlighting in the fields. Not for long: when the USSR shattered into its constituent republics in 1991, and market economics were introduced to some of them, commuting came riding in triumphant. By 1995, Stalin's ring road was choked with armoured Mercedes limousines and other luxury vehicles carrying converts to capitalism to their offices and meetings.

Communists everywhere seem to have been prejudiced against commuting in particular and freedom of movement in general. Both were anathema in the People's Republic of China in the era of Mao Zedong, and in so far as commuting was permitted at all it was restricted to movement on two wheels. China's first five-year plan (1953–57) focused on bicycle factories rather than a grandiose pocket-metro system. Imperialist tramways were removed from the streets of Beijing to make way for pedal power.

Although China had started to plan a metro system for Beijing in 1953, the project was shelved during the Great Leap Forward (1958–61) when ideology ruled economic practice, and there was neither the desire nor the resources to build an underground railway. In the event, construction didn't start until 1965, and when the first twenty-one kilometre stretch opened on 1 October 1969, a twentieth-birthday gift* to the people from the party, most people weren't allowed to use it. They had to show their IDs and submit themselves to questioning before they were allowed to buy a ticket – a state of affairs that persisted until 1981. Progress in private transport was equally feeble: China didn't get its first home-made passenger car until 1958. This was the Hongqi, or Red Flag, a sedan model based on a '55 Chrysler, with a V8 engine, wrap-around windscreen and chromed bumper intended to represent a Chinese fan, such as a courtesan might have held

---

* The People's Republic of China came into being on 1 October 1949.

over her mouth while she dallied with a mandarin. It was built to carry party officials and visiting dignitaries, and most Chinese never got to see one.

In consequence, the only way to get to work that the average Chinese could imagine, apart from walking, was by bicycle. Comrades needed permits to buy or ride a bike, and became model communists in order to win them. The bicycle they all wanted, which cost two months' salary and had a three-year waiting list, was the Flying Pigeon, a single-gear, sit-up-and-beg affair with giant wheels and primitive brakes,* and which, like the Model T Ford, came only in black. At least 500 million Flying Pigeons have been built since the brand was born in 1950, making it the most popular wheeled vehicle in history. It is one of the few artefacts of the Cultural Revolution that evokes nostalgia in China. When Deng Xiaoping became 'Paramount Leader' in 1978, he defined prosperity as 'a pigeon in every household'. Brides-to-be took him at his word, and often refused to accept their suitors until they could afford a Pigeon.

When China started to admit Western tourists in the early 1980s, rush hour in Beijing (which then consisted of several million Flying Pigeons and only a handful of vehicles equipped with combustion engines) was accounted one of its wonders. Fleets of cyclists ghosted over intersections a hundred or so abreast in the morning mist, tinkling their bells. Most wore identical trouser suits – grey men on black bikes – and their apparent sameness contributed to the strangeness of the vision.

---

* The Flying Pigeon was modelled on a Raleigh design from 1932.

It was hard for an outsider to understand the individual sacrifices and the massed pride in ownership that such a sight represented.

Deng's vision for China stretched beyond a Flying Pigeon in every household, however. Starting in 1978, a series of reforms were introduced that allowed a ray of capitalism to shine on the economy. Agriculture was de-collectivized and entrepreneurs were permitted to start businesses. The reforms were extended during the 1980s and 1990s, and growth rocketed. Commuting was encouraged: the general public were allowed to use the Beijing Metro, and in 1982 it carried 72.5 million passengers. A new line was added, and within six years annual ridership had risen to 300 million. By 2012, it had seventeen lines, 456 kilometres of track and carried nearly 2.5 billion passengers per annum. Similar rates of growth occurred on other transit systems as China switched from collectivization to commuting. The country now has four of the top ten busiest metro systems in the world, and nearly 100 million Chinese get to work by rail each day.

Progress in private transport was also rapid. In the 1980s brides-to-be raised the bar and demanded that their suitors had motorbikes rather than pedal power. The vehicle they all wanted was the Honda C100, which was to become as iconic a commuter vehicle as the Flying Pigeon. The C100, also known as the Super Cub, had been developed in Japan in 1958 with two specific target markets in mind: commuters and couriers. While Japan's railway system at the time was second to none, its roads, beyond the major arterial routes, were medieval. A motorbike built for Japanese conditions needed larger tyres than European scooters, and had to be easy to use, fuel and maintain. Equally importantly, it should be capable of operation one-handed, in order that it might replace bicycles in its second target market. Bicycle couriers employed by Soba* restaurants in Japanese cities to deliver their noodles to offices had to carry lunchboxes in one hand while steering with the other. The Super Cub met these criteria through innovative engineering and a friendly design. The bike's automatic centrifugal clutch meant that it could be operated with the left hand alone, and its 19" wheels were big enough to cope with suburban potholes. It had a step-through profile, so that women could board it without having to hitch up their skirts (or soba waiters without having to put down their trays) and it was the first motorcycle to boast a plastic fairing. Target sales were 30,000 per month at a time when total Japanese motorcycle sales were 40,000 each month. The market was there, as public transport was choking on the commuters who were busy rebuilding Japan, and the only affordable way to get on the highway was on two wheels. The production target was exceeded in year two. The C100 in various variants has gone on to become the world's best-selling powered vehicle (73 million to date) and, as Honda boasts on its website, 'the standard in commuter models'. It is also a contemporary design icon – both the British Museum and the Guggenheim have an example in their collections.

LINE SP

The C100 lifted millions of Japanese, and tens of millions of other Asians, onto the first rung of automobility. Many have stayed there, for commuting by motorbike is the norm in much of

---

* Soba noodles, a type of thin noodle made from buckwheat flour, are a popular fast food in Japan.

Asia. Thailand, for example, has ten times as many motorbikes as cars, and Thais venerate them in much the same manner as Americans loved their motorcars in the 1950s. Teenagers race their customized Hondas the wrong way down freeways late at night, lying flat on the saddles with their legs stretched out behind them, and bikes are celebrated in Thai pop songs as symbols of liberation. The *Mor lam sing* genre, for instance, an amplified version of traditional Isan music from the north of Thailand that features bamboo mouth organs and electric guitars, derives its name from its association with motorbikes: *sing* is abbreviated from the English word 'racing'. Many of its songs revolve around the themes of leaving the village, moving to the city, finding love and buying a motorcycle.

However, even with such nimble vehicles, commuting times in Bangkok are among the longest in the world. In sufficient numbers, bikes and tuk-tuks (motor-tricycles with a bench seat under a metal awning over the rear axle) will gridlock just like cars. And in this South Asian city, not far north of the Equator, motorbikes are a challenging as well as uncomfortable way to commute. In the tropics, where the length of daylight varies less than in northern latitudes, hard-working travellers who start for work before dawn are likely to find themselves riding home in the dark also. Their trips to and from work take them through a smog of exhaust fumes, and during the rainy season they are blitzed by Thailand's monsoon downpours. In consequence, bikes are now seen as stepping stones in Thailand, and as soon as commuters can afford a car they buy one, with air conditioning and tinted windows. Indeed, Thai government surveys show a clear divide in commuting patterns between rich and poor. To get to work, those at the bottom of the ladder sweat it out on public transport or on foot for an hour or more each way; those halfway up zap around on two wheels and in tuk-tuks, and travel greater distances in similar times; while the affluent, especially those with university educations, drive or are driven in their own cars and cover the most miles as they retreat into villas in the suburbs after working during the day in the centre of Bangkok.

A similar pattern is apparent in India, where there are even more variables at play in commuting. The rules of the road are governed by religion and custom as much as the desire to help traffic flow in safety. Sacred cows take precedence at intersections; certain castes should not share the same stretches of pavement. Moreover, there are forty-eight types of transport on the roads during rush hours, ranging from camels and elephants through rickshaws to 4x4s. Just like the Thais, Indian commuters also aspire to escape from the chaos to the sanctuary of an motorcar. This widespread longing, and the rapid increase in wealth, have choked the streets of Indian cities. Car parks are few and far between: Mumbai is projected to need 3,750 kilometres of road just for parking by 2015 and has only 2,045 kilometres of roads at present. The competition for places is intense, and can even lead to bloodshed. In Ahmedabad in July 2010 a commuter named Himmat Pargi was beaten to death with iron rods by his neighbours, after stealing one of their parking spaces.

The pattern established in India, and indeed Italy before it, suggests that commuting in democratic countries follows a natural progression from two wheels and/or public transport to motorcars, and that commuters will trade up to them as their wealth increases. However, in developed countries where the process is complete a counter-trend is emerging, and commuters are regressing from V8s to pedal power. In flat or small European cities such as Amsterdam and Copenhagen, a full third of commuters now cycle to work and scorn motorized transport as being the product of a less enlightened era. The current head of transport in Frankfurt, once the epitome of a car-friendly city, with a series of autobahns built in the 1950s running right into its heart, is a Green who cycles everywhere and is determined to convert some of its internal motorways to cycle tracks.

In Britain, cycling to work is the fastest-growing form of commuting. Its practitioners now fight for the cycle lanes that they so furiously opposed in the 1930s. These first appeared in Britain in Milton Keynes, which introduced Redways – red tarmac cycle paths – in 1970 as part of its master plan for development. They have since spread, albeit slowly. After decades of lobbying, cycle lanes were included in Transport for London's (TfL) planning, and in 2008 the then mayor Ken Livingstone introduced a £400 million initiative to create twelve new cycling superhighways, four of which are currently in operation, as well as bike racks at major railway stations. Two-wheeled commuting has boomed since: the number of journeys by bike in London rose by 150 per cent between 2000 and 2011. When TfL measured traffic flow over central London's eight principal bridges during rush hour, it found that 'bicycles made up 27.7 per cent of the almost 35,000 vehicles crossing northbound between 7 a.m.

and 10 a.m. compared with 28.2 per cent for private cars'. In 2006, in contrast, 'with similar overall levels of traffic, bikes were just 19 per cent of the total'. Their number has since been supplemented by the so-called 'Boris bikes', which are publicly owned bicycles available for short-term private hire and named after Livingstone's Conservative successor as mayor, Boris Johnson. In 2013, the Boris bike scheme owned 8,000 cycles that could be picked up or dropped off at 570 docking stations, and registered up to a million rides a month.

Cycle commuting has also been encouraged at the national level. The 'cycle2work' scheme, introduced in 1999, enables cyclists to reclaim tax on money spent on a new machine and any related safety equipment. Dedicated routes and tax breaks have encouraged a number of longer-distance commuters to include cycling as part of a multi-legged journey into work. Many cycle from home to a railway station, or from the station to their offices, rather than driving or using public transport. Brompton bikes, which can be folded up and carried on a train, or stored beside one's desk at work, are now the largest bike manufacturer in Britain.

As well as being the fastest growing class of commuters, cyclists are the most positive about commuting. They see themselves as empowered, as taking control over the dead time spent getting to and from the daily grind. Unlike most other commuters, they celebrate the practice in web forums, and some even boast of adding extra miles to their route just for the fun of it, or of moving further away from the office to get a longer ride. Surveys of their motivations for cycling reveal why they enjoy their commutes. The exercise floods them with endorphins, as does the pleasure of engaging with their surroundings. For many, the excitement is enhanced by a sense of righteousness: 81 per cent cycle because they think it is good for the environment. *mapmyride*, the favourite commuter cyclist app, allows its users to calculate distance travelled, calories burned, money saved in petrol and parking, and the micrograms of CO_2 emissions they've offset while pedalling to and fro. Indeed, such are the potential benefits of commuting on two wheels that it's been taken up by people who don't need to commute. David Barter, author of *Obsessive Compulsive Cycling Disorder*, which celebrates 'the madness that engulfs those who descend into cycling obsession', decided to become a virtual commuter when Rob, his training companion, started cycling to his work eighteen miles away. The idea that Rob might get to cover an extra thirty-six miles each day made Barter so jealous that, even though he worked from home, he decided to ride out and meet Rob at his house, then cycle back into town with him. He found the experience compelling. When he returned after his virtual commute, peeled off various layers of Lycra and sat down to work, he confessed to feeling 'the fatigue of the sanctimonious. I was tired, but I'd earned the right to be tired, and that sort of tired felt good. I was ready for the day ahead. If you understand that, then you probably cycle-commute already.'

◆ ◆ ◆ ◆ ◆

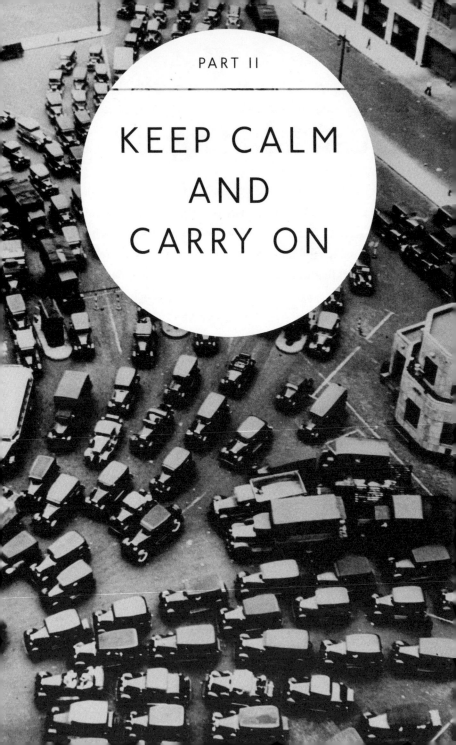

PART II

KEEP CALM
AND
CARRY ON

CHAPTER VIII

Crush Loading

...travellers routinely find themselves subjected to levels of overcrowding that are not simply uncomfortable, but positively frightening... people expect their journeys to be difficult and unpleasant.

House of Commons Transport Committee,
Overcrowding on Public Transport, 2003

The conversion of commuting into a leisure activity by cyclists marks, perhaps, its zenith: from a pursuit practised by a fortunate few it had grown to become a near universal part of many people's working day, in both developed and developing countries. Indeed, for most of the twentieth century, commuting served as a barometer of both freedom of movement and economic progress. In places where it had been restricted, such as the USSR, it triumphed with the downfall of the system that had opposed it. It had, moreover, been assimilated into a host of different cultures, often displacing customs that expected people to remain in their traditional stations. Above all it was aspirational: commuting gave people the freedom to live where they wanted, to work where they wanted, and to change their lives for the better.

However, it had also become a victim of its own success, associated with overcrowding on public transport and congestion on the roads. Commuters have had to learn to tolerate each other en masse, in perhaps unnatural proximity. In the UK, for example, rail commuters are allocated a theoretical 0.45 metres of space each, which they rarely receive during rush hour, and which is substantially less than the minimum that European law mandates for the humane transportation of farm animals. The temperature in the carriages, moreover, can exceed 30 degrees centigrade in summer, which is above the legal maximum for livestock. From a global perspective, however, UK commuters on public transport are relatively loosely packed. Their counterparts in places like Japan and India are crammed together in far higher densities during rush hour. 'Crush loading', the technical term for such overcrowding, is one of the mysteries of commuting. It's perhaps the greatest challenge that commuters have to face each working day. How do we tolerate, indeed voluntarily submit to, being stuffed into spaces deemed unfit for pigs? Does it force us to change our behaviour, and if so how?

The first research into the effects of overcrowding on behaviour was carried out on zoo animals, which were expensive to buy, but lucrative to display. It seemed there was no use stuffing as many as possible into one cage as they grew moody or defensive, and shed their fur or pecked off each other's plumage. The notion that this might be because they were programmed genetically to compete for territory occurred to Heini Hediger, a Swiss biologist, who advocated in 1942 that instead of treating zoo animals as captives, they should be thought of as the owners of their cages, and if given the right space, and just enough of it, they would preen happily all day long. In his opinion overcrowding had a negative effect on the behaviour of captive animals, and should be avoided at all costs.

The anthropologist Edward T. Hall extended Hediger's work to humans in 1963. Hall thought that our perception of territory was different from that of most other creatures because we relied on our senses of sound and vision rather than our sense of smell. This dependence had arisen because our ancestors had been forced to take to the trees at some point in our evolution, and, 'arboreal life calls for keen vision and decreases dependence on smell, which is crucial for terrestrial organisms. Thus man's sense of smell ceased to develop and his powers of sight were greatly enhanced.' Crucially 'the loss of olfaction... may have endowed man with greater capacity to withstand crowding'. Hall pointed out that if people lived by their noses like rats, such resilience might be impossible: 'they would be forever tied to the full array of emotional shifts occurring in persons around them. Other people's anger would be something we could smell... The psychotic would begin to drive all of us mad, and the anxious would make us even more anxious. To say the least, life would be much more involved and intense.'

Hall broke down our need for personal space into four categories: *intimate distance*, i.e. how close we allow our kin and lovers to be, which emphasizes contact rather than separation; *personal distance* – how close we stand to people at a drinks party before the drink takes over; *social distance*, which roughly corresponds to how close we like to get to strangers when doing business with them; and *public distance*, which politicians and pop stars and other performers enjoy when on stage, where they communicate with their audiences through gestures and postures. He labelled his new science *proxemics*. Proxemics seems obvious when explained on human scale – people we hug, people we shake hands with, but otherwise stay at least a few feet away from, and people absolutely out of reach like the players on a football field. Hall's various classes of personal space are even reflected in everyday speech. We talk about keeping others at arm's length, or not wishing to touch them with a barge pole.

If the theory of proxemics is valid, then how do we tolerate its violation, especially when we do so voluntarily when we commute? Tube travellers, for instance, know they run the risk of being squashed up against strangers while stuck in a tunnel that runs through the middle of a medieval plague pit until London Underground sorts out, say, a signal failure, yet nonetheless consent to the discomfort. The answer may lie in the so-called 'fight or flight' theory, first proposed by the American physiologist Walter Bradford Cannon in 1932, which explains that when faced by a source of danger people are hardwired either to run away from it or confront it. The theory has since been expanded to become the 'freeze, fight or flight' hypothesis. In some circumstances, instead of fleeing or fighting, staying still and trying to minimize one's physical presence may be the best response. Many other species of animal 'play dead' when threatened. Moreover, through isopraxism (mimicry), we sometimes all freeze together. Perhaps, therefore, commuters on a crowded train are, unbeknownst to themselves, paralyzed with fear, and this is why they avoid eye contact and stare instead at each other's feet.

The theory of objectification, however, offers a better explanation for our ability to tolerate overcrowding. It posits that we have evolved density-specific patterns of behaviour, and will treat other people as inanimate objects that don't require an emotional response when we get packed too closely together. The other person pressed against your front or back could be a chair for all you care. Although we might objectify our fellow travellers for most of our commutes, we don't shut them out entirely, and are ready to help if needs must, particularly in a crisis. Rather than turning into a panicked mob, where it's every man or woman for themselves, it seems that the presence of a common danger will unite us. According to psychologist Stephen Reicher, while 'the classic view of crowd psychology, which is still widespread, talks about the loss of selfhood, leaving people at best out of control and at worst generically violent... the "mad mob" is not an explanation, but a fantasy'. Reicher's research suggests that when rush hour is disturbed by disaster or emergency, such as a crash or a terrorist attack, the event 'far from dividing people into instinct-driven competitive individuals, can serve to create a powerful sense of unity and hence mutual support amongst survivors'. People begin to think in terms of 'we' rather than 'me' and the shift 'means a greater commitment and loyalty to the group, who are now seen more like "self" than as "other"'.

This phenomenon is called 'collective resilience' and was evident in the cooperation displayed by tube-goers caught in the London suicide bombings of 7 July 2005. In the aftermath of the blasts aboard three Underground trains and a bus, amidst the bodies and smoke, survivors said the tragedy had made them feel far more connected than usual, as the following transcript from an interview with one of them demonstrates:

> INTERVIEWER: *Can you say how much unity there*
> *was on a scale of one to ten?*
> SURVIVOR: *I'd say it was very high, I'd say it was seven or*
> *eight out of ten.*
> INTERVIEWER: *OK and comparing to before the blast*
> *happened, what do you think the unity was like before?*
> SURVIVOR: *I'd say very low – three out of ten, I mean you*
> *don't really think about unity in a normal train journey*
> *… you just want to get from A to B, get a seat maybe.*

When asked to elaborate, the survivor explained: 'I felt that we're all in the same boat together and… the feelings that I was feeling could well have been felt by them as well cos I don't think any normal human could just calmly sit there going oh yeah this is great… It was a stressful situation and we were all in it together and the best way to get out of it was to help each other.'

In the opinion of psychologist John Drury, who conducted research into the bombings, collective resilience is so strong that rather than expecting crowds to behave like headless chickens during an emergency, 'governments should treat them as the "fourth emergency service"'.

It seems, therefore, that a combination of objectification and collective resilience goes a long way towards explaining how commuters manage to get so close to each other without running amok. They tolerate overcrowding on a day-to-day basis by treating fellow travellers as if they were inanimate objects rather than strangers penetrating their personal space, and during exceptional circumstances by facing up together to a common threat.

There is, however, a final theory to consider, one that posits that we tolerate crush loading because we, or part of each of us, actually likes the compression and that we ride public transport during rush hour because it makes us happy. According to Paul Bloom, professor of psychology at Yale University, 'we used to think that the hard part of the question "How can I be happy?" had to do with nailing down the definition of *happy*. But it may have more to do with the definition of *I*. Many researchers now believe, to varying degrees, that each of us is a community of competing selves, with the happiness of one often causing the misery of another.' Perhaps we develop a commuting identity that prevails in between our personalities at home and at work, an identity that loves commuting? Maybe there is a part of us that is in the ascendant during transit and navigates us through the discomfort with ease, and possibly pleasure, before handing back the controls to the model worker or the perfect spouse? Perhaps because crush loading is a special experience that requires a suspension of existing mores and the adoption of unusual behaviour, the only way we can achieve these is by creating a distinct identity – a commuter avatar – to deal with it all.

There are cultural as well as biological explanations as to how we manage to put up with overcrowding. The British, for example, have been commuting for the past 170 years, long enough for it to become a part of the national identity. Matters such as not speaking until one is spoken to, giving up seats to ladies, or maintaining a stiff upper lip are therefore conditioned rather than reflexive. If this is true, then commuter behaviour ought to vary between cultures. Perhaps the desire to stare at one's footwear on a crowded train isn't universal, and different habits prevail depending on where one is travelling. Edward Hall, the father of proxemics, thought that people who speak different languages 'inhabit different sensory worlds', and that the concentric circles of trust around us swell or shrink according to our native tongues and where in the world we speak them.

This may be the case in Japan, which was a caste-ridden society run on medieval principles, and where, in the period immediately before commuting commenced in the second half of the nineteenth century, people were required to dress and act their parts on pain of death. Japan got its first passenger railway in 1872, four years after feudalism was swept away in the Meiji Restoration. The new regime aimed to move from the medieval to the modern in decades rather than the centuries it had taken in Europe, and, for most Japanese, the shock was great. Anyone and everyone's first steps onto mass transport represented a breach with tradition. Although change was encouraged, custom was still venerated, and commuting was on the fault line between what had been and what was on the way. New standards of behaviour had to be formulated to bridge the gap between the old-fashioned ceremonies that were performed when strangers met, and crush loading in Meiji Japan, for its budding railway system was packed from the start.

In order to accept change, the Japanese needed new idols to

stand for the future, figures that possessed enough of the past in their veins to make them credible. These appeared in the shape of *Sarariman* (salary man) and schoolgirl in the first decade of the twentieth century. This pair of stereotypes represented two very visible classes of traveller in rush hour – a new wave of white-collar workers dressed in Western clothes, and the daughters of the elite who commuted to school in their kimonos. The girls were pretty, the salarymen ambitious, and Japanese commuting developed an erotic side. The novelist Tayama Katai's *Shojobyo* ('The Girl Fetish'), a short story published in 1907 that features a thirty-something lecher and nubile schoolgirls, set a tone that has continued into the present millennium.

Tokyo now has the biggest, most modern and most efficient transit system in the world, carrying 14 million passengers on thirteen underground and ten overground lines every day. It's too complicated to show on a single map, and even partial representations generate puzzlement or panic in a visitor wanting to get from Ueno to Roppongi for the first time. It's more crowded than London's Underground during rush hour – *average* loadings are 200 per cent of capacity as against 150 per cent on the Tube at its worst – and it's still riddled with schoolgirl fetishists.

It's possible that 'super crush loading' (as the Tokyo variant of overcrowding on public transport is called) is responsible for the persistence of eroticism, rather than traditions invented during the Meiji Restoration to support modernization. Maybe one more turn of the screw turns us on, and people are prepared to put up with a little more overcrowding for the flushes and tumescence that it provokes. Tokyo commuters can certainly tolerate a great deal more compression than Londoners. Ever since the 1960s, Japanese train operators have employed *oshiyas* ('passenger arrangement staff'), or pushers, who literally squash commuters into carriages. YouTube clips of them at work are reminiscent of animal charity ads highlighting cruelty in transit, and if they showed the Japanese treating livestock the same way, people in the British shires would boycott Toyota and Sony. The *oshiyas* wear paramilitary uniforms in the company colours of their employers, peaked caps and white gloves. They start one to each door and work with a mixture of power and delicacy – one instant bending their backs to shove someone aboard, the next leaning down solicitously to tuck in a handbag or scarf. As the second for departure approaches, they work together. Any *oshiya* with a closed door rushes up to the next carriage and helps jam in its complement. It's all neatly choreographed, and when the train is ready for departure the head *oshiya* salutes its driver, mops his brow and signals that it's safe to pull away.

While such treatment would be unthinkable on the Tube, *oshiyas*' victims don't resist. They keep stony faces, and as far as is possible practise 'ventral denial', i.e. stand back-to-back. Even though, by Japanese standards, manners collapse during rush hour, cultural conditioning is too strong for commuters to feel able to face each other in such unnatural proximity. Those next to windows look outwards, even if this means that their faces are squashed against the glass. The photographer Michael Wolf has captured their expressions in *Tokyo Compression*, a series of portraits of super-crush-loaded commuters seen through the frames of train windows taken in 2010. These range from misery to despair, as if the trains were carrying the commuters to hell and it was beyond their power to save themselves. Indeed, the only glimpse of a smile in the book is on the face of a salaryman some distance from the door, who appears to be sizing up a girl pressed against the window in the adjacent frame.

The habit – or tradition – of salarymen ogling or even molesting young women, especially schoolgirls, has flourished since the 'The Girl Fetish' was published. It's an established subject for both literature and movies, and has its own pornographic sub-genre, *Norimono poruno*, which includes such works as the film *Molester Train* (1975). Its practitioners are known as *Chikan*. Many Chikan are surprisingly open about their perversions. Eminent men are said to belong to the *Chikan Tomo-No-Kai* – the Brotherhood of Molesters. Some of Tokyo's *Imekura* ('image club') brothels offer commuting or super-crush-loading themes, with sex workers dressed as schoolgirls and rooms decorated like carriages, 'where to the recorded roar of a commuter train, men can molest straphangers in school uniforms'. There are even sub-categories of perversion inside chikanery: for some, a spot of frottage, or acting out their fantasies at an image club, is not enough. In August 2012, for instance, Takeshi Furusawa was caught spraying mayonnaise over a seventeen-year-old schoolgirl on a commuter service, and confessed that he had done the same to at least a dozen others, sometimes with yakiniku sauce instead of mayonnaise, because he 'got a rush from dirtying their school uniforms'.

The common-or-garden Chikan, however, is a deviant salary-man who spends weeks inching towards his target across super-crush-loaded carriages, with a game plan that would seem intricate to a Go master. His every move is premeditated: left leg six inches to the left this week, right leg ditto next week, develop a stoop, and so on, and then, after taking a month to reach a victim, presses himself against her until the next stop. If the girl quivers in anger, fear or indignation so much the better, though it's just as likely she'll pretend not to notice – Chikans are so common that it's possible she's been groped on the train to school ever since she started as a junior. A 2001 survey of the girls at two private schools in Tokyo found that more than 70 per cent had been abused in transit; in 2005, a survey of young Japanese women in general recorded that a similar percentage had been fondled on 'trains, subways or at stations in Tokyo'. Riyo Yamamoto, for instance, a twenty-one-year-old college student, told *The Atlantic* magazine that she'd been molested during her commute more than twenty times since junior high school. Although she stamped on the feet of her assailants or punched them, she didn't report them: 'If I go to the police, it could get them fired and divorced and ruin their lives,' she explained. 'I feel sorry for them, even though they're disgusting and annoying.'

Tokyo transit operators have been fighting Chikans since they first appeared on their systems. Women-only trains, nick-named *hana densha* ('flower trains'), were introduced in 1912, and after fading away in the 1950s were reintroduced throughout Japan in 2000, specifically to combat sexual harassment. According to Shogo Nakatani, a spokesman for the Osaka Metro, 'we decided to have women-only cars to protect women from gropers,' and in his opinion the strategy has worked. Nakatani is supported by surveys that show women like them not only because they are

Chikan-free but also less crowded and malodorous.

The war against Chikans is being fought with propaganda as well as flower trains. The Tokyo Metro launched a manners crusade in 2008 with a poster campaign whose strapline 'do it somewhere else' aimed to remind travellers that they were in a public space while in transit. Although the posters, which featured cartoon caricatures of typical sorts of annoying traveller, didn't show explicit *Sarariman*-on-schoolgirl action, their message was that it was as wrong to lust as it was play music too loudly on your headphones, apply make up, pass out in a pool of your own vomit with your last empty bottle by your side, or practise your golf swing in a train carriage. In 2010, however, Tokyo Metro shifted its tone, and changed its slogan to 'please do it again'. Its new propaganda featured acts of altruism, such as a young man giving up a seat to someone holding a crutch, who looks both flabbergasted and suspicious, with the aim of indoctrinating commuters via positive rather than negative messages.

Finally, there are signs that chikanery is becoming stigmatized. Conscientious salarymen can buy fake hanging straps to hold aloft to prove their hands aren't wandering. Some also splash out on deodorizing underwear, lest they molest the noses of their fellow commuters and drive women out of mixed carriages. Developed by Professor Hiroki Ohge of Hiroshima University, the Inodore range of underwear incorporates nanoscopic particles of ceramics, whose pores and ions absorb and neutralize bad smells. Inodore boast that their pants cut 'old age smell' by 89 per cent, 'sweat, armpit, feet smell' by more than 95 per cent, and 'fart, faeces, urine smell' almost completely. Its website features testimonials from happy commuters: 'Seeing it advertised on TV I thought I'd give it a try. I tried farting [in a pair of the underwear] as an experiment and I was truly shocked! The deodorant effect is outstanding!'

However, male neurosis and countermeasures such as women-only carriages and Psy-Ops have not entirely succeeded in taming lust during rush hour in Japan. As a last resort, several railways have introduced animal station managers at automated stops, hoping that a daily shot of sentimentality might stabilize their customers. The trend began with Maron, a miniature Yorkshire terrier who was nominally responsible for Okunakayama Kogen station. Maron was dressed for duty in a navy blazer with gold piping, a peaked cap, and wore his armband of office around his left forepaw. He not only cheered commuters up, but increased traffic to his fiefdom. His example has been followed elsewhere with various other creatures, including monkeys, penguins, a tortoise, and lobsters, all in uniform, except the lobsters, which are really crayfish, and have corporate ribbons around their tank. The most famous of Japan's animal stationmasters is Tama, a tortoiseshell tabby, who rules at Kishi and enjoys a cult following. She has a special train – the *Tama Densha*, decorated with whiskers and kitty graphics – named after her, and Tama cuddly toys, fridge magnets and commemorative stamps are sold in the Kishi gift shop.

The Japanese associate rush hour with death in addition to progress, crush loading and sex. The ancient and venerable tradition of *jisatsu*, or suicide, has been kept alive with the help of trains and their operators' obsession with punctuality. About 800 people kill themselves each year on Tokyo's transport systems. They are referred to as *jishin jiko* ('human accidents') and irritate the railway companies, who resent the delays they entail, which they consider a far greater blemish on their reputations than running instruments of death. Train drivers think the same way and some will crash their trains rather than dishonouring themselves by arriving late: in 2005, for example, a driver trying to make up ninety lost seconds on the West Japan Line went so fast that his train derailed, killing him and 107 passengers, and injuring a further 540.

Casualties in Japan, whether caused by suicides or obsessively punctual drivers, are light in contrast to India, where fatalism rules rush hour. In Mumbai, there are ten deaths every day on the commuter lines of the Mumbai Suburban Railway. The Mumbai Suburban began life under the British Raj as the Great Indian Peninsula Railway, which opened in 1853 and was the first train system in Asia. It grew at the same pace as the city it serves and now has the dubious distinction of operating the most overcrowded trains in the world. Its 'local' commuter services carry three times their rated load during rush hour, at theoretical densities of up to sixteen people per square metre, or nearly eight times the recommended maximum on British passenger trains. The compression is so extreme that even a Japanese salaryman who'd spent all his working years being shoved onto the Tokyo Metro by a man in white gloves would hesitate before boarding. It has acquired a technical name of its own – Super Dense Crush Loading.

The arrival of a super-dense-crush-loaded train at a Mumbai commuter station is an arresting spectacle. The crowd on the platform is a trembling mass of humanity dressed in brightly coloured clothing, As the train pulls in, even before it has come to a halt, people start leaping from the doors and onto the platform, sometimes colliding with similarly impatient passengers trying to board it. There are trips and slips amongst both sets of travellers, and exactly a minute later the whistle blows twice and the service departs, having picked up two 2,000-odd passengers and set down as many, and having also, perhaps, left a casualty behind.

More than 36,000 people have died on the Mumbai Suburban over the past decade, and a similar number have been badly injured. Most deaths result from people trying to cross the lines and miscalculating how far they are from an oncoming train and how fast it is going.* The second ranking cause of death on the rails in Mumbai is commuters falling out of trains or off their roofs. It is as if the extra degree of compression inherent in super dense crush loading changes their characters and makes them, when trying to catch trains, indifferent to the danger of losing life or limb.

There are both cultural and behavioural explanations for their unconcern. According to Hindu theology, *dharma* governs destiny, and for those with a certain *karma*, being run over by a

---

* This inability to judge is known as the Leibowitz Hypothesis, after Herschel W. Leibowitz, the renowned visual psychophysicist who formulated it in 1965. It is unlikely that we ever travelled at more than 35 mph in the first several million years of our evolution; or encountered any animal as big as a train that was as fast as a cheetah; and hence we underestimate closing speeds and overestimate our ability to sidestep them.

train can be their *moksha,* or liberation from the treadmill of re-incarnation. Indeed, each full moon, Mumbai train drivers pray to Durga, an avatar of the goddess Kali, mistress of destruction, to keep people off the lines in front of them. Some drivers run over dozens of people during their careers.

The behavioural explanations for such cavalier attitudes rely on the theory of objectification. During boarding, Mumbai commuters really do treat each other as inanimate obstacles that are there to be shoved aside, landed on or clambered over. In addition to deaths and serious injuries, there are broken bones and cuts and bruises aplenty. The objectification, however, is transient. As soon as everyone is settled in or on top of a carriage, humanity returns and it is as if they have reverted to their normal selves after letting another of their personalities take control for a few seconds at the beginning and end of each train journey.

The Mumbai Suburban Railway is both sympathetic and fatalistic towards the hordes that board its trains and endanger themselves and each other in transit. While it carries over seven million people every day, and is a miracle of efficiency – 97 per cent of its services are on time even during the monsoon season – it has to choose between operating overcrowded services for pragmatic reasons, or not running them at all on humanitarian grounds: 10,000 new people arrive to settle in Mumbai and its suburbs every *day*. Even with unlimited funds and the power to bulldoze new lines into the city, it would be impossible to accommodate the increasing quantity of traffic in total safety.

Like its counterpart in Tokyo, the Mumbai Suburban has tried to keep its passengers in check with a combination of etiquette posters and safety notices. It has had to become more inventive, however, as simple messages such as 'Danger!' have failed to make an impact in the maelstroms that spin around every train on every platform during rush hour. In order to make its passengers less careless of their fate, in 2007 the Mumbai Suburban commissioned Final Mile, an Indian 'behaviour architecture' consultancy that tries to shape the conduct of massed individuals through the application of cognitive psychology, to formulate a safety strategy. Final Mile began with the assumption that people are above all irrational: once they've seen them more than once, they treat caution signs as part of the landscape and disregard their messages. In consequence, the consultancy designed three 'interventions', each aimed to correct a defect of human perception. The first was to paint perpendicular yellow lines over the rails, so that commuters crossing them could have a frame against which to judge the velocity of approaching trains, and therefore not succumb to the failure of vision identified by the Leibowitz Hypothesis. The second intervention was to replace the stick figures getting skittled on existing safety posters with close-ups of an actor's face grimacing in pain as he is being cut in half. This focused people's thoughts on what it might feel like to be dismembered by a train, on the basis that empathy is a greater motivator than rationality. The final intervention was to change the warning whistle on trains from one long to two short blasts. According to Vinod Menon, a behavioural scientist at Stanford University, 'brain activity – and hence alertness – peaks during short silences between two musical notes'. Apparently, 'the silence sets up a kind of expectation in the brain', and hence two blasts on the whistle should make commuters more vigilant and less likely to lapse into an irrational reverie when their train pulls into the station.

Sex and death are intertwined and Mumbai's commuters are seized not just by objectification but also by sexual objectification. As is the case in Japan, its services are plagued with molesters, who take advantage of the overcrowding to indulge themselves in a little 'Eve teasing'. The euphemism was coined in Indian English post-independence and applies to behaviour that is much more aggressive than its wording implies, including gang rape and murder. Public sexual harassment of women is a growing problem on Mumbai's railways: 5,984 offences were registered in 2012, against 3,544 the year before. However, its proliferation isn't limited to rush hour – the problem is acknowledged to be a cultural one rather than a result of overcrowding on public transport and the Indian press speaks of a national epidemic. Perhaps cultures that limit encounters between the sexes are more prone to having problems in public spaces, and molesters on the lines. Commuting is a chance to interact outside the fetters of custom. In the absence of such restraints, anything goes.

The Mumbai Suburban has been fighting 'Eve teasing' ever since its first incarnation as the Bombay Metropolitan Railway. Women-only carriages have been available since the nineteenth century, and in the twenty-first, as in Japan, there are women-only trains. These are patrolled by the Railway Police Force, a paramilitary body with the power to shoot to kill. The railway even has its own magistrates who punish men proved to have entered carriages reserved for women. They hold their sessions in a cavernous room in a wing of the Chhatrapati Shivaji Terminus, each with a typist by their side to record their verdicts.

It is interesting to compare the situation in Mumbai and Tokyo with London, where sexual assaults on public transport are rare and convictions even rarer. 'Eve teasing' and chikanery are thought to be un-British rather than inevitable, and when newspapers cover cases they tend to focus on their humorous aspects. In March 2012, for instance, the *Daily Mail* reported that a commuter from Basingstoke had been acquitted of outraging public decency. He explained to the jury that he'd thrust his leg against a woman in the seat next to him, jiggled with his hands beneath the newspaper covering his lap, and alarmed her with his heavy breathing and 'snarling' because he had been 'strumming an imaginary banjo' and was so lost in music that he hadn't even noticed that she was there. The judge, himself a train commuter, pointed out to the jury that they should take it into consideration that men often 'reorganized' themselves in the presence of women, and that in some cases this was a symptom of prostate cancer.

The idea that London's men are more likely to improvise on imaginary instruments than objectivize women and behave indecently isn't borne out by surveys. A recent study of London women aged eighteen to thirty-four found that 40 per cent of them had 'experienced unwanted sexual attention' (the definition of which included strange men staring at them). However, only 30 per cent of respondents claimed that they had experienced it on tubes, buses or trains, and many said they felt safer while in transit than they did in the streets, suggesting that a degree of restraint is indeed practised on British public transport.

For the transport operators of the developing world, however, safety rather than sexual harassment is the principal concern. They have deployed a variety of different strategies to protect commuters from both the inherent dangers of travel and their own reckless behaviour. In Jakarta, the capital of Indonesia, for example, where crush loading is becoming super dense, rather than following Mumbai's attempts to solve the problems of rail-hopping, door-hanging and roof-riding commuters using cognitive psychology and visual psychophysics, the authorities have chosen to suspend curtains of concrete balls the size of grapefruit on chains over the tracks, which leave no clearance for anyone trying to travel on the roofs of train carriages. The balls were introduced after prior deterrents, including barbed wire, greased train roofs and live performances of safety songs on the platforms, had failed to effect change. Jakarta's commuters, however, are a spirited lot. While some roof-surf into work because there's no room inside, others do it to avoid paying for a ticket, or for the thrill of dodging power lines and low-hanging bridges en route. They take each new countermeasure as a fresh challenge.

'I was really scared when I first heard about these balls,' a roof-surfer who commutes between his hometown of Bogor and Jakarta told a reporter from Associated Press. 'It sounds like it could be really dangerous. But I don't think it will last long. They have tried everything to keep us from riding... but in the end we always win.'

The roof-surfers' cavalier attitude towards danger is perhaps an example of collective resilience. The threat that they are united against is the attempt by the rail operator, KA Commuter

Jabodetabek, to circumscribe their behaviour. I think that this perception of the operator as the enemy is, to a degree, common to commuters everywhere, whether fuming on the Tube, or super-dense-crush-loaded on a Mumbai suburban service. While cultural differences and varying degrees of overcrowding account for the diverse strategies that commuters around the world have evolved in order to cope with spending an hour or so each day squeezed up against strangers, having someone or something – in the shape of the service operator – to blame for the discomfort gives us a degree of unity. So instead of venting our frustrations on each other, or giving up commuting altogether, we keep calm and carry on.

♦ ♦ ♦ ♦ ♦

CHAPTER IX

Road Rage

The chariots shall rage in the streets,
They shall jostle one against another in the broad ways.

Nahum the Elkoshite, c. 620 BC

R oad congestion is the counterpart of crush loading for commuters who travel by car: it forces them likewise to be closer to their fellow travellers than they would wish to be. And it has mushroomed around the world at the same pace as overcrowding on public transport: traffic jams have multiplied and worsened on every continent in every year of the twenty-first century. Its progress is monitored by IBM's Commuter Pain Index, which measures congestion and suffering in twenty major cities, including London, Moscow, Mexico City, Los Angeles, Bangalore and Beijing. The index takes a sadistic pleasure in revealing the hardships its respondents endure in terms of hours wasted going nowhere, and implies that traffic jams are an inevitable consequence of automobility. Surprising though it might be to that city's inhabitants, London is second to bottom of the index, which is topped by Mexico City, where commuting is over five times more painful than in the capital of the UK.

Having commuted to London by car as well as train, I find

it hard to imagine just how awful Mexico City must be. My route included a section of the M25, which was built to accommodate 88,000 cars, but was by then (2008) carrying over 200,000. When it was completed in 1986, it was lauded as being the 'longest city bypass in the world'; it has since been nicknamed the 'world's biggest car park'. Even though the M25 has been broadened almost continuously since its opening, the traffic has grown with it, especially during rush hours. It used to be purgatory in winter, when one always drove, or rather inched, home in darkness, in what seemed to be a perpetual traffic jam. Conditions have since got worse, and are expected to become worse still. In March 2014, the Highways Agency issued leaflets admitting that 'the strain is beginning to show' and advised motorists to 'stay off the M25 in rush hour'. The leaflets had a similarly hectoring tone to the Second World War poster campaigns aimed at needless rail journeys, and provoked a furious response. 'This is ridiculous, it is like a bad joke. How are commuters supposed to travel? The M25 is there precisely so that motorists can use it at rush hour,' Kevin Delaney of the RAC Foundation told the *Daily Mail*. The problem was compounded by the parlous state of other forms of London transport: 'The Tube is in trouble, bus lanes are often clogged, the trains are still not running properly* and the centre of London is now more congested and roadwork-bound than ever before.' If commuters had to keep off the M25, alternative ways to get into work were likely to be equally frustrating.

Congestion is not only unpleasant but also wasteful. In

---

* After three months of floods and storms between December 2013 and February 2014.

America, where auto-commuting rules and 87 per cent of all commuters drive solo to work, against a mere 29.8 per cent in London, an estimated 4.8 billion hours of productive, or leisure, time are lost to traffic jams each year. The costs of such enforced immobility are astronomical – commuters fritter away over 100 billion dollars in fuel and needless wear and tear on their vehicles each year while caught up in congestion, and if the human and monetary costs of accidents (32,788 deaths in 2010 and nearly $300 billion over the same period) are factored in the cost would be even higher.

Indeed, the problem that the highways and freeways built in America in the 1950s were going to solve – according to the propaganda of the auto companies – has instead become worse. Most of them now host traffic jams that are far more severe than those they were intended to end. The grand failure of the 'more roads equals less congestion' theory has reversed the poles in thinking among traffic analysts. Nowadays, according to economists Gilles Duranton and Matthew A. Turner, 'roads cause traffic' and 'building new roads and widening existing ones only results in additional traffic that continues to rise until peak congestion returns to the previous level'. This theory of congestion suggests that it is impossible to prevent or cure, short of forcing people to give up their cars. Even roads to nowhere will draw traffic, which will grow until it chokes them.

So how do car commuters deal with the challenge of apparently inevitable congestion? Does it force them, like crush loading, to change their behaviour, or even switch personalities? Traffic jams aren't quite equivalent to overcrowded trains. Their participants are prisoners of each other, rather than hostages to a common enemy. Moreover, if you're on your own in your own car the laws of proxemics aren't violated. Instead of having the equivalent of twenty people in the average family saloon, as there might be on a Mumbai Suburban local service, there's only one. You travel in a bubble and can even take your cuddly toys with you if that makes you happy. Indeed, solo drivers tend to think themselves invisible behind their windscreens and are shameless in their behaviour: they will pick their noses, scratch dandruff out of their hair, smoke, and sneeze explosively without a care.

However, while drivers are insulated from each other by their high-tech shells, they have to expand their intimate space to take account of the dimensions of their vehicles, with suitable margins for error, especially in America, where the average 'midsize' car, although a minnow in comparison to the Ford Edsel, is nonetheless fourteen feet long and weighs nearly 3,000 lbs. Drivers also have to defend this expanded space more vigorously. Motorcars are faster, less flexible, and less forgiving than human flesh and can become death traps as well as a slice of home on wheels. Other vehicles need to be warned off, and quickly too, before they make contact. Moreover, drivers cherish their machines as well as their own safety. According to the American Automobile Association (AAA) 'the car is a prized and symbolic possession which is uniquely able to provoke personal offense and territorial defense if any perceived threat occurs.'*

---

* The British have a similar, if more muted, affection for their vehicles. In the crescent where I live now, where everyone who works drives to work, the weekend begins with a ritual Saturday morning car wash.

This means that car commuters are far more likely to turn violent than passengers on public transport, and the phenomenon of 'road rage' is the result. It's something that every driver has to face in others, and manage in themselves.

The notion that a special sort of anger descends on people in charge of wheeled vehicles predates commuting, indeed it stretches back into antiquity. The Old Testament accuses Jehu, king of Israel, of driving furiously; the Romans encouraged such behaviour during chariot racing; Lord Byron, the Romantic poet, boasted of attacking someone in a carriage who had been 'impudent' to his horse; and the Victorians legislated against it by making it an offence to cause 'bodily harm... by wanton or furious driving'. More recently, after the advent of commuting by motorcar, it featured as a fantasy in the 1932 movie *If I Had a Million*, in which a retired actress who runs a tea room and has just had her new car destroyed by someone running a red light is chosen randomly by a dying tycoon to receive a million dollars. She uses the manna from heaven to buy eight cars and hire chauffeurs working both solo and in unison to crash careless drivers off the road.

Road rage, however, was rare until it exploded into the public consciousness during the 1990s, at the same time as congestion was reaching unprecedented levels. The term first appeared in America in 1986, and is thought to have been a corruption of 'roid rage', which was a distinctive sort of anger that afflicted bodybuilders who had taken too many steroids. According to the cultural historian Joe Moran, it made its debut in Britain in 1994 in an article in the *Sunday Times*, which reported that an elder at a London synagogue had assaulted a Buddhist monk while in the grip of this novel kind of anger, which it claimed was 'a problem that police, motoring organisations and psychologists say is sweeping the country'.

At first it seemed that road rage was a media phenomena. You couldn't turn on the TV or open a newspaper without finding it mentioned. There were even instances of celebrity road rage. In 1994, for example, the actor Jack Nicholson smashed in the windscreen of a Mercedes with a golf club, insisting that its driver had cut him off. However, when road rage led to murder, it became a matter of horror rather than entertainment. In May 1996 Kenneth Noye became so infuriated with the driver of another car that he forced her to stop on a slip road of the M25 and stabbed her passenger and fiancé, Stephen Cameron, to death. The incident altered the treatment of road rage in the media, which subsequently treated it as a serious problem in need of a solution.

The notion that road rage is a special type of anger brought on by congestion has received the most attention in America, where citizens can carry firearms and the potential of road rage to lead to murder is far greater than elsewhere. In 1997 the federal government launched an inquiry into the phenomenon. At a Senate hearing in the same year, Republican congressman Merrill Cook testified that:

> *Three years ago, road rage… was unheard of in Utah, but my District was shocked recently by two murders on I–15, which runs through the heart of Salt Lake City. One young mother*

was shot and killed while driving up a freeway on-ramp by a man in another car who was angry at her for cutting him off. Another man, a husband, father, and notably kind man in our community, was shot and killed only a few months ago on his way to work by another angry driver who got out of his car in stalled traffic, walked back to this man's car, and shot him repeatedly.

Other senators had similar stories, and when the American Automobile Association examined 10,000 road-rage incidents that had occurred between 1990 and 1996, they found these 'resulted in at least 218 murders and another 12,610 injury cases'.

Not only were the statistics shocking, but some of the motivations cited for individual outbursts of road rage were chillingly trivial. 'He practically ran me off the road – what was I supposed to do?' asked one man who had killed his victim. When Donald Graham, deacon of his local church in Massachusetts, shot a stranger with a crossbow because he'd seen him tailgate another car, he displayed a similar detachment. Even though his victim bled to death en route to hospital, the deacon was unrepentant. 'I'm not gonna apologize for doing the right thing,' he told a reporter.

Some even boasted of their road-rage exploits, as if they were not merely justifiable, but also noble. In 1997 Tracie Alfieri, a twenty-four-year-old office worker who forced a pregnant woman to crash into a truck during rush hour, causing her to lose her baby and break nearly all her bones, bragged to her colleagues when she reached work that 'No one cuts in front of me and gets away with it!' and 'I don't take any shit when I'm driving.' Tracie even said it was unfair that she should have to go to prison after she was convicted of Aggravated Vehicular Assault and Aggravated Vehicular Homicide for killing her victim's unborn baby. She appealed her sentence on the grounds that it amounted to 'cruel and unusual punishment in violation of the Eighth Amendment', because while 'a woman and a doctor may freely abort a woman's pregnancy', she had been penalized for 'the same act of terminating the pregnancy.'

While Alfieri apologised to her victim on release from jail in 1999, the denial she displayed at the time is typical of road-ragers, as is, in some cases, a cold-blooded streak. Indeed, many of its sufferers seem to perceive themselves as vigilantes, above the law because they serve a greater cause. People talk about their road-rage experiences as if they were fistfights – one-on-ones rather than general mêlées with themselves against every other car on the road. They also dream of rough justice for drivers who cross them. AutoVantage, an American motorists' association, publishes an annual *Road Rage Survey*, which rates the relative anger of drivers in various cities. Most years, New York and Miami trade the number-one spot, with Portland, Oregon and Cleveland fighting for the last place. The survey asks its participants to identify what causes road rage, and whether they suffer from it. Most blame it on the inconsiderate behaviour of other drivers. Eighty-four per cent said that seeing someone else talking on a phone in another car was enough to set them off. Other aggravations were driving too fast, tailgating, eating, drinking, texting or emailing at the wheel, and driving too slowly.

The idea that road rage is a justifiable response to provocation, and therefore inevitably someone else's fault, ties in with general surveys of driver confidence. Two-thirds of all drivers 'rate themselves almost perfect in excellence as a driver (9 or 10 on a 10-point scale), while the rest consider themselves above average (6 to 8)'. In their own minds, they can't put a wheel wrong when they're on the road. As a consequence, while '70 per cent of drivers report being a victim of an aggressive driver', only '30 per cent admit to being aggressive drivers'. Such mismatches between perception and reality suggest that cognitive dissonance rules the highways. Drivers operate in a parallel universe where they are perfect and everyone else is bad and dangerous.

The territoriality, belligerence, vindictiveness and, above all, double standards that typify road-rage sufferers have been investigated in depth. It's now treated as a problem in its own right that claims hundreds of casualties each year, and is in urgent need of solution. In 2006, it was diagnosed as a serious medical condition by the American Psychiatric Association (APA) and christened Intermittent Explosive Disorder, or IED for short. The APA thinks IED may affect up to 16 million Americans. Its symptoms are 'repeated episodes of aggressive, violent behaviour that are grossly out of proportion to the situation'. While IED is not limited to drivers trapped in traffic jams, they are its most recognizable class of sufferers.

The anger that defines IED is attributed to stress. Stress stimulates our freeze, fight or flight reflexes, and since we can't fly our cars out of congestion, and stopping them in the middle of a busy road might cause even more rage among other motorists, we fight. Dr Leon James, professor of psychology at the University of Hawaii, has identified fifteen ways that driving causes stress. In particular, he focuses on the effects of our being – metaphorically – chained to the driver's seat: 'Tension tends to build up when the body is physically restricted and constricted,' which is then aggravated by the constraints of having to drive in lanes in the same direction, obey speed limits and deal with jams. We also get stressed that we might damage our cars in the chaotic rush-hour traffic, whose unpredictability is yet another source of stress, as are the heat, noise and smells that it generates. Already on edge, if we make an error, or someone accidentally cuts us up, our inability to set things straight is also stressful. As James explains: 'motorists don't have an accepted or official gestural communication language. There is no easy way of saying "oops, I'm sorry!" as we do in a bank line. This allows for ambiguity to arise: "Did he just flip me off or was that an apology?"' In his opinion, 'it would no doubt help if vehicles were equipped with an electronic display allowing drivers to flash pre-recorded messages'. One wonders how many would flash 'Oops, I'm sorry!' if they could choose what messages to pre-record.

Stress leads to a state called 'venting', which is also known as 'rage rush'. We see danger in everything and, once provoked, our limbic systems* release organic compounds called catecholamines that make us ready to either run or brawl. Rage rush doesn't last,

---

* Structures in the brain that govern our emotional responses.

but while it does it also serves to wake up the nervous system, which gets angry in turn, so that 'successive anger-provoking thoughts [cause fresh] surges of catecholamines, each building on the hormonal momentum of those preceding it... [so] that the body is rapidly in a state of extreme arousal', i.e. very angry indeed. This is a bad place to be. According to Daniel Goleman, author of *Emotional Intelligence*: 'Anger builds on anger; the emotional brain heats up. By then rage, unhampered by reason, easily erupts in violence. At this point people are unforgiving and beyond being reasoned with; their thoughts revolve around revenge and reprisal, oblivious to what the consequences might be.'

However, it's not just stress that makes us angry in traffic. Behaviourologists have identified another, primal, cause for it: when we're stuck in congestion, 'we're looking at everyone's rear, and that's not how human beings were set up to maximize [our] communicative potential'. When we turn our backs on people, it's a gesture of dismissal and it leaves our victims fuming. Other apes use the same tactic to assert dominance. And while you're sitting on someone else's tail, there's also someone on yours, edging up to your bumper, and the behaviour of the people on our own tails also ignites our primitive wrath. Our discomfort is further exacerbated by 'asymmetrical communication', which we likewise find infuriating: however hard we curse and howl when our engines are revving but our wheels are still, no one else can hear us, and we're conscious of our impotence. It's like being struck dumb at a moment when you have plenty to say. You can scream the air blue, while the target of your abuse laughs at your silent show. Although Dr James's suggestion that cars could be fitted with message boards might reduce the asymmetry, they might also be even more provocative, and feed people back into the rage-rush loop.

It may be, however, that road rage isn't simply caused by the problems of stress and asymmetric communication. According to the economist Rick Nevin, the tetraethyl lead that was added to petrol as an anti-knock agent from the 1920s until its use was banned in the 1990s, addled the brains of the road-rage generation. Lead is a neurotoxin that the body can't excrete, and cumulative exposure to it via exhaust fumes can result in severe lead poisoning, whose symptoms include aggressive behaviour. It also retards children's mental development and turns them into backward and unstable adults. In Nevin's opinion, 'if you add a lag time of 23 years, lead emissions from automobiles explain 90 per cent of the variation in violent crime in America. Toddlers who ingested high levels of lead... really were more likely to become violent criminals.'

Dr James also suspects that road rage may derive from childhood conditioning. Every lead-head had a mother and a father whose behaviour behind the wheel influenced their perceptions of what constituted proper driving. Nurture, as well as nature, can make us mad. 'Drivers grow up being socialized into a highway of hostility rather than mutual support and peace,' he explains. 'The back seat of the car is what I call road rage nursery. From childhood in the car... we are prepared for competitive hard-nosed driving.'

So what can we do to protect ourselves against an attack of road rage – assuming we didn't get too much lead in our youth? The condition endangers our health as well as shaping our behaviour and disturbing our heads. Too much venting, for instance, wreaks havoc on our hearts. When Professor John Larson of Yale University interviewed more than a thousand heart attack patients, he found 80 per cent of them 'had a long history of violent anger behind the wheel'. Dr Arthur Agatston, meanwhile, eminent cardiologist and inventor of the South Beach Diet, believes that 'being stuck in traffic raises blood pressure and triples heart attack risk'.

According to a Canadian survey published in 2013, the best way to steer clear of road rage is to avoid driving on Tuesdays in September between 6 a.m. and 9 a.m. This is when recorded incidents of the malaise are at their peak. This solution, however, would be impractical for most commuters, and the first line of defence that many have opted for instead is to buy a Sport Utility Vehicle, or SUV. SUVs started life as car/truck hybrids, invented by the auto industry to get around America's Corporate Average Fuel Economy laws.* Trucks didn't have to be capable of doing as much as twenty miles per gallon, so the manufacturers bolted auto bodies onto truck chassis and sold the result to city dwellers as a taste of the wilderness – or of refinement to farmers. However, SUVs didn't really take off until road rage became a story in the media, after which sales soared from 1.8 per cent of new American vehicles in 1980 to over a quarter of all sales in 2002. Incidentally, SUVs in the guise of 4x4s or 'Chelsea Tractors'† have also been a

---

* Instituted in 1973 after the first oil crisis to force US car-makers to build more fuel-efficient vehicles.
† Their archetype is the Range Rover, built by the corporate descendant of the manufacturers of the revolutionary safety bicycle.

hit in Britain, where they are used principally for metropolitan and rush-hour driving. A 2005 survey found that only 12 per cent of 4x4 owners had ever taken their car off road, and 40 per cent had never even taken them out of the city.

While the surge in SUV sales has also been attributed to re-masculinization and growing militarization among American men, the most likely reason for the rise in their popularity is their size in comparison to normal cars. People feel threatened by larger vehicles, so it is less stressful to be in one than surrounded by them. SUVs evolved to meet this perceived threat, supported by adverts that emphasized their ability to win any challenge. The result was an arms race on the freeways that reached its zenith with General Motors' Hummer H1. Adapted from an all-terrain military vehicle, and powered by a 6.2-litre V8 that managed in the low teens in terms of miles per gallon, the Hummer weighed nearly 5 tons. According to Clotaire Rapaille, the French-born marketing strategist behind the vehicle, the Hummer was perfectly suited to the spirit of the age: in the road-rage era, drivers conceived of their vehicles as 'armoured cars for the battlefield'.

Rapaille's reputation as a marketing guru rests on his insight that much of our behaviour is governed by what he calls the lizard portion of our brain. This is its most ancient component, which is responsible for our survival instincts and, in Rapaille's opinion, for many of our purchasing decisions. If the lizard speaks, reason has to take a back seat. When, for instance, Rapaille was asked by the media theorist Douglas Rushkoff if people should balance their desire for a giant SUV against the damage they caused to the environment in terms of emissions, he was confident, in a somewhat cryptic manner, that the lizard would always win:

> RUSHKOFF: *What about the environment? If the lizard wants the Hummer?*
> RAPAILLE: *Right.*
> RUSHKOFF: *Then… the lizard's not going to listen to the environmentalist.*
> RAPAILLE: *Right.*
> RUSHKOFF: *Then isn't it our job, as aware people, to get the reptile to shut up and appeal to the cortex, to appeal to the mammal?*
> RAPAILLE: *Now, you see, the problem is that… the people who want to do good [do] not always do good… So the people that want to do good… say, OK, we need to make smaller cars… to protect the environment. Then nobody buys the smaller car. Why? Because they're too small.*

Rapaille's insight echoes Shakespeare's King Lear: 'O, reason not the need! Our basest beggars are in their poorest things superfluous.'

A similar sentiment is apparent in Hummer adverts – one of which includes the line 'Need is a very subjective word' – and time after time in Hummer web forums, especially if the topic is commuting. While many threads on the forums start with inquiries as to whether it's worth squandering so much gasoline for the sake of inching a monster through congestion, they usually turn into a celebration of the irrational after a few posts, as the following example demonstrates:

I commute every other day from New Jersey to near
Washington DC (240 miles roundtrip). There is nothing
like riding in a Hummer when you get into traffic, which
is most mornings past Baltimore. The first half of my
commute is sane, setting the cruise control @ 73 mph
with nothing but road. It is absolutely 'Pure Love'
riding in this truck...
This will be my last vehicle in life. No matter what it will
take in the future to fix, new engine, new transmission,
whatever, there will be nothing else I will ride other than
*an H2... ***
Those are my thoughts. Get it if you can, you won't
be disappointed.
Oh, and if your spouse ever gives you grief about your H2,
get rid of them and keep the H2. You'll make out better in
the long run. Lol.

Unfortunately, rather than alleviating anger on the roads, the SUV craze may have exacerbated it. 'Combine road rage with congealed traffic with bloated, ego-inflating SUVs and you have a recipe for more angry, *dangerous* confrontations,' claimed a 1999 article in the *San Francisco Business Times*. Normal cars usually come off worse in collisions with SUVs, whose higher, stiffer front ends lead to so-called 'crash incompatibility', whereby SUVs' bumpers hit smaller vehicles at the head height of their drivers. According to America's Insurance Institute of Highway Safety, the fatality rate

---

* A slightly lighter and marginally more fuel-efficient model than the H1.

in serious accidents is 'lowest for occupants of SUVs weighing over 5,000 pounds' and 'highest for small and very small cars'. This potential to injure other drivers together with the vehicles' prodigious thirst for gasoline has turned sectors of public opinion, including some Christian groups, against SUVs. In 2002, for instance, the Revd Jim Ball of the Washington-based Evangelical Environmental Network launched the advertising campaign *What Would Jesus Drive?* on television. 'We have confessed Christ to be our Saviour and Lord, and for us, that includes our transportation choices,' he told reporters. In Ball's opinion Jesus wouldn't have driven one, and nor should his followers.

How else, then, might Christian commuters – and other innocents – protect themselves against road rage? Should they, perhaps, take inspiration from Genesis 4:9–10, 'am I my brother's keeper?' and try to steer their brethren back onto the path of righteousness by alerting them to the error of their ways? There has been a rise in internet vigilantism on websites like platewire.com, where people list the number plates and misdeeds of drivers who have offended them. The sites usually allow anonymous posts, and thanks to the 'online disinhibition effect' many of these are 'Web Rage' pure and simple, a condition that is as vituperative as the highway variety. Web rage, like road rage, arises in part from isolation: being alone in front of a computer is much the same as commuting solo and staring at a windscreen. We feel invisible and take advantage of it to let go. Some of the release also comes from naming and shaming, for shame is a powerful influence on our behaviour: we're born hardwired to censure people who act against the common good – we voice our objections in the hope of recruiting other people to our sides, and when we succeed our status is elevated and that of our opponents is diminished. No matter that it's unlikely that a road rager will actually read their indictment by a web rager, the fact that discontent has been expressed is enough to compensate the victim for the feeling they've been violated, and help them believe that they've won, by having the last word. Naming and shaming online has been enhanced in recent years by videos from dashcams – dashboard and rear-view mounted cameras – which allow people with web rage who are posting about road rage to supplement their tirades with images.

Commuters who do not wish to end up substituting web rage for road rage could do worse than to follow the guidelines issued by the AAA, which believes that the best way to fight IED is with self-control. In its opinion, although the reptilian part of your brain may have made you buy your car, you need the limbic to drive it, and the cortex to be able to comprehend it at all, which should therefore be listened to over the saurian din. The AAA's safety campaign offers three principles of behaviour to people fearing road rage in others and themselves. All are defensive, and require a step up in self-control from the SUV owner's passive-aggressive state of mind. The principles assume that rage is natural, indeed inevitable, in the average head and is best not provoked. They are:

1 DON'T OFFEND: *'be a cautious and courteous driver'* – *avoid angry gestures;*

2 DON'T ENGAGE: *'one angry driver can't start a fight unless another driver is willing to join in'. Above all avoid eye contact. Looks can kill; and*

3 ADJUST YOUR ATTITUDE. *Forget winning: instead of trying to 'make good time' try to 'make time good'.*

If the AAA's principles fail to keep a lid on rage, psychologist Steve Albrecht advises that any commuter about to boil over should ask themselves, 'What Would the Dalai Lama Do?' ('WWDLD'?). In Albrecht's opinion, a sermon on the subject delivered by his Holiness Tenzin Gyatso might run thus: 'Go forth down the road and be yourself, with compassion towards others. Stop caring about your "space." Tint your windows. Get a subscription to satellite radio and enjoy your music without commercials. Realize road rage is ridiculous, life-threatening, and not something you have to participate in, ever.'

There is even road rage in the Dalai Lama's place of exile in Dharamsala in northern India. In July 2012, the *Times of India* reported that the driver of a Maruti 800 was severely beaten by four youths after his car touched theirs. The roads gridlocked for an hour while a member of the traffic police 'remained a mute spectator' to both the jam and the anger, as if they were but Maya, or an illusion. The incident is unremarkable for India, where 1.3 million people were injured in traffic accidents in 2010 and where road rage is rampant. The nation even has examples of celebrity road rage: the former Indian Test cricketer Navjot Singh Sidhu was convicted in 2006 of the road-rage killing of a fellow driver in the Punjabi city of Patiala.* As in the 1990s in the UK and USA, there is plenty of soul-searching on the subject in the Indian media. Delhi is acknowledged as the national capital of IED: ten million motorized vehicles are on the streets each rush hour, dodging potholes, pedestrians, tongas (horse-drawn wooden carriages), herds of goats and sacred cows. Many busy intersections don't have traffic lights, few cars bother with staying in lane, and every horn is blaring. Meanwhile, 1,400 new cars are added to the chaos every day.

The violence and insecurity that these conditions generate are all too familiar: 'I used to laugh and say that everyone driving slower than me is a moron and everyone faster, a maniac,' Rakesh Verma, a pseudonymous ex-road rager, confessed to the *Hindustan Times*. Then Verma became a victim himself. When his car broke down at a traffic light, he found he had a truly dangerous driver on his tail. 'I heard loud honking from behind me… this person in a Maruti 800 was focusing all his attention on me… before I knew what was happening a man started beating on my window and windshield.' Both the driver of the Maruti and his passenger then attacked Verma with baseball bats and broke his ribs, knocked him out and only held back from finishing him off when bystanders intervened. In the opinion of Satyendra Garg, head of Delhi Traffic Police, such incidents are unremarkable. 'In our country there is no respect for law. Physical encounters are considered macho.'

This is a far cry from Gandhi's ideal that one should 'be the

---

* Sidhu's conviction was later 'stayed' by the Indian Supreme Court, allowing him to stand as a Member of Parliament.

change you wish to see in the world' – i.e. lead by example and indeed non-violence – but rush hours are changing India. Even sacred cows fall victim to road rage. There are about 40,000 of them wandering around Delhi, living off garbage and what they can scavenge from food stalls. It is illegal to kill one for the sake of it, but not a crime to run one down by accident. In 2003, writing in India's *Financial Express*, the economist Bibek Debroy labelled them the 'greatest traffic hazard in Delhi today' and suggested that they be fitted with reflectors and licence plates. His levity can be contrasted with Gandhi's opinion that 'cow protection' was 'the most important outward manifestation of Hinduism'.

In order to prevent too sharp a collision between India new and old, Delhi has created a municipal caste of sacred cowboys whose job it is to round up strays and take them to one of five 'gaushalas' – cow sanctuaries – around the city, where they'll be cared for until they reincarnate. Sacred cowboys don't have the glamour of their Western counterparts. Most come from the rural suburbs, and commute to work on super-dense-crush-loaded trains. The job is dangerous, as the cows are street-smart, and though their horns are small their points are sharp. There is also the risk of being stoned by cow worshippers, or attacked by the owners of Delhi's numerous unlicensed dairies, who put their cows out into the streets to forage, or by the poor people who drink their cheap milk. The cowboys persist, nonetheless, so as to protect the occasional mounts of Shiva from congested commuters suffering from road rage.

Indian pundits who look for physical explanations for the incandescent fury that makes Delhians betray their culture believe that the noise and heat of the city's traffic go a long way towards explaining the combustibility of its inhabitants. When it's 50 degrees in the shade and the humidity is running close to 100 per cent, and every vehicle is revving its engine and blowing its horn, the cattle are lowing and pedestrians are shouting, it's impossible to keep one's head fixed on the wheel of fate.

Heat has also been posited as a trigger for road rage in America, though the present state of research suggests that it's at best a contributory cause of inter-traveller violence on the highways. Indeed, evidence from Russia proves that road rage runs equally hot in a cold climate. YouTube hosts many 'Russian Road Rage Greatest Hits' compilations that show that both IED and dashcams are alive and well in the kingdom of the bear. The compilations feature spectacular acts of aggressive driving, and fights between drivers who are often armed. While such episodes may seem extreme to non-Russian viewers, road rage is no mystery to the Russians themselves: violence was associated with wheeled vehicles under the tsars, when landowners and government officials thought nothing of running down their serfs. During the communist era, cars remained under the control of the rulers of the USSR, and were driven with an equal disdain for the workers, with the consequence that when private citizens were at last allowed to own them in the wake of perestroika, IED was a cultural norm. Violence on Russia's roads is also compounded by circumstance: when commuters have vodka in their bellies, there's ice on the roads, and, according to the 2011 IBM Commuter Pain Index, nearly half of all drivers have suffered delays of more than three hours on their way to work, it's unsurprising that they think everyone else is in the wrong.

There are nonetheless a few local peculiarities to дорожного гнева* that mark it out from the Western paradigm. For instance, car commuters in Moscow have a virulent hatred of cars with *migalkas*, i.e. flashing blue lights on their roofs, whose owners assume they have precedence over other traffic. These lights, a relic of Soviet days – when they were given to officials so important that the interests of the USSR might be threatened if they were delayed by congestion – were sold to the highest bidders in their thousands post-perestroika. Whether people had bought or earned their *migalkas*, they behaved with the same contempt for other road users as both tsars and apparatchiks had done before them. When, for instance, the rush-hour traffic failed to part in front of emergency situations minister Sergei Shoigu's flashing blue light in June 2010, his chauffeur pulled out a megaphone and asked the driver in front 'whether his not getting out of the way meant that he wanted to be "shot in the head, dumbass"'.

Commuters have been fighting back against *migalka* owners via the Society of Blue Buckets, which organizes four-wheeled flash mobs, involving motorcades of cars with toy buckets on their roofs, and posts dashcam and mobile-phone clips of blue-light owners breaking laws online. At first the Kremlin vacillated on whether to shut down web ragers or road ragers but decided that public opinion was with the buckets. After a particularly outrageous example of *migalka* abuse in December 2010, when 'three men smashed the windows of a Lexus car in an attempt to

---

* The Russian term for road rage.

drag out the driver who failed to give way to a VIP convoy they were travelling in', and it turned out that the blue light was owned by a billionaire with prior form for dangerous driving (he had allegedly been whisked out of Switzerland in a private jet after hospitalizing a pensioner when racing his sons in luxury rented cars), the then interior minister of Russia, Rashid Nurgaliyev, stepped in. 'Such impudence, especially accompanied by unlawful actions, is simply inadmissible on roads, regardless of who is behind the wheel and what status he has. Especially in Moscow, where the traffic situation is already extremely complex,' he told a reporter from RIA Novosti news agency. Cars were re-registered and the number of *migalkas* reduced from 7,500 to 977. However, rumour has it that they can still be bought and that their numbers are creeping back up.

There is, however, one place in the world where courtesy on four wheels is making its last stand and road rage, while not unknown, doesn't even have a name in the local tongue. *Ka ka unten* ('aggressive driving') is the nearest phrase the Japanese have to describe the kamikaze behaviour that seizes drivers in other places when they're jammed too closely together. Although Japan has millions of car commuters, the vast majority of them practise Zen behind the wheel. It is as if cars have restored the traditional distance between people, and drivers take pleasure in exchanging courtesies: they let each other out at intersections and flash their hazard lamps to signal their appreciation. Perhaps driving takes them back to a more formal mindset, which they act out via their cars. It is possible too that the Japanese keep a lid on road rage through science. Every student at an officially certified driving school has to sit a Minnesota Multiphasic Personality Inventory (MMPI) test similar to that faced by CIA recruits. While learners cannot fail, the results are used to 'encourage *hansei* (self-reflection)' in those who might be inclined towards *ka ka unten*. 'Those who score low on the "emotional stability" scale are exhorted to focus on driving' and nothing else.

The idea that learner drivers should be taught how to control their emotions as well as their vehicles is gaining traction elsewhere. In Singapore, learners now sit a practical examination as part of their driving test to assess 'their reaction to verbal abuse and physical confrontation'. In Britain, meanwhile, the RAC has lobbied for lessons in anger management and how to cope with irate drivers to be included in the UK driving test. The Scottish Campaign against Irresponsible Driving (SCID) wants to go further: it recommends that every driver should be forced to re-sit their test every five years, and that anyone convicted of road-rage offences should 'undergo psychological assessments' before being granted a new licence.

However, until changes in driver education programmes become universal, or road rationing a reality, the only surefire way to avoid road rage during rush hour is by walking. Commuters who cycle are also victims of road rage. Indeed, to judge by their web forums, it is their principal concern when on the roads. Cyclists are a uniquely vulnerable group of road users: unprotected in comparison to the cars and buses with which they compete for space, many of them wear headcams in rush hour, both to film dangerous motorists and to signal to them that they should drive in a more considerate fashion. Cyclists themselves are thought to be a major cause of anger on the road. A 2013 survey by specialist cyclist insurers Protect Your Bubble found that cyclists who overtake on the inside, jump red lights and change lanes without indicating were 'the biggest cause of road rage in Britain'.

In contrast, there is no such phenomenon as pedestrian rage: strangers rarely start feuds on the pavements. The Scandinavian psychologists Risto Näätänen and Heikki Summala pioneered research into this important difference in 1975, and came up with several explanations. The first was that people who walked got rid of pent-up aggression via exercise: a vigorous walk burns almost 270 calories per hour whereas drivers in jams use up only half that amount. The second was that pedestrians don't gridlock like vehicles – they can keep moving in denser concentrations, and can duck and weave around each other with greater fluency than cars. Furthermore, they don't have to obey speed limits and traffic signals, which aggravate every driver's sense of victimization. And finally, if they bump into one another by accident, damage is rare and it's easy to apologize.

◆ ◆ ◆ ◆ ◆

CHAPTER X

Quo Vadis?

> Our nature lies in movement;
> complete calm is death.
>
> Blaise Pascal, *Pensées*, 1669

Road rage is not the only emotional disorder blamed on commuting. The act of travelling to and fro between work and home, whether on public or private transport, has also been credited with causing depression and insomnia by the medical profession, and accused of triggering obesity and impotence. According to the critics of commuting, the journeys themselves, even if they were carried out on empty roads or in a club carriage on the rails with a mini library of good books and a decent bar for the homeward leg, would be more than the human frame was meant to bear. Moreover, commuting is portrayed in the media as a kind of hell, albeit spoken of in sympathetic tones, as many of its audience are commuters. There are floods of indignation and grief in the British newspapers every January, for instance, when rail fares rise and travelling on public transport is at its most miserable. Each rush hour takes place in dusk or darkness, and the rain and the cold outside and the dirt that people trample into the carriages make it feel all the more dismal. Finally – possibly because of all the negative press – non-commuters make a show of taking pity on people who do commute, which at times is patronizing and at others offensive.

Is commuting really so unpleasant – the worst part of every working day? Is it worse than being bored at work or arguing at home? Is it really a nightmare on wheels – something you wouldn't do if you didn't have to? Or is it closer to my experiences – something you'll never love and sometimes hate but nonetheless a discrete part of each weekday, which offers solitary pleasures that neither office nor house can supply? Commuters have been placed under the microscope by a host of experts, including biologists, psychoanalysts, town planners and economists, each of whom has examined why people are willing to spend so much time in transit. While their answers differ wildly – we commute because we're nomadic carnivores, we waste petrol as a gesture of power, commuting facilitates infidelity, we all want small identikit houses etc. – they are almost unanimous in believing that commuting is a bad thing.

This presumption of misery is reinforced by surveys like IBM's Commuter Pain Index, which is widely publicized and is used to market IBM's electronic traffic management systems. The Commuter Pain Index is based on a survey of drivers in the cities that it covers, which asks them about ten issues, all of them negative: if they get angry or stressed during rush hour, if petrol costs too much, if they spend too long getting to work, and so on. So it's unsurprising that the index finds suffering wherever it goes, albeit in lesser quantities where IBM's traffic management systems are installed. IBM's index also investigates what people would do with the extra time they would have if they didn't need to commute, offering them choices from a list as short as that in its driver survey. Its conclusions are that most would 'devote it to personal relationships and improving their physical health'. Any time left over would be used for recreation, and 'nearly three in ten drivers (29 per cent) would sleep more'.

If commuters really resent their time spent in limbo to the extent that the Pain Index suggests, and feel that the practice steals some of their lives, why do they keep doing it? There are three main reasons why people might commute: (a) to find better work; (b) to live in a nicer home; and (c) because it's an expression of a natural or conditioned urge to travel every day. Looking at each in turn: does commuting enable people to find better work? The answer – if better job equals both more money and power – is a resounding yes, and has been since Victorian times. Both locomotivity and automobility enabled people to sell their talents to the markets where they had the most worth; current surveys of rail and tube commuters into London reveal that they earn more than the national average, and are more likely to be executives, team leaders and the like. They're also better educated, and live longer. Last but certainly not least, they can afford season tickets. Objectively, all the numbers are on their side.

However, economists nowadays also try to measure 'quality of life' as well as median incomes when determining the relative health of nations. The importance of this intangible and the fact that it had been neglected in the past were first highlighted in a speech that Robert F. Kennedy, American senator and younger brother of President John F. Kennedy, delivered at the University of Kansas in 1968:

For too long, we seem to have surrendered personal excellence and community values in the mere accumulation of material things. Our Gross National Product... if we judge the United States of America by that... counts air pollution and cigarette advertising, and ambulances to clear our highways of carnage... It counts the destruction of the redwood and the loss of our natural wonder in chaotic sprawl... And the television programs which glorify violence in order to sell toys to our children. Yet the Gross National Product does not allow for the health of our children, the quality of their education or the joy of their play. It does not include the beauty of our poetry or the strength of our marriages, the intelligence of our public debate or the integrity of our public officials. It measures neither our wit nor our courage, neither our wisdom nor our learning, neither our compassion nor our devotion to our country, it measures everything in short, except that which makes life worthwhile.

Kennedy's speech inspired economists to try to quantify the elusive elements that made up the 'quality of life' and determine their influence over GNP. Their first step was to devise new ways of measuring how people really felt throughout the day, and measure their fluctuating emotions against their productivity. They began with the technique of Experience Sampling, which involved bleeping people every other hour or so to ask them what they were doing and if they were happy. Some of the subjects also swabbed their armpits at fixed daily intervals and the swabs were used to establish their cortisol levels, whose release correlates with stress. Economists also developed the Day Reconstruction Method (DRM), which required its subjects to keep journals and to fill in a daily questionnaire about their activities the previous day. Both Experience Sampling and DRM came up with some interesting results. Playing with the children was, for many, an unpleasant rather than joyful experience – much less fun than watching TV; some surveys showed that many people actually liked their work, while others showed the opposite; and almost all suggested that commuters hated commuting. In consequence, when the results of such surveys were collected into well-being indexes, commuting was deemed to be a negative influence on people's lives. The Gallup-Healthways Well-Being Index, for instance, shows a 10 per cent decrease in the well-being of people with long commutes, who, it claims, are more likely than those who walk to work to suffer back and neck conditions; to have raised levels of cholesterol; and to be prone to negative sentiments. The OECD Well-Being Index of thirty-six countries also rates commuting badly. Denmark, which tops its chart, wins partly because average commutes in that country are very short, and 34 per cent of Danish workers travel to their offices by bike. This combination boosts its scores on three counts – health (bicycle commuters have a 28 per cent lower mortality rate than the population average), environment and 'work/life balance'.

So are commuters all suffering from cognitive dissonance and, like smokers, addicted to a habit that will inevitably make them sick and possibly kill them? Some experts think so, and describe such blindness as a 'weighting mistake'. We humans mess up our priorities: we invest our passions in trivia, and overlook important matters – we splash out on a new pair of shoes, and forget to pay our taxes. When it comes to commuting, we dream of having houses with gardens in the suburbs and sending our children to good schools, but forget that we're spending a fortune on season tickets or fuel, and will seldom have time for our gardens or money to pay for private educations for our kids. In essence, we overvalue the rewards and underestimate the costs to our health and sanity. Economists Alois Stutzer and Bruno Frey have labelled this miscalculation the 'Commuter's Paradox' and estimate that we'd need a 20 per cent salary rise to compensate for an extra half hour on our commutes each way. They also note in passing that the 'strain of commuting is associated with raised blood pressure, musculoskeletal disorders, lowered frustration tolerance and increased anxiety and hostility, being in a bad mood when arriving at work in the morning and coming home in the evening, increased lateness, absenteeism and turnover at work, as well as adverse effects on cognitive performance'.

Interestingly, such doom-and-gloom-laden assessments of commuting are contradicted by the facts: with regard to our well-being, figures from the Office for National Statistics (ONS) in Britain revealed that in 2013 the Home Counties commuter belt, comprising Surrey, Buckinghamshire, Hampshire and Oxford-shire, was the best part of the country in which to enjoy 'a life free from health problems or disability'. In prime commuter territory such as Elmbridge in Surrey, less than 4.9 per cent of residents were 'severely constrained by health issues' in comparison to a national average of over 10 per cent, and 15.3 per cent in deprived parts of Liverpool where few commuted (or indeed worked at all).

Commuters may also be happier than their critics claim: on careful reading, some of the principal papers that label commuting hell actually show that most of its practitioners are contented for much of their journeys. Daniel Kahneman's influential DRM survey of 700 Texan working mothers, for example, which has been used extensively in well-being indexes to support the contention that the practice is all pain, found that its subjects were happy for 72 per cent of their road time, and although this was less than when they were having 'intimate relations', it wasn't very different from the pleasure they derived from looking after their children.

Indeed, there's a substantial body of research that suggests that many people actually enjoy their commutes, just like the residents of Levittown in the 1950s. A 1993 study of 1,557 health maintenance organization employees in America, for example, discovered that '94 per cent of those commuting for less that 32 minutes were "satisfied or very satisfied"' with their commutes. In 2001, a survey of a similar number of commuters in the San Francisco Bay Area also got affirmative numbers. More of its respondents liked commuting than found it uncomfortable, and a remarkable 7 per cent said they wished their journeys (by either car or public transport) were longer. The paper concluded that for most 'the ideal commute time is something greater than zero', i.e. some commuting is better than none at all. This implies that its subjects either wanted some separation between work and home, or some sort of journey every day. Two types of personality were identified as having an especial longing for commuting. These were (a) 'status seekers' who agreed with statements in the survey such as 'to me the car is a status symbol' or 'the one who dies with the most toys wins'; and (b) workaholics who counted their journeys as agreeable extensions of their working hours.

Such findings tallied with research into what was hitherto a neglected topic – why commuters might like commuting. According to the prevailing consensus, people travelled solely 'to attain the benefits of being at a different destination' and the journey itself had no pluses at all. This was turned on its head when David Ory and his colleagues at the University of California Transportation Center suggested in a 2004 paper, *When is Commuting Desirable to the Individual?*, that 'positive utility can reside in activities that can be conducted while traveling, as well as in the act of traveling itself'. On public transport these activities included 'opportunities to think, converse, listen to music, read, or even sleep'; when driving solo they were the 'enjoyment of variety, of speed, or even just movement; the acquisition of first-hand information about one's surroundings; and opportunities to exhibit a skill or a status vehicle, or to escape'.

There were, it seemed, plenty of cerebral attractions to commuting. It was meat for the cortex as well as for the lizard portion of the brain, especially for people who drove to work. Indeed, in a 1997 survey of their feelings, '45 per cent of American drivers agreed with the statement "driving is my time to think and enjoy being alone", and 85 per cent agreed with the statement, "I like travelling by private vehicle"'.

Canadians are as gung-ho about commuting as Americans, and their enthusiasm for the pastime includes travelling on public transport. In a 2005 survey carried out by the evolutionary ecologist Martin Turcotte, more people liked commuting than disliked it and one in six of them 'even said that they liked commuting a great deal'. In Turcotte's opinion, his findings raised 'the question of whether commuting workers are people who are "positive" by nature and enjoy a wide variety of activities, including commuting to work'. What, indeed, if they were a race apart – a breed of super humans, better and bolder than their sedentary counterparts, who thought nothing of being in crowds of strangers each day if the journey gave them adventures and had a pot of gold at its end?

Rather than assuming that all commuters are always unhappy and would give it up if they could, and believing that an extra half hour each day in transit makes people's 'life evaluation' ('is it worth it?') plummet to the extent that they need medication, it is more instructive to look a little deeper and see what parts of commuting irritate the most. Are there any minor inconveniences, for example, which if removed would make it more agreeable? Passenger Focus, an independent body established by the British government to look after the interests of the country's rail travellers, has surveyed them in detail to find out what they like most and least about rush hour. Passengers were asked whether their 'reasonable expectations' on eighteen different matters ranging from punctuality to luggage space had been exceeded or not. If so, that part of the experience was graded as positive, and, if not, negative. The 'helpfulness and attitude of staff' was chosen as the sunniest part of each journey and at the bottom of the list, worse than delays and overcrowding, was the state of the toilets on the trains. Indeed, the presumption that commuters have the bladders of elephants or the self-control of martyrs, unless they are disabled, seems to rule the provision of toilets on trains in Britain and throughout Europe, and commuters resent it. It's all very well to assume that every adult has perfected bladder control long before he or she began commuting, but unfair to build carriages for robots who never get caught short. In Holland such resentment bubbled over when Nederlandse Spoorwegen, the national rail carrier, introduced 131 new trains to its commuter routes that had been built without any toilets at all. 'It's unbelievable, nearly all trains offer internet access, but you can't take a pee,' representative Ineke van Gent told the Dutch parliament. In order to stifle the outcry, Nederlandse Spoorwegen responded by offering to install caches of TravelJohn gender-friendly disposable urinals in each carriage. TravelJohns are twenty-first-century versions of the India-rubber travelling lavatories used by Victorian commuters, and consist of a flexible tube connected to a leakproof plastic pouch that contains a urine-absorbing gel. They're considered a godsend by long-distance truckers in the USA, who leave dazzling testimonials on the company's website.* Dutch passengers were allowed to use them in the privacy of the vacant driver's compartment at the rear of the train, as long as they removed them and disposed of them responsibly.

The importance of the presence or absence of toilet facilities to commuters suggests that it would be relatively simple for the operators of public transport to make their passengers happier, and thereby boost the well-being index of the country in which

---

* 'My wife and I drive team in a tractor/trailer throughout the US and Canada. Your product has been a lifesaver a few times when we get stuck in metro rush-hour traffic… Thank you for developing the Travel John. It is long overdue and greatly appreciated.'

they operated, by making minor changes to their services. Commuters, it seems, have jollier dispositions than their critics in the media and among economists allow, and since the economic case against them usually rests on their presumed misery, it would fall apart if it were proven that they were generally in high spirits while crossing no man's land.

And what of the 'nicer home' reason for commuting? Do commuters have more agreeable accommodation than their town or country cousins? Looking at it from the point of view of suburb versus town, commuters seem to win. People who live in cities can never rest. According to Attention Restoration Theory, pioneered by the psychologist Stephen Kaplan in 1989, urban environments require too much concentration. City-dwellers need to have their wits about them in order to avoid bumping into one another, or getting run down by a bus, tram, car, motorbike or even sacred cow. They need to keep their heads up, scanning for threats, at all times. Natural landscapes, in contrast, are undemanding. The difference results from our having two sorts of attention – 'directed attention', when we have to concentrate on something; and 'involuntary attention', when something that excites or pleases us captures our gaze. The directed variety is both demanding and enervating, and whereas cities require plenty of it, natural landscapes don't. Green scenes are packed with 'soft fascinations' that keep the people who live in them calm and act as balm on the brains of visitors from the big smoke. Commuter suburbs usually have far more greenery than towns, and although they're no wildernesses, there's enough nature in them to let their residents relax in a way that true urbanites can't.

What, then, of the country mice? Are they happier in their farms and glades? They're generally poorer and poverty correlates far more strongly with unhappiness than with commuting. There's also the lack of facilities. Suburbs tend to have golf courses and shopping centres nearby and a better choice of schools and hospitals. Moreover, rural life is also perceived to be less salubrious than the suburbs or the city centre. In Britain, for instance, in 2003 there were more than 15,000 complaints to local authorities that the countryside smelled bad, suggesting that people who are used to paved environments find the real country unpleasant. It may look pretty through the windows of a car or train, but it's increasingly seen as a place to visit rather than to put down roots. In Germany, there's even a market in the cities and suburbs for authentic country smells. A company named Stall Luft ('stable air') sells cans of cow farts emitted in a traditional straw-lined stable at £5 a pop to nostalgia-ridden rural émigrés who've traded their milk pails for laptops.

Suburbs, therefore, are a Goldilocks solution: greenery without the inconveniences of a truly rural way of life. They also enhance the economic case for commuting, as houses in suburbs and dormitory towns tend to be significantly cheaper than those in the hearts of the cities to which people commute. According to Savills, the upmarket British estate agent, prices fall substantially as one travels outwards through London Underground's concentric zones. Whereas the average price of a family house in zone 2, which is closer to the centre, was £1.2 million in 2012, in zones 3 and 4, where commuting times are half an hour, it was just over £500,000, and dropped to around £360,000 in the outer zones, where commuting times are nearly an hour and a half. A commuter based in central London willing to put up with more time in transit could therefore buy themselves a house outside it and 'free up sufficient equity to fund major family commitments such as school fees, or a London bolthole that would make it easier to maintain links with the capital'. They'd also have a larger family home, in surroundings that required less directed attention, which would compensate for any additional discomfort occasioned by a longer commute.

In addition to enjoying better jobs and more congenial homes, it has been argued that commuters live a more natural way of life than people who are bottled up in cities or hoeing turnips in the countryside. For most of our existence as a species, we've lived as hunter-gatherers, foraging and killing to obtain our food, and hence we're programmed biologically to travel to win our dinners. Ten thousand years of agricultural sedentariness hasn't been enough to extinguish this instinct – and it has been resurgent ever since the Industrial Revolution gave people the means to express their wanderlust again.

Meta-surveys of traditional hunter-gatherer societies suggest that their way of life is a happy one. Although they work shorter hours, they spend an hour or so each day on the hoof – or about the same as the average OECD commuter. The similarity in daily travel time between such radically different lifestyles inspired Cesare Marchetti, the Venetian theoretical physicist, to suggest that there was a 'quintessential unity of travelling instincts around the world' and that this unity resulted in a fixed 'travel time budget' that he named after himself as Marchetti's Constant. He tested his theory against a variety of cultures past and present and decided that it has shaped our behaviour since the dawn of history. The territory associated with ancient Greek villages, for instance, whose inhabitants went about on foot, was about twenty square kilometres, which was about as much as they could manage within their travel time budget, and this pedestrian limit continued to restrict the size of towns and settlements until the Industrial Revolution. Once the railways gave people the chance to extend their ranges, they did so, but, as a rule, kept within Marchetti's rule of an hour or so of travelling each day. He thought, moreover, that if people tried to violate his constant, and turn the ancestral meander into a route march, they would feel uncomfortable. Such discomfort, he argued, had been a major force in innovation: people had responded to increases in their travel time budgets by inventing or perfecting forms of transportation, including trains, automobiles and airlines, that would let them range further while remaining within the limits of his constant.

Marchetti was convinced, too, that innovation would continue whenever his constant was threatened or breached. He predicted that this would occur in earnest around the year 2000, and suggested that Maglevs – trains powered by magnetic levitation which could in theory carry hundreds of thousands of people vast distances within his magic travel time budget –would be the solution. Ideally, the Maglevs would run through a network of tunnels filled with partial vacuums that would enable them to travel at Mach 5 or 6. The idea has its drawbacks: humans can only stand about 5 g of g-force (equivalent to accelerating at 49 m/s^2) without losing consciousness, although training and g-suits can extend this to 9 g, so the Maglev would have to accelerate and decelerate relatively slowly. After allowing for such biological limitations, Marchetti calculated Maglevs could carry commuters of the future between Paris and Casablanca (1,173 miles) in twenty minutes, enabling Moroccans to work all day in France and be home in time to cook dinner. Half the journey would be spent accelerating at the speed of 'Ferraris and Porsches', the other half braking at an equal rate. Such futuristic transport systems would not only offer commutes more thrilling than any theme-park ride, but they would also, in the opinion of Marchetti, enable a kind of reverse multi-culturalism by allowing different cultures to keep their distances from each other and thus preserve their diversity. While Maglevs have yet to appear in numbers, and the constant, as Marchetti predicted, is being violated by tens of millions of commuters all over the world, it is gaining traction among town planners. The Australian city of Perth, for instance, has restructured its public transport around half-hour journey times, and has become something of a poster child for neo-urbanists in consequence.

Commuting and hunter-gathering are linked by more than a similarity in travel time budgets. Both have a sexual bias. The division of labour by sex is ubiquitous among surviving hunter-gatherer tribes. In most, men do the hunting and women the gathering, and the men spend longer each day on the trail. The men of the Hadza tribe of Tanzania, for instance, who believe they are descended from hairy giants who could kill game just by staring at it, walk 11.4 kilometres a day – nearly twice as much as their wives, mothers and daughters. The same division is apparent among commuters. The latest (2014) figures from Britain's ONS show that men, on average, have longer commutes than women. A 2009 report, meanwhile – 'It's driving her mad: Gender differences in the effects of commuting on psychological health' – led by Jennifer Roberts of Sheffield University, noted that women, especially those with children, suffered more stress in transit than men, and suggested that the added trauma had biological roots.

The similarities between twenty-first-century commuters and hunter-gatherers continue at the outermost edge of the commuting spectrum. Some tribes practise 'persistence hunting' that requires them to spend many hours in transit between hearth and hunting grounds. Persistence hunting consists of running down a large game animal in the heat of the day, when the animal is handicapped by its inability to sweat, and – although it can run much faster than its hunters – has to halt to pant. The more it's pushed, the more often it has to stop, until it can't run at all and is speared at close range. Persistence hunts can take all day. More meat is the reward for more travel. The hunter's counterpart in the world of commuting is the so-called 'extreme commuter', who travels either great distances or for many hours to get to work each day. In America, where average trips are short, the Census Bureau defines 'extreme commuting' as more than ninety minutes each way and reckoned that 2.5 per cent of Americans fell into that category in 2012. The media has crowned various champions of the genre – including Dave Givens, who won Midas Muffler's*

---

* Midas, Inc. is a US chain of automotive service centres.

2006 extreme commuting title by spending an average of seven hours travelling to and from his home in Mariposa, California, to his work in San Jose in Silicon Valley, a round trip of 372 miles. He leaves at 3.30 a.m. and gets back at 8 p.m. He sleeps for five and a half hours of the seven and a half hours that he's at home, leaving only two hours for everything else in his life. When asked how so little could be enough, Givens said: 'it's worth it to me to come home and, you know, see my wife and pet the dogs, see the horses and enjoy where I live, even if it's just for a few hours before I go to bed'. He also thought the journeys themselves to be 'exhilarating... when I get in I'm pumped up, ready to go!'

Givens's efforts wouldn't necessarily impress British commuters, a number of whom travel by train between London and Scotland, and spend over eight hours on the rails each working day. Even my trips on the 07.01 from Botley to Waterloo would have placed me in the category of extreme commuter, alongside every other traveller already on the train, and the tens of thousands of Britons who commute to London from the Midlands, Cambridgeshire, Oxfordshire, Kent and further afield. In a 2014 feature on extreme commuting, the BBC identified a number of Britons who travelled even further than Givens, including Stuart Williams, an IT project manager, who covers 218 miles each way between his home in Ramsbottom, Lancashire, and his office in London. His journey includes a twenty-five-mile drive to Stockport railway station, followed by two and a half hours on the train and half an hour on the Tube. His travel costs the same as it would to rent a place in London, and the long commute, in his opinion, is the 'better option'.

The desire to commute may have cultural as well as biological roots. Many children travel to school on public transport and are conditioned from an early age to spending time in transit. In the UK, a third of all secondary school children travel by bus, and spend an average of seventeen minutes on the road each way. A further quarter travel by car – indeed, school runs are estimated to account for nearly 10 per cent of morning rush-hour traffic. Hence more than half of Britain's children will have between five and seven years' experience of commuting by the time they're old enough to do it for themselves. For many, these formative journeys are pleasant, at least in retrospect. Every school bus story I've ever heard, bar one (a cautionary tale my mother told me about a girl who stuck her arm out of the bus window to wave at a friend and had it ripped off by a passing lorry), has been laced with affection. The time spent on school buses is usually remembered as an anarchic interlude between the rule of parents and that of teachers, and the bus itself as a place where the only adult eyes were those in the driver's mirror, which couldn't see everywhere, and didn't look up often.

The nostalgia that characterizes reminiscences of the school bus seldom translates into a preference for public transport in later life. Over two-thirds of all British workers commute by car. It seems that while school trips might imbue us with a tolerance for the practice of commuting, they also instil the desire to do so alone in our own vehicles. The position is similar in the USA, whose yellow school buses are something of an icon. Fanatics obsess over them and believe they are as important to the national vehicular culture as Model Ts and the Indy 500. The yellow bus legend keeps growing. In 2012, 480,000 yellow buses carried 25 million children to and from school each day, a figure which, according to the American School Bus Council (ASBC), is 'more than half of America's schoolchildren' and makes 'the school bus industry the largest form of mass transit in the United States'. The ASBC also claims that its buses reduce congestion in the morning rush hour, with corresponding environmental and other benefits: 'every school bus on the road eliminates approximately 36 cars… that's 36 fewer cars clogging the morning commute and 36 fewer cars polluting the atmosphere. In 2010, school buses saved the United States 2.3 billion gallons of gasoline, representing $6 billion in savings at 2010 fuel prices!' Such benefits notwithstanding, Americans, like Britons, tend to buy their own wheels when they grow up, and the ambition to possess a car overrules any childish affection for the yellow icon.

In Japan, in contrast, many people continue on the same kind of transport through childhood, adolescence and all their working lives, and spend up to sixty years using public transport. While the country's schoolboys don't attract the same level of fetishism as its girls, they're equally numerous during rush hour. After graduation, many become the salarymen in suits with whom they shared trains when they were dressed in uniforms and carried satchels. Their example supports the notion that commuting can be conditioned into people from an early age. According to the poet William Wordsworth, 'The Child is father of the Man', and it seems in the twenty-first century that a child reared on train timetables will grow up to be a good commuter.

CHAPTER XI

Limbo Rules

You don't discover new lands without consenting to
lose sight of the shore.

André Gide, *Les faux-monnayeurs* (*The Counterfeiters*), 1925

I f commuting is a positive, perhaps even natural, activity for its
participants, who may also have been conditioned to it since
their schooldays, it might be expected that it has influenced their
behaviour outside of as well as during rush hour, and perhaps
also that of their peers. This is indeed the case: the cultural impact
of commuting on behaviour in general has been immense and is
accelerating. Commuters haven't just shaped the landscape with
their railways and suburbs and highways, they've also changed the
way people think and act, and how they communicate with each
other and entertain themselves. Rather than being (as their critics
would have them) a huddled mass of zombies or psychotics who
turn the roads into slow-motion demolition derbies, commuters
as a group are alert, discerning and influential. Behavioural
patterns born in the cauldron of crush loading or the logjam of
gridlock have been adopted outside rush hour. Far from being a
dead time where nothing happens and people suffer in silence, it's
a proving ground for technologies and styles of communication

that later spread to society at large. We are all commuters now.

The cultural influence of commuters derives in part from their consumption patterns. The desire for gadgets that demonstrate portability, miniaturization and connectivity has driven innovation in many fields. Take mobile telecoms, for instance. The first commercial cell-phone service was introduced on Metroliner trains running between New York and Washington in 1969, and while we're now used to seeing children with mobiles, and even some parts of the Hadza territory in Tanzania have network coverage, commuters were the first volume market for them. In addition to taking the lead in consumption, commuters have forged ahead in establishing new behavioural norms when using their gadgets. They were, for instance, the first social class brave enough to make a telephone call a public act. As late as the 1950s in Britain telephones were disliked by the upper class, and the notion that people one day might have intimate conversations on them at the tops of their voices in public spaces would have sent tremors through their upper lips. Now, in contrast, taking or making a call is a kind of performance art. Research has shown that people speak more loudly to their mobiles than in face-to-face conversations. We've become disinhibited, perhaps unnaturally so. We're cautious animals, forever second-guessing each other's intentions, and hiding our own, while we're jockeying for primacy. Such flamboyance could only have emerged on commuter services, where people are accustomed to being alone together, but forget they aren't solitary, and tell their telephones and the world their secrets. This change in attitudes has since spread beyond rush hour.

After mobile calls came texting. Once again, commuters were the first to enjoy regular access to texts. Their messages were used in the main for business – to arrange meetings, confirm contracts and relay market information. But texting, like making calls on the wing, has had a knock-on effect on manners in the world beyond commuting. People accustomed to rearranging meetings at short notice via text became brazen about cancelling dates at the last minute. It's much easier to lie when the offended party can't hear your voice, or, for that matter, see your face. It is, however, harder to convince. According to Dan Goleman, author of *Emotional Intelligence*:

> *…when we talk in person, massive numbers of parallel neural circuits process emotional signals and let us decide instantly what to say or do… a fleeting frown or a lilt in tone of voice is the basis for 'mind sight,' which lets us sense what the other person feels and thinks… Without those cues, we become 'mind blind' – unable to sense what the other person thinks and feels – and thus more prone to send a response that seems 'off '.*

In order to gild lies and salve consciences, text users evolved 'emoticons' – keystroke combinations that, with a little imagination, resemble a human face, and can be used to express a disappointment you might not really feel: ☹.

Notwithstanding its limitations as a method of communicating, texting has been a godsend to commuters in Japan, who have added a literary dimension to it, in the form of text novels.

In 2002, a Tokyo mobile service provider offered its subscribers access to the Shinsho Keitai Bunko – a library of books that could be read as a series of text messages – and promoted them as a pleasurable way to while away time when in transit. As well as reading prepaid fiction on their mobiles, commuters began to write their own stories with their thumbs, and by 2006 text novels dominated the Japanese bestseller lists, both in electronic form and as printed books. *Koizora: Setsunai Koi Monogatari* (*Love Sky: A Sad Love Story*), for instance, a tear-fest par excellence with a plot that streaks along at the speed of a bullet train – schoolgirl narrator endures forbidden love, gang rape, a stillbirth, a cancer-stricken boyfriend, attempts suicide but is dissuaded by the sight of two white doves, finds she is pregnant again by her now-dead boyfriend, and achieves resolution by laying a pair of gloves on the grave of her stillborn daughter, all in her first two years at high school – attracted 20 million subscribers, sold 2 million copies in paperback, and was turned into a hit movie and a manga cartoon series.

The episodic style of Japanese text novels is reminiscent of Victorian commuter fare in Britain. Dickens's novels and the Sherlock Holmes stories were serialized and sold at train stations – each instalment or story being just long enough to entertain the reader on their journey home. Japanese text novels also highlight the continuing and benign influence of commuting over reading habits. Public transport gives its riders detentions twice each day, and many use these chunks of compulsory immobility to escape into fiction, and carry on reading long after their sedentary counterparts have given up the habit for television.

Commuter demand for mobile entertainment continues to drive innovation. Both the Kindle and BlackBerry were targeted at nine to fivers, who also embraced the iPad in their millions while the media was still wondering who would want one. Anything that keeps the eyes, fingers and thumbs occupied in a crowded train, or that expands the range of pleasures available during rush hour has been welcomed. And now that there's mobile internet access even underground, the rat race has acquired an extra dimension. We can both consume and create. We can pretend to be caring on Facebook and make friends with machines. We can watch films and tap out potboilers in real time. Such diversity would have staggered the commuters of fifty years ago, who had little beyond printed matter, whist and smoking with which to entertain themselves.

Here's an example from real life. In the railway carriage where I'm writing this, there's an elderly lady to my left playing Patience on her mobile, and a man my age across the table is locked into a session of iDestroy, busy creating and exterminating species of vividly coloured insects. Across the aisle, there's a student reading on his Kindle, a woman in a business suit tapping figures into a spreadsheet on her laptop while playing online poker in another window on its screen, and a burly man with a shaven head is standing in the aisle between us scrolling through Russian mail-order brides on his iPhone. There are also half a dozen copies of free newspapers – *Metro* and the *London Evening Standard*, both of which are bucking the trend in declining circulation for print publications – lying around.

The *Standard* and *Metro* target commuters, and both papers are long on emotional matters – romance, gossip and star signs. Their audience, it seems, are as keen to read about love affairs as stock prices. Indeed, commuting has been as disinhibiting for lovers as it has for people who love talking on the phone. When it started in Victorian times, commuting hastened the decline of traditional communities and the establishment of new ones, where parochial taboos no longer ruled. Commuting allowed singletons to have lives in two places and to meet a wider range of potential partners. Hence it increased their chances of finding love. Moreover commuting blossomed in tandem with the Victorian discovery of romantic love, and the offspring of its love matches, who were the first-generation natives of suburbia, found it to be a rich hunting ground.

People still think about love during rush hour. Their sweet musings are explained in part by demographics. On the London Tube, for instance, two-thirds of passengers are male, with an average age between twenty-five and thirty-five and average income well above the median, and one-third are women five years younger with lower-paid jobs. About half of each sex is single. Statistically there's no better place to find a good match than underground. This potential is recognized by dating agencies and other advertisers looking to sell to the hopeful or the smitten.

Early adverts on the Tube highlighted the fact that it brought strangers together. The first poster commissioned by Frank Pick, the man responsible for the publicity and marketing of the Underground Electric Railway Company of London in Edwardian times, showed escalators of elegant men and women dressed up for a night out, with the motto 'Brightest London is best reached by underground'. Face-to-face encounters on passing escalators, both inside and outside of rush hour, have since become iconic scenes – like adorations or crucifixions. I remember the posters for Dateline on the Tube in the 1980s, for instance, which showed a couple gazing at each other across a pair of up and down tube escalators, he rising, she descending, above the slogan 'Don't let love pass you by'. There was such a yearning in their eyes as they passed that they evoked Romeo calling out to his Juliet on a summer night in Verona. On bad days, however, they made one feel like Orpheus in the underworld, who loved and looked and lost.

Nowadays, there are a host of apps and live online services for people seeking love in transit, which make it easier to put inclination into action: there's no need to wait until we get home to ring a dating agency. Grindr, for instance, the gay geosocial meat market app, and its hetero/bi-curious equivalent Blendr (motto 'Social networking just got social'), will alert us if there are others nearby wanting affection and offer up their profiles. According to an editorial at Queerly.com, 'some of us only have time to do our mobile cruising during morning commutes', and the missed trysts Dateline used to taunt us with can now be fulfilled.

There are, however, limits to disinhibition when it comes to love during rush hour. Watching pornography on British public transport seems to be taboo.* A recent thread on Mumsnet, for instance, the UK's largest parental website, which began with the post, 'A colleague told me today that the man sitting next to her on the train was watching graphic porn on his iPad. She

---

* In contrast to Japan, where even comic books are pornographic.

did ask him to stop but he refused. I think she was brave to do that. WWYHD?'* received hundreds of responses, the majority in favour of intervention, either by telling the watcher to desist, or alerting the transport police. Indeed, a common morality – to keep it prim – has arisen among the first crush-loaded generation to have hardcore at their fingertips. How can you watch porn and not think about sex? And if you are thinking about sex, then everyone around you could be a target for your lust – which breaches the commuter compact that we travel together but pretend to be alone. Commuting can reinforce inhibitions as well as freeing us from them: as one of the contributors on Mumsnet pointed out, a train carriage 'is not a private space'.

Rush hour has altered attitudes towards infection as well as romance. We crowd together with strangers in a way that would have surprised our ancestors, who were wary of such contacts. Strangers were often suspected of possessing evil powers in pre-scientific societies, for the very good reason that they might be carrying a new disease. According to James Frazer, the godfather of anthropology, and author of *The Golden Bough* (1890):

> *To guard against the baneful influence exerted voluntarily or involuntarily by strangers is... an elementary dictate of savage prudence... Thus, when the ambassadors sent by Justin II, Emperor of the East, to conclude a peace with the Turks had reached their destination, they were received by shamans, who subjected them to a ceremonial purification*

---

* What Would You Have Done?

for the purpose of exorcising all harmful influence. Having deposited the goods brought by the ambassadors in an open place, these wizards carried burning branches of incense round them, while they rang a bell and beat on a tambourine, snorting and falling into a state of frenzy in their efforts to dispel the powers of evil. Afterwards they purified the ambassadors themselves by leading them through the flames.

On the Tube, however, we've made a bonfire of our taboos over infection. Instead of fumigating outsiders and their possessions, running from people with coughs, or belling lepers, we squeeze up against strangers without giving a second thought as to whether they might be carrying some contagious and fatal disease. Although such casual attitudes may strengthen commuters' immune systems by exposing them to a greater variety of everyday pathogens than people who live in isolated communities enjoy, 'Far from the madding crowd's ignoble strife', the conditioning comes at a price. Nearly 90 per cent of London Tube-goers, for instance, catch flu and other viral infections each winter, as opposed to only 50 per cent of walkers or cyclists.

Public transport, moreover, is a haven for bacteria. Microbiologists from Birmingham's Aston University took swabs from the seats, door buttons and handrails of various metro and rail carriages around Britain, and found them everywhere. The average square centimetre of seating on the Tube yielded 1,390 micro-organisms. This, however, was nothing in comparison to a Cardiff bus seat, which had 4,600 in the same area, and a desert when compared to the Newcastle Metro, where the seating hosted an amazing 190,500 bacterial cells per square centimetre – or nearly 1,250,000 per square inch – equivalent to the human population of Newcastle and its suburbs. There's quality as well as quantity among bacteria on commuter lines. A recent sampling of the micro-organisms on New York's subway came up with such exotica as *Aerococcus viridans,* which causes gaffkaemia in lobsters, *Acinetobacter radioresistens,* which, as its name suggests, is radiation resistant, *Corynebacterium glutamicum,* which eats arsenic and is thought to have a promising future as a bio-remediant, and *Shigella boydii,* which gives New Yorkers diarrhoea.

Although commuters on public transport are exposed to more minor ailments that their country cousins, they're much less likely to catch a new disease: '60 per cent of emerging human pathogens are zoonotic' (i.e. 'microbiologic infections acquired from animals'). Life in the sticks, with its constant exposure to domesticated and wild animals, is the frontline of our biological war with nature. A Dutch goat farmer, for instance, is far more likely to contract Q fever than his or her contemporary who commutes on the Nederlandse Spoorwegen and has to use a TravelJohn rather than the nearest hedge.

Commuting has also exerted a disinhibiting influence on our eating habits. Before rail time appeared, people used to order their days around meals. In Britain, the middle and upper classes ate a hearty breakfast early, and did not eat again until dinner time, which, just before commuting was born, was at three or four in the afternoon. The period before dinner was referred to as 'morning' and when dinner finished it was night-time. Dinner was a heroic affair that lasted anything from two to eight hours, sometimes with a break for a visit to the theatre if its participants lived in town. The rich ate seven courses, and even the middling sort had both quantity and variety on their tables, with menus such as 'boiled chicken and a pig's face, a bullock's heart and a rich plum pudding'. Dinner might be followed by supper at about ten at night, which consisted of cold cuts washed down with a bowl of alcoholic punch.

This rhythm changed quickly after commuting appeared. While there was already a trend towards dining later, which had been advancing at a rate of about forty-five minutes per century between William the Conqueror (who ate his dinner at 9 a.m.) and Oliver Cromwell (1 p.m.), the meal leapt into the evening once Victorians started commuting en masse. They worked from nine till five, Monday to Saturday, and ate breakfast before they left for the train and dined when they returned home. So long a stretch without food was alien to a British stomach that had traditionally needed food every six hours. Workmen solved the problem by carrying interim sustenance with them, and broiled kippers or warmed up slabs of beef in railway waiting rooms. Clerks and cerebral workers, meanwhile, relied on chophouses, taverns or cafés to keep them satisfied. Throughout the old-style morning these places sold simple meals that were kept hot and served as soon as they were ordered – the fast food of their era. There were also the infamous railway sandwiches that Dickens had satirized for the benefit of anyone tempted by stale bread, sawdust and gristle. Little by little, lunch – a meal eaten in a hurry and alone among strangers – crept into both the working day and the vernacular.

This was an important change. Hitherto in Britain – at least among the upper and middle classes who formed the first waves of commuters – meals had been as much social events as opportunities to sate hunger. Eating on the hoof was thought to be brutish, and until lunch became a fixture some seem to have preferred to starve rather than debase themselves during the working day by stuffing their faces in silence and solitude. In *Movable Feasts*, a study of changes in English eating habits, the example is given of a nineteenth-century solicitor's apprentice who breakfasts at 8.30 a.m., dines at 7.30 p.m., and has nothing more than a biscuit and a glass of sherry in between. Presumably sneaking off to a chophouse would have been a black mark against him for ungentlemanly behaviour, and solicitors aspired to be gentlemen.

The passing of such dignified self-restraint is now lamented, especially when it comes to eating on public transport. Transport for London and its predecessors have long run campaigns intended to dissuade passengers from offending others by eating odoriferous food in a noisy and messy manner. Its latest programme is the Travel Better London Campaign, which sets out its message as a poem on a poster that shows a faceless passenger munching on a burger while a traveller on the facing seat looks as though she's trying not to gag:

There is a special type of beast
Who likes to sit down and feast
On the train and on the bus

Unaware of all the fuss,
That Takeaways (although easy)
Can make others feel quite queasy

The message has popular appeal. Passenger surveys show that having to watch other people eat ranks high on the list of irritants. The *London Evening Standard* fulminated against it in a 2013 article on the 'Underground commandments'. In the same year a piece in *Esquire* magazine entitled 'The Real Rules of Using London Underground', aimed at 'anyone who fights their way through the underground jungle every day', included a warning against gobbling down junk food as rule number nine: 'a discreet sandwich or packet of crisps is fine, but anyone eating anything hot or smelly is an enemy to us all'.

Commuting in motorcars has also influenced life beyond rush hour. We've seen how it fashioned the settled environment in America in the decades when the nation rose to be a superpower, how it gave freedom of movement to the average citizen, and how it helped turn cars into cultural icons. As John Keats observed of his countrymen back in 1958, 'The automobile changed our dress, our manners, social customs, vacation habits, the shape of our cities, consumer purchasing patterns, common tastes, and positions in intercourse.' These changes are still afoot and car commuting has been as disinhibiting on behaviour in general as crush loading on public transport, albeit in different ways. When we're packed together in tube carriages, we aim to stand aloof; when we're really alone, gridlocked in our isolation cells and banging on our horns, we engage with strangers and even pick fights with them.

Indeed, instead of hiding our identity on the roads, we tend to assert it, perhaps out of pleasure as much as necessity. Car commuting gives us the chance to be individuals in an otherwise conformist society – to get a rush out of rush hour. It allows us to let off steam with an enthusiasm that would be difficult at work where we're expected to be model team players, and impossible at home where we have to display affection, intuition and the patience of martyrs. It's a twice-daily dose of freedom, a little bit of licence that helps keep us stable for the rest of the day. According to Tom Vanderbilt, author of *Traffic: Why We Drive the Way We Do (and What It Says About Us)*, 'it can be quite therapeutic to act like a yelling maniac once in a while, and the plush, leather-seated interior of a car provides a nice, semi-private environment in which to do that. Remember, in traffic, no one can hear you scream.'

In addition to acting as a safety valve, commuting by car also offers its practitioners the opportunity to compete in a much more immediate way than they do at work, where progress and promotion happen over years rather than the few seconds it takes to cut up a rival on the highway. Even simulated commuting can get people revved up. An experiment intended to prove that the rat race was bad for the heart found that this might be because of over-excitement rather than a slow-burning form of stress. David Strayer, psychology professor at the University of Utah, 'ran a simulation where people drove under the assumption that they were late for a meeting, and there was a financial incentive to get there before other people. One group drove in high-density traffic, another had an easier traffic environment. Some people were told there was a time limit.' Strayer found that his virtual commuters, especially those chasing the clock through busy roads, started 'driving by cars and flipping them off and honking at them' even though they were only pretend-driving in a laboratory booth. He concluded that an 'aggressive, combative, competitive frame for driving' may have deep roots in our evolutionary past, suggesting that driving to work can help us to stay true to our competitive natures in a world where chances for contest are otherwise few and far between.

Like their counterparts on public transport, people who commute by car have become disinhibited in their dietary habits. There's a current trend among commuters to stretch out their travel times in order to incorporate things they used to do at home, eating and drinking in particular.* Many leave for work earlier than they need to in order to enjoy a morning coffee and bagel on the road rather than at the breakfast table. Starbucks, which once declared that it would never sell to motorists, now has 800 drive-throughs in America to satisfy this new demand. Some of its outlets face each other across the same roads so as to catch both the morning and evening rush hours, for commuters are proving just as eager to extend their journeys on the way home. Cars have been adapted to accommodate their appetites, and fitted with supersize drink-holders and fold-out trays so speed freaks can pig out while at the wheel. Every year, millions are spent researching the ideal portion sizes for in-car eating and drinking. Will a 12-ounce burger shed its filling on a 30-degree

---

* Some German and Swiss commuters also visit drive-through brothels.

bend? Will a 16-ounce skinny latte with a shot of maple syrup leap out of its holder and scald the driver, maybe for life, and blind them with its froth so that they hit a telegraph pole or a school bus? Although the potential for lawsuits is dizzying, car-makers nonetheless bow to what they perceive to be their customers' wants and compete to offer them better facilities for eating and drinking during their commutes.

The automobile is now an official 'Food and beverage venue' in the opinion of *Food and Drug Packaging*, and home to a majority of the 4.4 billion 'on-the-go' 'eating occasions' that took place in the USA in 2008.* According to Datamonitor, the business intelligence provider, eating 'is no longer considered a primary activity' in the sense of being an end in itself, but rather is something we do while driving or working or watching television. Food on the go has become 'ingrained in our lives', and fast-food manufacturers have altered their products to suit the new Zeitgeist. 'One-handed convenience' is the contemporary mantra. A commuter should be able to grip a burger or taco in one hand without spilling bits of it into their lap. The Taco Bell Gordita Supreme Beef, for example, 'warm, pillowy flatbread filled with seasoned ground beef, reduced-fat sour cream, crisp shredded lettuce, a three-cheese blend and diced ripe tomatoes', is designed to be a single-fisted eating experience.

Success, however, has created a burden of expectation. Datamonitor believes that 'consumers will increasingly view the "convenience" aspect of on-the-go formats as a given', and look

---

* Americans spend more on fast food than on education.

for their big snacks not only to satisfy their hunger but also to offer 'fun, interactivity or variety that fit with their motivations at different times of the day'. They want some of the ceremony or pleasure that surrounded eating in a pre-industrial world: food should be more than fuel. While even the most Mitty-esque driver would have trouble transforming in their imagination their on-the-go eating occasion into a Georgian dinner party lasting many hours, with seven courses, songs and multiple libations, they're still suckers for a whiff of romanticism in their takeaways. Snack-makers have responded by trying to imbue their offerings with mystery via the use of exotic ingredients and suggestive packaging.

In Britain, for instance, BP created 'Wild Bean Cafes' within its petrol stations in an attempt to trade on the traveller's desire to find spiritual nourishment in fast food. Wild Bean's offerings focus on purity and nature, in the sense of using clearly identifiable ingredients such as blue cheese in salads and free-range egg in egg mayonnaise sandwiches, while still providing the calories snack-eaters need to compensate for the absence of formal meals. Its lead has been followed: both Waitrose and Marks and Spencer, who together represent the upper crust of British food retailing, now have franchises at service stations.

Fast-food vendors are also targeting British service stations. According to *British Baker* magazine, the voice of the convenience-food sector, drive-through outlets are 'an exciting new channel' for sales and are expected to offer major opportunities for growth. Starbucks has commenced a programme of building 200 new drive-throughs in Britain by 2017, McDonald's is launching them at the rate of thirty a year, and the Krispy Kreme doughnut chain is also opening UK roadside outlets. Most are sited along busy commuter routes. However, the increase in 'dashboard dining' has led to problems. Research conducted by psychologist Conrad King for the RAC suggested that the smell of fast-food wrappers could increase a driver's propensity to road rage, by making them hungry, irritable and impatient. 'More than any other sense, the sense of smell circumnavigates the logical part of the brain and acts on the limbic and emotional systems,' King told the BBC, and when cars were brought into the equation, 'the ability of various smells to over- or under-stimulate us as drivers can have catastrophic results.'

Fast-food packaging is a threat to the environment as well as to the peace of mind of motorists. Drivers have become disinhibited over its disposal, and some of it leaves cars through their windows. Solo drivers, who make up the majority of car commuters, are the worst offenders. After collecting more than 150,000 sacks of litter from British roads in 2013, the Highways Agency launched a 'Bag it. Bin it!' campaign aimed at persuading motorists to keep a rubbish bag beside them that they could fill while in transit, and dispose of in safety at their destinations.*

Rush hour has influenced its participants' listening habits as much as their diets. The motorcar was established as a music venue long before it became a place to eat one's breakfast. Who

---

* Any driver worried that accumulated fast-food packaging might give them road rage should buy a peppermint air freshener. According to Conrad King's research, the smell of peppermint has the opposite effect on a driver's brain to the scent of junk food, and thus may counteract it.

had time for a Double Bacon & Egg McMuffin® when they were speeding down the freeway singing along to 'Born to be Wild' and banging out the rhythm on the steering wheel? Listening to music is the most popular diversionary activity of people who are driving alone. Their favourite source is radio, which is still the 'undisputed champion of in-car entertainment in America' and indeed in Britain. It has outlived eight-track, cassettes, CDs and MiniDiscs, and has kept its market share in an age of smartphones, podcasts, satnavs and Pandora streams. Eighty-four per cent of American drivers listen to their radios while commuting, and two key spells of each day's programming are dedicated to commuters – the a.m. and p.m. 'drive times'. These are the most expensive periods in which to advertise, implying that their audiences are attentive, suggestible and more valuable than any other class of American listener. This is in part because auto-commuters are believed to trust their radios as well as love them. Surveys, and brain scans, show that both their happiness and energy levels are raised when they hear a favourite station. Radio is a companion that offsets isolation, connects the driver to the great world beyond the car, and provides him or her with uplifting music and familiar voices and prejudices. Commuters, moreover, believe that radio presenters care for them. They warm to any voice that is trying to cheer them up when they're tied up by congestion, and even appreciate the tones of commiseration feigned by traffic reporters when they mention five-mile tailbacks. Indeed, it has been suggested that listening to traffic reports is an exercise in self-pacification rather than news-gathering: 'the traffic bulletins really are about collective solace, an invitation to fatalism, and even masochism – for the jams, like the poor, will always be with us'.

Drive-time radio is, however, a fickle and changing market. Broadcasters have made and lost fortunes trying to second-guess what combination of music, news, polemic and traffic reports is irresistible to commuters. A good drive-time DJ knows if and when and why they might want to hear the news, their horoscopes, or 'Won't Get Fooled Again'. Successful formulas developed during rush hour have proved equally so outside it: drive-time trends have been a decisive influence on radio broadcasting to non-commuters, and have represented both a picture and a prophecy of tastes in audio entertainment over the past fifty years.

Preferences have shifted since mass-market car radios first appeared in the 1960s. Drivers on the free-moving highways of that era, the descendants perhaps of the founding members of the Chicago Automobile Club, that 'virile and fearless' association of motorists, seem to have had substantial attention spans and could listen to the same music shows for hours on end, without being overcome by the need to hear a snippet of celebrity gossip or news. However, as the traffic snarled up over subsequent decades, impatience bubbled into commuters' heads. Their diminished ability to focus was first addressed by the 'morning zoo' style of radio show, which made its debut in America in the 1980s, and used multiple hosts who teased or abused each other in between songs, phone-ins, tittle-tattle and traffic reports. The format is now standard throughout the Anglosphere. *The Chris Evans Breakfast Show* on BBC Radio 2, which is the most popular radio programme in Britain, has a mini-menagerie of presenters, as does its evening counterpart led by Simon Mayo. Even Jack FM, a new commercial station in the south of England with an otherwise DJ-free business model, has Bam Bam, Hayley and Welshy to guide its listeners through rush hour. Although it is happy to play pre-recorded messages in between tunes and adverts for the rest of the day, it won't risk it during the peak, when authenticity rules.

Every morning zoo has its king of the beasts, and in the USA these evolved into shock jocks. It seems that commuters became bored of their favourite menageries, and sought greater thrills from the airwaves. DJs like Howard Stern gave them the kicks they missed. Stern made his name with a routine called 'Bestiality Dial-a-Date', was censured in court for his 'frequent and explicit' references to genitalia and coitus, and set a record for fines for indecency. After fifteen years at the top, he moved to Sirius Satellite Radio, where he still raves in his inimitable style, deals in smut and delights a seven-figure audience of commuters.

Indeed, the 'mass-marketing of outrage' to people stuck in rush-hour traffic with 'blood-pressure levels already approaching the blowout range' has proved popular with audiences at all times of the day. Once again, commuter tastes have leaked into the mainstream. The most popular radio programme in America, the *Rush Limbaugh Show*, takes its inspiration from drive-time slots and peddles a mix of snap judgements and adrenaline-charged rants to its 15 million listeners.

The drive-time radio advertising market profits from the trust that commuters place in their favourite presenters and shows. Messages can be wrapped around the traffic reports that they're listening out for. The biggest advertisers, in fact, are car-makers, used-car dealers and insurers. It seems that when we're driving, our minds as well as our eyes are on the road: research suggests that we meditate on buying faster, more elegant or more comfortable machines while we're stuck in traffic. Maybe the lizard truly does rise, and inspires us to lust after the largest and least practical vehicles even at a time when we might be expected to hate them. By rights, adverts for cars should jar if we feel imprisoned behind the wheel when we hear them. Perhaps we're receptive because the automobile still has some of the cultural aura that grew up around it in the first half of the twentieth century: it's still a mythical steed like Roy Rogers's Trigger. We want to keep a little fantasy in our road time, even if it's only of owning dream cars and possessing the freedom of the roads, rather than sailing to the South Pacific or conquering Everest. Such wistfulness is also apparent in our choice of motoring apps. Trapster, for example, which has nearly 20 million users, cries out warnings from your phone when you're getting close to speed traps, sobriety checkpoints and red-light cameras. *Time* magazine voted it one of the 'Ten Best iPhone Apps for Dad' in 2009 – 'If your dad has the soul of an outlaw.'

Auto-commuters are creatures of beauty to billboard as well as radio advertisers. When drivers are stuck in a jam, they're immobilized in much the same way as tube passengers, and likewise are looking for something to stare at other than their fellow unfortunates. Hence billboards have 'dwell times' similar to those of posters in underground carriages, in the sense that their viewers may have little else to look at. Although their detractors label them 'visual pollution', and lament the waste of an acre or so of fertile ground on a tubular steel frame carrying 60" by 100" boards, commuters appreciate them as distractions and read them. Advertisers, in their turn, try to titillate their audiences with inventive and extravagant displays: giant fibreglass McMeals, real Mini Coopers, neon crosses, slogans – 'What Would Jesus Drive?' Indeed, everyone wants their message in front of the eyes of the auto-commuter, or shouted into their ears. Politicians all over America buy billboard space and airtime in drive time, and beg to be interviewed by stations that they think are sympathetic to their platforms. Drivers are voters and tend to be swayed by what they hear between home and work. Hence drive time can be an important factor in elections, especially when local issues are at stake. In New Jersey, for example, which relies on New York and Philadelphia TV stations for its local news, the 1993 gubernatorial contest was decided on the strength of shock jocks' advice over the radio on how to vote. The incumbent, Jim Florio, was pilloried as 'Flim-Flam Florio' in rush-hour shows and the winner, Christie Whitman, acknowledged her debt to the DJs and their four-wheeled voters by christening a toilet block on the New Jersey Turnpike after Howard Stern.

British politicians also exploit drive time. In 2010, in the months leading up to the general election, the Labour administration bombarded the airwaves during rush hours with public-service advertorials. Listeners were given advice on how to lose weight, claim benefits, have a free health MOT, and see off door-to-door salesmen who might defraud them. The announcements gave the impression that the government cared for the well-being of the voters, and would lavish money and attention on them if they voted the right way. They were also a perfect way to get around strict limitations on spending during British elections. While the Labour Party could spend no more than £19 million in total on selling itself to voters, the Labour government spent £34 million a month on radio propaganda. In its defence, it claimed that it had to take up the slack in advertising revenues, which had fallen during the recession. As a listener, it was a novelty to hear feel-good messages instead of the usual warnings about being fined if you didn't buy a television licence or pay your road tax. As a driver, it was disheartening to be taken for a fool.

British motorists contribute over £30 billion in petrol duty and road taxes each year, while the government spends only a third of that on the roads. Indeed, it seems that politics, on a national level, is the exception that proves the rule when it comes to the influence of commuting over both its participants' lives and society at large: although they're courted, it's as a loose social class rather than a coherent lobby with specific demands. Commuters aren't as significant a collective force in politics as they deserve to be.

◆ ◆ ◆ ◆ ◆

CHAPTER XII

Controlling the Flow

> It was a Monday morning rush hour at an underground station. I can picture myself walking down the stairs, standing near the edge and then stepping forward into nothing as the train approached.
>
> Anonymous [attempted suicide], *Guardian*, 27 January 2012

Imagine hurtling along a pitch-black tunnel in the cab of a tube train, whose headlamps bite just far enough into the darkness ahead to illuminate the shining rails beneath and the soot and encrustations on the circular walls either side and overhead, which seem scarcely wide enough to pass between. Suddenly, the tunnel divides into twin barrels like those of a shotgun, and before you know it, you've taken the left-hand one and it curves sharply away and you brace yourself against the centripetal force. You straighten out in time to see a blinding disc of light ahead, then a row of posters with pictures of coconut palms and footballers flashes by on one wall and a crowd of faces stare at you from a platform on the other side as the brakes squeal and the train halts. There's a strange look on all of the faces – a mix of resignation and aggression – that is genuinely disturbing when you see it for the first time. Tube drivers see it every working day, and enjoy a privileged view of commuters, being with us but not of us. They're members of a 18,000-strong army of London Underground employees whose job it is to get everyone else to their desks – to stage-manage rush hours and cart around herds of shoppers, sybarites and tourists in between.

There are over half a billion commuters around the world. Their journeys are choreographed by millions of workers, ranging from train drivers and ticket collectors, through control-centre operatives, to civil servants and transport ministers. Entire industries, moreover, are dedicated to the business of getting people to work. The people on the other side of the barrier, so to speak, have different perspectives on commuting from its participants, and vast responsibilities. They see, and have to manage, all our individual journeys in the collective. The driver of a crush-loaded tube train, for example, carries the burden of delivering over a thousand passengers to their destinations day in and day out. So what's it like from their perspective? Is it the same, more or less, as distributing parcels? Or do drivers and other transport personnel feel that they have a bond with their charges: that they are our shepherds and we are their sheep? We commuters seem to treat them as being on the same side. Surveys of tens of thousands of UK rail travellers by Passenger Focus always rate the kindness and helpfulness of staff highly. In Tokyo, meanwhile, fetishists pay their controllers the ultimate compliment by dressing up as station staff in uniforms bought under the counter,* and memorize their announcements. But are such compliments returned? Do transport personnel think of commuters as being placid flocks, easy to control and please, or unpredictable collections of lunatics who will make a mess of both their own trips and the entire system unless supervised with the utmost diligence? Do they notice traits in our behaviour that we ourselves can't detect? And finally, do we cause them as much stress as we are said to suffer ourselves?

Underground train drivers certainly see their charges as human beings, albeit not entirely rational ones. From their point of view, passenger indifference to whether the carriage doors are open or closing is infuriating as well as hazardous. In his autobiography *Mind the Doors!* (2002), Robert Griffiths, who worked on the Tube as both platform attendant and train driver for more than thirty-five years, noted that 'many passengers have been dragged to their deaths as a result of their clothing or bags becoming caught in the doors', and thought that the best way to prevent such tragedies was via verbal bonding between driver and travellers. A quick and witty announcement over the intercom was worth a thousand safety notices. The notion that passengers will respond to humour as much as hectoring seems to be common among drivers, who are renowned for making the occasional, sardonic statement on the PA to keep passengers in check. Messages such as: 'Next time you might find it easier to wait until the doors are open before trying to get on the train'; or 'This is a customer announcement, please note that the big slidey

---

* Their sale to the public is prohibited.

things are doors, the big slidey things are doors' might make us hold back from committing fatal errors.

A recurrent theme in tube drivers' accounts of commuters is their unpredictability. One minute they might be streaming along in peace, and the next turn into a pack of zombies, either absolutely careless of their own and others' safety, or utterly irrational. They dive into closing doors, try to climb out of carriages if they're stopped for more than a few minutes in a tunnel, then, perversely, refuse to get off if they are told that the train is on fire. Bus drivers on duty during rush hour note similar traits among commuters. The driver-turned-novelist Magnus Mills describes the same impulsiveness among the passengers he had to pick up from a tube terminus in *The Maintenance of Headway* (2009):

> From 7 o'clock until 9, swarms of them emerged from the escalators in a continual surge. Woe betide a bus that happened to arrive just after a train had come in. Within seconds it would fall victim to the sort of feeding frenzy usually associated with the jungle: a grazing beast laid low by predators. Even when the bus was full the people kept trying to get on, and the besieged driver could do little to relieve the situation.

Platform staff and station managers have a slightly different view of the commuters from drivers. They don't share their journeys: instead of seeing passengers only when they pull into stations, as if they were picking them up from harbours on an otherwise hidden coast, they encounter, or monitor via CCTV, flowing masses of humanity coming at them from all directions during rush hour. They have a golden rule that, whether rational or not, travellers must be kept moving, 'like sheep' according to John Hodges, a control-room assistant at Bank Station, speaking to the BBC in 2012. Bob Weedon, the station's manager, however, has a more humane view. 'If people have almost forgotten that they've travelled on the [Tube]... if you can make it as painless and speedy as possible then you've done a good job.'

There are plenty of tricks to keep people moving, including sending them on dog-legs around the communication tunnels between platforms, and reversing escalators, so that more passengers can get out of a station than into it or vice versa. The signage in the Underground has also been designed to keep the crowds in a liquid state. The location and size of every notice that commuters encounter, and what each says, are determined in accordance with the principle of phased disclosure. Its prophet, Paul Marchant, who advises London Underground how to guide people from station entrances to their trains, believes that information should only be released on a need-to-know basis. Too much choice will make crowds freeze and the Tube's tubes congeal. Therefore sign sizes and the information they include are matched to 'decision-making points' that offer commuters simple A or B choices when they're reached, such as turn left, turn right, go up, go down. There are also comfort signs that reward travellers with a little thrill when they arrive at their target platform or exit. The font size of the lettering on signs is determined by a simple formula linking sight lines and distances. The blurs resolve into information at precisely the right ranges.

The Tube has long been an innovator in signage. Frank Pick commissioned the typographer Edward Johnston to design its iconic sans-serif font in 1913, briefing him that it should be bold, authentic and 'unmistakably' twentieth century. At the time, sans-serif fonts had 'plebeian' associations. Formal signs were expected to be in capital letters and decked with serifs. The clarity of sans-serifs, however, led to their adoption, in title case, on road signs, railway stations and bus blinds, as well as on the Underground over the course of the next fifty years, albeit after a minor cultural war in the 1960s. Emotions ran so high between pro and contra serif-istas that the conflict made national news. A debate was televised between Jock Kinneir, who described himself as a 'visual engineer' and thought serif notices in capitals were 'symptomatic of authoritarian government', in the sans-serif corner, and David Kindersley, a stone letter-carver with an opulent beard, who wanted hooks and tails on every letter of transport signage, which should also be in upper case wherever possible. The Worboys report of 1963 eventually settled in favour of sans-serif fonts. The serif-lovers weren't graceful losers and comforted themselves with visions of a future where their typefaces ruled once again and Underground and motorway signs were sneered at as 'brash reminders of an aesthetically impoverished age'.*

Visual engineering and sending commuters along dog-legs aren't always enough to keep rush hour flowing. Station personnel also have to deal with intra-commuter competition, as well as sheer bloody-mindedness. While we commuters on

---

* The march of sans-serif fonts continues: they're reckoned to be easier to read on computer screens and therefore dominate digital publishing.

public transport may think we're meek and mild beyond the call of duty, our behaviour appears otherwise to the average platform attendant, who sees things in us that we can't, including a competitive streak. If you're on duty on the same platform every day you notice individuals as well as hordes, and watch them struggling not just against the system but also each other. There are people who fight their way onto a train as soon as it arrives, others who time their runs for the doors late but shimmy around their fellow commuters as if it was an exercise in balance and coordination that gave them pleasure, and a few who use blocking tactics and take up as much of the door frame as possible when boarding.

While intra-commuter competition was denied or discouraged in the past, and visible only to the people responsible for controlling our flow, its existence is now recognized. In a 2004 experiment, the technology company Hewlett Packard fitted caps with electrodes to the heads of rail commuters to measure their heart and brain activity. It found that the excitement and anxiety they experienced when jostling for space were as intense as the emotions felt by fighter pilots during combat or riot policemen confronted with a violent protest. Commuter vs commuter action even has its advocates, who think that competition adds a certain spice to rush hour. Brendan Nelson, for instance, a digital strategist who believes that winning a place to sit should be the first goal of any rush-hour traveller, has devised a seat-acquisition formula that draws on game theory, Sun Tzu's *The Art of War*, and statistical analysis. Nelson treats the carriage as a tactical space, with three classes of occupants, each of whom poses a different kind of challenge to seat-seekers whom he calls 'Aspirants'. 'Civilians' are people pretending they'd rather stand; and 'Occupants' are the guilty or smug-looking individuals sitting down. If you follow Nelson's advice, you can deal with all three types of traveller and get the weight off your feet within a couple of stops. There's even an app for super-competitive commuters that tells them which carriage to join on the train so as to be closest to the exit at their destination.

Platform workers dislike rivalry among commuters because it creates turbulence in the flow. They're similarly perturbed by the frequent intransigence of their charges. Rush-hour travellers lock into surprisingly precise routines during their daily odysseys. Some will only get onto a certain train, even if it is crush loaded and they have been promised an empty one in two minutes, while others will insist on standing on exactly the same spot on the platform every day, even if it means burrowing into a scrum to get there when there's plenty of space on the wings. It's as if they believe there is only one true formula for tube riding, and any deviation, however small, will result in catastrophic failure. Such obstinacy can affect entire carriages as well as individuals. Robert Griffiths laments in *Mind the Doors!* how difficult it can be to persuade passengers to abandon the train, even when faced with a real and present emergency like a fire.

Bus commuters are also intransigent. Magnus Mills describes them standing by a stop covered with a yellow hood saying NOT IN USE and waving mournfully at passing buses. Similarly, many look only at the number of the bus and not at its destination blinds. In Mills's opinion, 'I firmly believed that if a bus was destined for HELL AND DAMNATION the people would still blithely climb aboard. Equally, they would moan and groan if they were kicked off before they expected to be.'

Besides competition and stubbornness, there's another aspect of commuter behaviour that transport workers see and we don't, and that is its weekly rhythm. Our moods oscillate at several levels and this is reflected in the pulse of the flow, which changes as we cycle from Monday through to Friday. London Underground staff claim to be able to predict our behaviour simply by looking at a clock and a calendar. On Monday mornings women faint because they haven't eaten any breakfast in their rush to get to work; and on Friday nights men pass out in their own vomit because they've drunk too much on an empty stomach. Staff take up their positions before such key periods in the weekly cycle, ready for a rising tide of dizziness or inebriation, knowing that they will need to be ministering angels to one or other class of traveller. Platform attendant Jane Oakes, for instance, speaking to the BBC of the Friday night mayhem, feels that she has 'to be a bit of a babysitter… turn into mummy and daddy sometimes'. The parenting extends to cleaning up the messes that spoiled children leave in the trains and on the concourses. So as not to disturb other passengers, tube staff speak in code over the PA when planning how to deal with the substances that commuters eject while in transit. A number 1, for instance, means spilled blood; 2 = urine (or a number two); 3 = vomit; 4 = spillage; 5 = broken glass; and 6 = litter. There are even annual meta-cycles in commuter behaviour: crush loading is most intense in September and March; we're most likely to add a drink to our journeys in December; and to kill ourselves on a Thursday in February.

Finally, personnel need to contend with the commuter sense of fun. We can be playful as well as hell bent on getting from our beds to our desks, and this also disrupts the flow. When tube-goers celebrate 'No Pants Day', for instance, a flash-mob event that takes place on public transport in sixty cities around the world and is marked by people commuting in their underwear, the official line is that it is disruptive rather than a ray of sunlight in the underworld that allows commuters to show each other how beautiful or normal their bodies are below the waist. Officials are just as hard on the spoof signs that have been appearing in tube carriages, which are the same shape and size as some of the myriad safety notices but which have bogus rather than serious messages. The No-smoking stickers on some trains, for instance, have been replaced with: 'No eye contact – Penalty £200'. And the white on blue notices reminding passengers to ensure they have a valid ticket with: 'For a more efficient service, please alight at the next stop where a team of heavily drugged sloths will drag you to your destination.'

Although commuters like the odd blast of humour or whimsy in their trips, both are anathema to London Underground employees, whose enemy is anarchy. They are focused on getting people to work with the least possible fuss, and feel that commuters should keep their side of the bargain and concentrate on commuting. New media have aggravated the problem. Travellers tweet among themselves, and sometimes are better informed as to why a train is delayed than the staff, which undermines their authority and uniforms. Transport operators are fighting back by tweeting too. Every tube line has a personalized Twitter feed. The exchanges on these allow a glimpse of the creative tension that exists between operators and passengers, as the following example from the Central Line's feed demonstrates:

> *@centralline : A good service has resumed on the line.*
> HG: *Then please can you let me know why the 7.29 from West Ruislip has not departed? Says there is nothing for 17 mins?*
> *@centralline: I was informed this was due to a faulty train that was taken out of service. Apologies for the inconvenience to your journey.*
> HG: *Then why put good service on all lines? This is clearly not a good service. People rely on tfl site for up-to-date service info!*
> *@centralline: The status of the line relates to the overall service, if one train is cancelled it's not necessarily affecting this.*

Overground operators also tweet. Allison Dunn, head of social media at South West Trains, a self-confessed optimist who posts on behalf of its services to and from Waterloo, thinks that Twitter permits the operators and their passengers to bond in new ways: it 'allows us to talk to people in a manner we've never been able to, on a one-on-one basis'. She's unfazed by return tweets like 'Hang your head in shame', and says that, in general, it gives her 'a buzz'. However, she's not entirely shame-proof: 'If we're severely disrupted, sometimes it does impact on you, seeing what people are saying. The name-calling, that sort of thing', she confesses. 'You really do have to put yourself in their shoes and feel their pain, because they're the ones that are paying us to run this train service.'

As well as formulating its own strategies to control the flow, the Tube is receptive to ideas from outsiders. For instance, it has been donating advertising space inside carriages to the *Poems on the Underground* project since 1986. The motive for such largesse is that the odd poem in a display panel instead of yet another advert or safety notice suggests (to those trapped inside its carriages at rush hour) that London Underground is more than a machine built to rob and imprison people. It's prepared to sacrifice a little revenue in order to offer them food for thought. There's now a similar project on public transport systems in twelve other countries around the world. I'm a fan. Instead of being made to feel paranoid by an advert for deodorant, mouthwash or life insurance, one can read and meditate on inspirational poetry. Of the poems that I have encountered for the first time on the Underground, my favourite is 'Dreams', by the seventeenth-century English lyric poet Robert Herrick:

> *Here we all are, by day; by night we're hurled*
> *By dreams, each one into a several world.*

Poems on the Underground have yet to feature such twentieth-century anti-commuter classics as T. S. Eliot's *The Waste Land*, or Sir John Betjeman's 'Middlesex', a richly ironic portrait of the north London suburbs. Perhaps this is because there's a policy of optimism: poetry should take us away from the quotidian aspects of commuting rather than confront us with its misery or suggest that it is futile.

As well as encouraging poetry, the Tube has legalized busking. There are licensed, branded pitches at many stations. The free spirits who once braved guards and the police to howl at commuters for a hatful of coins, have been replaced with performers who audition for their pitches and the odd celebrity playing as a publicity stunt. Although, prima facie, busking disturbs the flow, it also has a soothing effect on commuters. Music makes the experience filmic, and so distracts us from violations of our various proxemic spaces.

In order to keep the pulse of commuting beating, London Underground's staff are trained at special institutions that include West Ashfield, which sometimes features on trivia quizzes as the answer to the question 'Which London Underground Station is forty feet above ground?' West Ashfield is on the third floor of an office block in Kensington and features 1:1 mock-ups of various sections of an Underground station, including a platform. Fans blow and the platform rumbles to simulate the imminent arrival of a train as trainees pretend they are standing at a real tube stop. This is where the people who choreograph our dances during rush hour learn their trade. West Ashfield also possess 'the ultimate' model railway, equipped with carriages the size of kittens whose sides have been painted with miniature graffiti to render them all the more authentic.

At West Ashfield, trainee drivers spend hours on simulators that teach them how to manage their trains, but never quite prepare them for the stress of the real thing, when they might be transporting a thousand people engaged in a silent war for one of only 248 seats through a narrow tunnel 120 feet beneath the pavements of London. The training is rigorous: drivers are required to be able to fix most common problems that might arise on a train – change fuses, conduct emergency evacuations and deal with suicides, as well as make perfect landings at every station. The responsibility is immense – like that of an airline pilot, but without the prestige – as is the pressure. Tube drivers record far higher levels of stress than the supposed neurotics they cart around. The stress is aggravated by the fear of a 'one-under' – tube-speak for running someone over. Even near-misses are hair-raising, not least because the driver feels powerless. 'You can't swerve to avoid someone… There's nothing you can do except hope… that you've got time to apply the brakes and stop the train,' driver Mohammed Mujahid told the *Guardian*. The experience 'can really freak you out, leave you shaking and some people can't handle it and have to leave the company'. Those drivers unlucky enough to hit a passenger are likely to be scarred for life: about 15 per cent develop post-traumatic stress disorder and 40 per cent suffer from other psychological problems including depression and phobia. Robert Griffiths describes hitting two 'one-unders' in *Mind the Doors!* Both were suicides. In each case he was placed on a manslaughter charge until the coroner's inquest had established that the traveller was seeking oblivion. On the second occasion, he needed three months' sick leave and counselling before he could work again.

The stress is as bad on a day-to-day basis among bus drivers. According to Professor M. A. J. Kompier, a Dutch psychologist, driving a bus is 'a high-risk occupation', cruel to both body and psyche, in comparison to office work, blue-collar work, taxi driving or working at a brewery or as a civil servant – or indeed almost every other occupation. Sitting down all day and driving a large vehicle slowly is more dangerous than it seems. The ergonomics of many drivers' cabs are poor – the steering wheels are too big, the seats are one-size-fits-all and the pedals are either not close enough or almost out of reach, with the result that most drivers have to twist, stretch or hunch up while they're being shaken by the motion of the bus, blasted with hot or cold air whenever they open the doors, and abused by their passengers.

The contrast between perception and reality emerges starkly in the testimony of one of Professor Kompier's subjects. In Holland, to sit behind the wheel of a bus is 'the dream of every boy: that large bus, the uniform and the cap'. There's also an initial sense of freedom: 'on the bus, no one tells me what I should and what I should not do'. However, after the first rush of living one's childhood ambition is over, the job wears drivers down: 'there are not many guys left that I started with fifteen years ago. Most of them disappeared, they got sick... And there is that violence these days, I have been assaulted twice and the public has changed... they are in a hurry, no time for jokes, and traffic has intensified terribly.' Many bus drivers give up before they reach retirement age, usually because of ill-health. They're particularly prone to heart disease and problems with their backs, knees, bowels and tendons.

Some are crippled mentally as well as physically. Their work is typified by high demands and low control. They may, in theory, be captains of their ships, but they are slaves to both timetables and their own consciences. On the one hand, they're under pressure from their employers to follow their routes like clockwork; on the other, they're bombarded with demands from passengers who might want to get on after the doors have closed, or take aeons to dismount because they're old or infirm. According to a Swedish study of public transport personnel, these conflicting priorities force drivers either 'to adopt an attitude whereby the passengers are regarded as freight' and sacrifice them to the timetable so that 'a person who is late and runs for the bus can be left behind without compunction', or to try 'to live up to demands for personal service' and treat passengers as fellow humans. But philanthropy can't be reconciled with the rat race. Drivers try to compensate by driving too fast: 'around 25 per cent of bus and tram drivers report that schedules are so tight that traffic safety is endangered almost daily' or are 'continually behind schedule, so that passengers complain and there may not be time for a proper break'. The authors conclude that 'whichever alternative the driver adopts, he or she will constantly have a conscious or subconscious feeling of inadequacy'. They try too hard to please everyone while they know in their hearts that they can't. This dilemma takes centre-stage in Magnus Mills's *The Maintenance of Headway*, which offers a Kafkaesque vision of bus inspectors in thrall to the dogma of the book's title, one that they try to impose on their drivers with a rigidity that would be realistic only in a clockwork world, and where the worst sin a driver can commit is to be early, as this disturbs headway as much as delays do.

Headway, in the technical sense, is the proper separation of trains or buses on their routes. Its maintenance is a problem that has been taxing the best brains in public transport since the Victorian era. As soon as it became desirable to run more than one train at a time on the same line, systems had to be put in place to stop them crashing into each other or piling up in tunnels. The first consisted of positioning men with coloured flags and lanterns at intervals along the track, and they then stopped a train if it was too close to the one in front. When telegraph lines were installed alongside railway lines, electric signals were used as well as visual ones, and the 'block system' of managing headway evolved. Every route was divided into chunks called 'blocks' and a golden rule was applied whereby only one train at a time was allowed in each block. This rule persisted until the appearance of automated, that is to say computerized, systems enabled transit operators to run more than one train per block, and hence both reduce headway and increase the frequency of services.

The controllers who run contemporary traffic management systems have a different view of commuters from that of drivers and platform staff. Instead of seeing people, they watch coloured rectangles representing trains inching along lines on their screens, and have to solve mathematical problems instead of human ones. It's a stressful occupation nonetheless. When the journalist Edward Simpkins visited the old control room at Waterloo railway station in 2001, he noted that it was run by real-life Fat Controllers whose chairs were 'surrounded by a black slick of trodden-in chewing gum that the overweight men munch to keep their cigarette cravings at bay during the long hours in front of the screens', and that the atmosphere was one of 'controlled tension'. New systems that are easier to operate have since been installed, but the tension remains. Simon Flatto, who controls the Metropolitan Line on the Tube, and is responsible for guiding 100 trains through 54 stations during rush hour, described his work to the BBC as being like 'juggling hot potatoes', for if the doors on a train close fifteen seconds late, the train behind it will be two minutes late and the fourth train in line ten minutes late. Every second is vital for every hour of his working day.

In addition to managing headway via automated control systems, transit operators have been moving towards driverless trains. These have been in service for nearly forty years: the Victoria Line on the Tube has been effectively driverless since it was opened in 1968. While drivers have always and still do sit in the cabs, the trains generally run on autopilot. Few of the 200-odd million passengers that the Victoria Line carries each year realize that a machine is controlling the great vehicle that bears them to and fro during rush hour; many would find it disturbing to know that there might not be anyone at the helm. Automation may reduce human error, but it also dispenses with human ingenuity, which may be the only salvation if an unexpected problem arises. Moreover, it's always good to hear the driver speak when the train's stuck. The reassurance that there's someone aboard who knows how it works, how to change its fuses and reset its circuit breakers, how to open its doors by hand, and how to evacuate it, is as important as whatever he or she might actually say over the intercom. The apprehension that passengers feel about riding driverless trains is illustrated by the fact that the first question on the FAQ page of the Docklands Light Railway* is 'Where are the drivers?' Instead of simply stating that there aren't any, the answer anticipates and deflects paranoia by pointing out that the system is still under human supervision:

> *While trains may appear to stop and start of their own accord, the DLR is operated through a computerised system that is closely managed and monitored 24 hours a day, 365 days a year at the DLR control centre. Control centre staff have access to a visual overview of the entire DLR network displaying exactly where each train is along the railway at any given time.*

While transit system owners are reticent about communicating the virtues of driverless systems to their passengers, they trumpet them from the rooftops to each other. Unattended Train Operation (UTO) systems enable them to work on the principle of the 'moving block', and greatly to reduce headway between trains. Less headway equals more capacity, and UTOs also benefit from lower labour costs. According to Claudio Andrade, for instance, the director of Yellow Line 4 of the São Paulo Metro in Brazil, which is totally UTO, 'Eliminating human factor interference brings the operational headway closer to the theoretical one.' Line 4 is designed to work with a gap of only seventy-five seconds between trains, compared with two minutes for the Victoria Line

---

* The first totally driverless system in London.

on the London Underground. Its 'turnaround time' isn't slowed by drivers having to change ends, or arriving late for work, and trains can be added during rush hour without having to find fresh pairs of hands to steer them around the tracks.

Although Andrade might not recognize that he's murdering the dreams of Brazilian children who want to be train drivers when they grow up, the genuine efficiencies offered by UTOs suggest that it's inevitable that one day all train systems will drive themselves. Machines rely on binary data rather than their senses. Humans would need telepathy and reaction speeds measured in milliseconds to be able to function at a similar level of competence. As long as passengers are protected from their own stupidity, for example by making it only possible for them to reach their carriages via an impenetrable barrier with an extra set of sliding doors, as is the case with Jubilee Line platforms on the Tube, rail commuters of the future are likely to be tended by robot shepherds that are both beyond stress and devoid of feelings for their sheep.

◆ ◆ ◆ ◆ ◆

PART III

FACE
TIME

CHAPTER XIII

Virtual Journeys

> We are entering an era of electronically extended bodies living at the intersection points of the physical and virtual worlds, of occupation and interaction through telepresence as well as through physical presence.
>
> William Mitchell, *City of Bits: Space, Place and the Infobahn*, 1994

I f it is possible to take drivers out of commuter trains, might it be feasible to take commuters off them too? Instead of people travelling to work, their work would come to them: leave its place of origin for the homes of workers every morning, and return at the end of each day to be integrated into whatever grand scheme it belonged. While this sort of arrangement would be impossible for occupations where both worker and work have to be together, like coal mining or hairdressing, in theory it's practicable for most contemporary white-collar professions. Is it really necessary to cram lawyers, call-centre workers, accountants, academics and council workers into middens in order to get the best of their productive potential? Why not substitute telecommunications for transportation?

Pundits everywhere, whether they love or loathe commuting, have been hailing telecommuting as its future for nearly forty years, especially in America. The idea that less of the real thing might be good, that people shouldn't aspire to driving oversized and overpowered cars to palatial corporate headquarters set in parkland, where they could put their feet up on desks the size of billiard tables between nine and five, was born in the 1970s and was very much a child of its times. The optimism of the 1960s – when gas-guzzling was part of the national mindset and small beer in comparison to sending rockets to the moon – had been strangled by the oil crisis of 1973. America was sombre. Its cities were dying, its rivers were polluted, its very air was tainted with acid rain and lead from petrol, flares were in fashion, and since public transport was a distant memory in most places, if you couldn't drive you'd have to walk.

Not everyone lost hope. Jack Nilles, professor at the University of Southern California, realized that an information revolution was going on amid all this misery and that it offered new paradigms to workers and employers alike. Principal among these was 'telecommuting', a word Nilles coined in a seminal 1975 paper, which he thought would 'enable employees of large organizations to work in offices close to (but generally not in) their homes, rather than commute long distances to a central office'. Nilles argued that by using ever-increasing computer power, and such novel technologies as fibre optics, the 'professional, technical, clerical, and sales workers, managers, officials, and proprietors who constituted about 50 per cent of the US labor force' could be decentralized, i.e. packed off to hubs in the sticks, where rents were low and restaurants few, but the absence of the latter wouldn't matter because employees would be compensated by living closer to home. Moreover, local telecom networks would enable employers to expand their labour pool by using people with useful brains but limited mobility, such as the physically handicapped, housewives with young children and college students on vacation.

The aim wasn't so much to eradicate commuting as to rationalize it. Most telecommuters would still go into an office every day, but to hubs rather than headquarters. Nilles hoped that his idea would have the side effect of rejuvenating city centres: remove the need for everyone to be in the same hive, and the 'monolithic office buildings' that dominated the skylines of most American towns in his time might be replaced by mixed-use spaces with shops and homes and flower gardens. Those telecommuters who lived outside town, meanwhile, would redevelop a 'sense of community', which had been falling since the glory days of the Organization Man, by working closer to home. Instead of treating suburbs as mere dormitories, they would turn them into villages and revive sewing circles, Bible classes, baseball teams, bowling leagues and all the other communal activities that people used to practise before they owned televisions. However, Nilles cautioned that telecommuting should not be a licence to ruin the country with ever more sprawling suburbs: 'Clearly, one of the potential results of the greater ability to relocate because of improved and less expensive telecommunications technology is that people will move to areas of great scenic beauty or recreational potential in such numbers as to destroy the resource they have moved to be near.'

Nilles further acknowledged that telecommuting would not

be perfect for executives who, in accordance with management theories of the era, needed 'face-to-face meetings to renew confidence in verbal cues, perceptions of attitudes, and similar imponderables not easily transmitted' over telephones. Finally, · he warned that there would be consequences for labour: if the unions and the courts decided that making people telecommute looked too much like divide and rule, then they would resist it tooth and nail.

Alvin Toffler was the next futurist after Nilles to back telecommuting. In his book *The Third Wave* (1980), he split civilization into three eras or *waves*: (a) agricultural; (b) industrial and (c) the coming one of information. Toffler was convinced that the third wave had arrived ('A new civilization is bursting into being in our midst!') and thought it would be closer in spirit to the agrarian era than that of coal mines, steam trains and mechanized warfare. His key concept was the 'electronic cottage', which offered 'once more on a mass scale the possibility of husbands and wives, and perhaps even children, working together as a unit'. Instead of rearing sheep and spinning wool like the crofters of old, electronic cottagers would perform administrative duties for multinational corporations. All they'd need was 'a "smart" typewriter... along with a facsimile machine or computer console and teleconferencing equipment' and they'd never have to wear a suit again except for a wedding or funeral. While the type of cottage office Toffler envisaged would have been exceedingly expensive to install in 1980 (as would the phone bills for running it) he was certain that prices would come down over time. One day, 'the cost of installing and operating telecommunications equipment' would be cheaper than driving to work, and 'the irrational, frustrating and absurd process of shuttling back and forth to the factory or office' would be history. Electronic cottaging, moreover, would rebuild the community spirit that had diminished even further when Toffler was writing. Like Nilles, he predicted a 'renaissance among voluntary organizations like churches, women's groups, lodges, clubs, athletic and youth organizations'.

Telecommuting continued to grow more as an idea than a reality until the 1990s, when Moore's Law, the internet, fibre optics, digital exchanges, concerns over global warming and shifts in the Zeitgeist made it both feasible and desirable. The power to work anywhere and everywhere – have laptop, will travel – or stay at home according to one's mood, seized the imaginations of Generation X: every day could be a No Pants Day. It also fitted in with the ethos of the green movement, which had become a mainstream political cause and counted physical commuting as one of its enemies. The hundreds of billions of euros, dollars and pounds wasted on fuel, on lost productive hours spent spewing out CO_2 during traffic jams, and poured away in funeral expenses and lawsuits after accidents, would be sufficient to reclaim the Sahara, save the Amazon, raise Africa out of poverty, load its adults with seed and contraceptives, and build them all windmills so that they could light their homes at night. Commuting represented all that was wrong with the West, and the sooner it was curtailed the better.

Governments listened, and started to encourage the virtual version as a substitute. America took a stick-and-carrot approach: the Clean Air Act of 1990 required every company with 100 or more employees to 'reduce solo driving' among them. Tax and other incentives, meanwhile, were offered for facilitating home working. The European Union was also enthusiastic about 'Telework', as it termed it,* and after drawing up a mound of policy recommendations in the late 1990s, it established a framework in 2002 that was endorsed by its 'peak social partners' and presented to European governments as a fait accompli. The resulting directive gave all the carrots to the employees and beat employers soundly. It aimed to enable people to 'reconcile work and social life', with the focus on the latter.

The EU Telework Directive was a qualified success. By 2005, according to official statistics, a full 7 per cent of European workers spent up to a quarter of their time teleworking, and a princely 1.7 per cent did it full-time. This was somewhat lower than projections, if, indeed, it was true at all. Advocates of telework/telecommuting have always been over-optimistic. In 2000, for instance, Jack Nilles had suggested that Europe would have about 10 per cent of its working population telecommuting all the time by 2004, i.e. more than five times the official number, which in itself was almost certainly an exaggeration. Problems tallying telecommuters derive in part from the difficulty in defining who they are. Should the classification apply only to people who work from home full-time for someone else, with whom they communicate digitally, or should it include those who are in

---

* There was a transatlantic divide with regard to what to call virtual commuting that lasted well into the new millennium. The dictionary on Microsoft Word 2003, for instance, didn't recognize 'teleworker' and offered 'steelworker' instead. Teleworking, meanwhile, might be 'teleporting'.

their offices for, say, three days a week and work at home for the remainder? According to Lars Qvortrup of Denmark's Aalborg University, 'counting teleworkers is like measuring a rubber band. The result depends on how far you stretch your definition'. In America, for instance, according to the Bureau of Labor, only 2.5 per cent of workers laboured all the time from home in 2011. If, however, you included people who spent the odd day there and people who glanced at their work emails outside office hours in your measure, the figure rose to 24 per cent. In Britain, for the sake of comparison, the percentage of the employed workforce who, in the words of the ONS, 'work mainly at or from home' was 5.4 per cent in 2013.

Differences between projections and the truth wouldn't have been quite so great if foreign telecommuters had been included in domestic counts. Advocates of virtual commuting overlooked the impact of globalization on their dream, and its unintended consequence of outsourcing, in the sense of sending jobs overseas. Employers in both the EU and the USA, obedient to the letter if not the spirit of pro-telework legislation, decarbonized (and gave their ex-workers more social time) by Business Process Outsourcing (BPO), i.e. relocating their call centres and sundry other corporate functions to Asia. In consequence, a Westerner looking to telecommute in their own country would be best advised to emigrate to India, Mexico, Bangladesh or some other developing nation, where literacy is high and talk is cheap. India, for example, is home to as many British telecommuters as actually live in the UK. It offers an articulate and educated pool of Anglophones, prepared to work for a tenth of the wages of their British counterparts. Bangalore alone has over a quarter of a million telecommuters, who keep British or American hours, and to all intents and purposes could be counted in the labour statistics for London or Los Angeles.

The growth in BPO commuting wasn't just the result of legislation, fear of global warming, and corporate penny-pinching: there was Indian push as well as Western pull. Sub-continental entrepreneurs went out and sold it to foreign multinationals. Raman Roy, 'the father of Indian outsourcing', was one of the first to pitch the benefits of BPO-ing to India in the USA. He found he had to deal with ignorance as well as prejudice: 'In the late '90s my favorite line at the beginning of a presentation was, "You probably think I come to the office on a bullock cart."' He had to point out India on the map to prospective clients, and show them pictures of the Taj Mahal, in order to reassure them that his proposals weren't all a giant Ruritanian scam. At home in India, meanwhile, Roy worked to persuade the government that telecommuting was a good idea, and that he should be allowed to build facilities to accommodate it. At times he had to overcome surreal obstacles:

I went to meet bureaucrats after they sat on our application for months. A government official said he could approve a call center, but could not approve a center to handle 'incoming and outgoing calls'. So we had to print definitions of a call center from the Internet and take them to him to show him that's what a call center did.

In keeping with the Jack Nilles vision of telecommuting – that it might employ people who were excluded from the labour market either because they couldn't get to it or weren't expected to be there – Roy pushed for the right to employ women on his so-called 'graveyard shifts' that ran from 7 p.m. to 3 a.m. (Bangalore time) for North America. He found there 'were laws that forbade employing women in jobs after 10 p.m. In each state that we planned on setting up call centers in, we had to persuade its government to change that law.' Billions of dollars of foreign investment in India later, 'now the shoe is on the other foot. If we raise issues, policymakers listen.' As was the case with physical commuting, the introduction of virtual commuting has resulted in legislative change and cultural liberation.

Competition is fierce in India for the chance to ask such small but important questions as 'is your computer switched on at the wall?' to furious and abusive people in foreign countries. The pay averages the equivalent of £200 per month, the job has a certain cachet, and the surroundings are often salubrious. Many call centres are laid out as campuses with cappuccino bars, chill-out rooms, and sports facilities, as well as partitioned rows of workstations. The address of IBM's Indian headquarters: 'Golf Course Links, Bangalore', says it all. Telecommuting aspirants borrow several months' wages in advance from their relatives to pay for elocution courses, so that they'll sound just right on the phone. The courses are designed to wipe out 'Mother Tongue Influence' ('MTI') i.e. Indian accents, and teach students to speak with absolute clarity, so that any English-speaker anywhere in the world can understand them, even over a bad line. The courses also teach tricks of the trade, like pretending that you're called Bob. As Deep, an ex-British Telecom call-centre worker and MTI trainer explained to *Forbes* magazine: 'Tell an American that your name is Raja and an F-word pops out. Better to use a fake name.'

Indians lucky enough to get a job on the frontline are hit by culture shocks from the instant that they boot up their screens and strap on their headphones. They're not allowed to choose whether or not to take a call – they hear a beep, a customer profile appears on their VDU, and a few seconds later they're with Sharon in Epping who wants to kill someone because she's spent more money than she thought she had and her cashpoint card won't give her any more. This is all very taxing: it's as if they'd been teleported to the same locations as the people they are servicing down the phone and online. While call-centre workers, according to Deep, are trained 'to think like Westerners, to talk like them, and to spend all day talking to them. The culture seep[s] through, but not all of the culture. Most of the people who work on the floor have never been to America or Great Britain… There are enormous gaps in their mental picture that they simply fill with their imagination and the movies.' Sometimes, such measures aren't enough. When Eve Butler, a seventy-six-year-old Welsh woman, was put through to an Indian call centre in January 2013 instead of to BT's Welsh Language Bureau, the operator she spoke to was forced to admit that he couldn't connect her to a Welsh-speaking service because the language, and indeed the country, were mysteries to him. 'I don't know what Wales is,' he confessed.

The disconnect is compounded by problems at home. Not only do Indian teleworkers have to deal with irate strangers all night, but they also get detached from their family roots, forget what sunlight looks like, have no time for friendships, and are led into temptation by their handsome incomes. There's a high churn rate among call-centre workers, and they burn out far quicker than Dutch bus drivers. Deep feels that this is because 'your mentality changes' when you work in a call centre. 'You try to think like an American, but you're not really an American, you're an Indian. And sometimes you make the wrong decisions… You're earning good, you're looking good, you're admired — that's outside. But on the inside, you have a void.'

Ironically, many Indian telecommuters not only have to face the stress of virtual travel but also have to endure the discomforts of commuting in the flesh. Although call centres may ease congestion in the West, they increase it in the places they are built. Bangalore has spectacular jams in rush hour, and its public transport systems are close to being swamped. As in Mumbai, there's super dense crush loading, and fatalities by the score. Indeed, to date, rather than eliminating physical commuting, telework has simply sent it overseas. This inconvenient truth tends to be played down by multinationals. IBM, for example, trumpets its commitment to virtual commuting on its corporate website: 'IBM was one of the first global companies to pioneer programs to reduce employee commuting. It has sustained these programs for nearly two decades. Two key aspects are its (a) work-at-home program and (b) mobile employees program. In 2012, 103,000 of over 430,000 global employees participated in one of these two programs.' However, it fails to highlight that these triumphs have been achieved by growing operations in India while shrinking them at home. In 2003, IBM employed 140,000 people in America and 9,000 in India. By 2010, in contrast, the domestic headcount had fallen to 105,000 and the Indian one risen to 130,000. The 2010 figures are estimates. IBM stopped disclosing who worked where in 2009. Its secrecy over the geographical distribution of its employees is, according to Sujit John, blogging for the *Times of India*, 'presumably because it does not want unemployed Americans to get upset that it is taking jobs out of that country. But that's exactly what it has done. Today, by most estimates, it has close to a third of its 4.3 lakh* employees in India'. As such, John argues, it should be labelled an Indian rather than an American company, as should Cognizant and Accenture.

British Telecom, which vaunts its telework scheme as much as IBM, is going the same way. While it trumpeted the fact that in 2011 it had 15,000 homeworkers out of 92,000 employees in the UK, and that the homeworkers were 20 per cent more productive and took fewer sick days, it omitted to mention that its British workforce had fallen by over a third by 2009, while its Indian operations and interests had blossomed over the same period.

Outsourcing has taken some of the lustre off telecommuting. Employees have become suspicious. Even if their employer hasn't BPO'd one or other corporate function, they come across it when they call a help centre or their bank. Doing your job from home might prove that someone else somewhere else could do the same for less money: far better to clock on and be a face as

---

* One lakh is a South Asian numerical unit equivalent to 100,000.

well as a function. The new buzzword in the IT community is 'presenteeism'. Employees think they need to put in 'passive face time' in order to survive the tail end of the recent economic recession. The theory is that it's harder to fire someone you've chatted to around the water cooler, especially if they've told you the names of their children. Besides, people go to the office to gossip as well as work. There's a pleasure derived from active face time as well as the passive variety and, for some workers, their job may be the only part of their atomized lives that allows them to participate in communal rituals.

Employers are also very enthusiastic about presenteeism, especially in the dotcom industry that has done so much to eradicate the need for it. While many of its participants have liberal telecommuting policies, they don't actively encourage their workers to take advantage of them. Twitter, for instance, defines its homeworking policy as a second best. According to a spokesperson, 'we believe there are significant tangible and intangible benefits when employees are working under the same roof. We also recognize that every so often it's important to be able to work remotely, and we allow for that flexibility.' Google, meanwhile, seems not to want to encourage its employees to work from home. CFO Patrick Pichette knocked remote working on the head in a February 2013 speech: 'The surprising question we get is: "How many people telecommute at Google?" And our answer is: "As few as possible"'. In Pichette's opinion, employees would both stunt their creativity and miss the wonder of sharing if they stayed at home: 'There is something magical about spending the time together, about noodling on ideas... These are [the] magical moments that we think at Google are immensely important in the development of your company, of your own personal development and [of] building much stronger communities.' A similar ethos prevailed in the City when I commuted to work there in 1986, just before the Big Bang. Officially, you had twenty days' holiday a year, but if you took more than two weeks of it in total, or more than five days at a stretch, your card was marked. Holidays were for people who didn't like their work enough. Why miss the chance to get rich just to lie on a beach somewhere hot?

Those tech companies that do encourage domestic tele-commuting, meanwhile, keep a tight rein on it. Apple, for example, starts its online advisers on a month-long training programme that is actually an extended entrance exam. If trainees don't get at least 80 per cent on a curriculum they don't even know they're taking, they're rejected. Apple monitors their mouse clicks during working hours, and if their mice are still for too long, it sends them prompts, or calls them on their mobiles. There are also online team-building sessions, where telecommuters are encouraged to send in pictures of what they're eating for lunch, or to participate in 'silly hat' days – anything to prove they're actually at their desks. Apple, moreover, is a prophet of the corporate ethos and believes that people will work harder for less if they feel they're part of a branded team with a good communal reputation in the wider world, rather than faceless drudges labouring away in anonymity. Its training programme/entrance examination includes time on corporate history and culture, complete with a taste of how it felt to work alongside Steve Jobs in Cupertino in the 1980s. Successful Apple telecommuters are expected to achieve near-perfect customer satisfaction records, for between US$9 and $12 per hour.

Indeed, even though telecommuting has never been easier, it's going backwards at present. It's a good idea that doesn't work. It assumes that virtual encounters are as effective as real ones: that people are happy to communicate by typing words or speaking to pictures or videos of each other. But this implies that both sensual and social contacts are irrelevant, whereas our need for them is in our DNA. We'll have to evolve into, say, *Homo virtualis*, a being that gets all it needs for its emotional well-being from a screen, before telecommuting beats the real thing. Both workers and employers want face time, whether to submit, dominate or for a spot of metaphorical grooming. Moreover, it's as if each sees the willingness to travel as a test of fitness, in the Darwinian sense.

While growth in domestic telecommuting has stagnated in the West, there's still plenty of goodwill pent up behind it. The Zeitgeist presumes that real commuting both scars people's minds and is a monumental waste of the planet's resources. In consequence, employers who insist that their employees drive into work, rather than logging on in their pyjamas, come in for plenty of flak. When, for example, Marissa Mayer, the CEO of Yahoo since 2012, recalled all her workers to their offices in February 2013, she broke a taboo, and caused uproar. The first ever Apple was built in a garage. Facebook was dreamed up in a college dorm. Yahoo itself was created by a pair of freethinkers at Stanford University who named their baby after the imaginary race of coarse and offensive halfwits in Jonathan Swift's *Gulliver's Travels*. The idea that the creative types who ruled the web should be required to gather at set hours in offices was unthinkable. It was the equivalent of calling in all the cowboys in late nineteenth-century Texas and telling them to give up their Colt 45s and spurs and sit together in a schoolroom. According to James Surowiecki of *The New Yorker*, Yahoo wasn't just 'tweaking an H.R. policy' but also 'trampling on the future'.

The memo announcing the recall, from Chief Development Officer Jackie Reses to Yahoos everywhere, avoided the subject of liberty to work solo wherever they wished and focused instead on the pleasures of cooperation. It began with the promise of more soma at the coalface: 'Over the past few months, we have introduced a number of great benefits and tools to make us more productive, efficient and fun... From Sunnyvale to Santa Monica, Bangalore to Beijing — I think we can all feel the energy and buzz in our offices.' But everyone had to be there to get the party going: 'To become the absolute best place to work, communication and collaboration will be important, so we need to be working side-by-side. That is why it is critical that we are all present in our offices. Some of the best decisions and insights come from hallway and cafeteria discussions, meeting new people, and impromptu team meetings... We need to be one Yahoo!, and that starts with physically being together.'

Responses to the recall ranged from fury to I-told-you-so. Opponents claimed that Yahoos were being forced to prove their survival skills in a Silicon Valley equivalent of *The Hunger Games*. Supporters, meanwhile, including ex and present Yahoos around the world, blogged about the culture of indolence that had sprung up around virtual instead of actual commuting. 'There's a ton of abuse at Yahoo,' claimed one who'd left, which had led to 'people slacking off like crazy, not being available, spending a lot of time on non-Yahoo projects'. A current employee, meanwhile, pointed out that 'we are fighting to stay relevant. So getting your ass into the office… is not too much to ask. If you don't like it, well too bad, the exit door is over there.'

The IT sector that's making 'a remote-access future possible for the rest of us' offers carrots as well as sticks to its workers to ensure they come into work. The industry is noted for its extravagant office complexes that resemble crosses between university campuses, cartoon sets and sweet shops, where employees can eat, sleep and play pool, golf and ping-pong as well as write code. Indeed, the excess apparent in some dotcom corporate headquarters is now on a par with that of auto manufacturers in the 1960s, when GM felt it ruled America. It's an interesting parallel and, perhaps, a parable.

Sir James Hanson, the notorious British corporate raider of the 1980s, used to consider over-palatial head offices to be a sign that a company was ripe for takeover and asset stripping. However, his favourite symbol of corporate decadence – a duck lake – seems limited and quaint beside, say, Google's current headquarters, the Googleplex in Santa Clara County, California. This behemoth has the skeleton of a *T.rex*; a replica of SpaceShip-One; two swimming pools; twenty-five cafés; a green building that uses recycled blue jeans for soundproofing; and random giant rubber balls, all crammed into its 56-acre lot. The food at the Googleplex is reputed to be spectacular. When *Gourmet* magazine investigated, it was impressed. Each café was 'helmed by its own chef, most hailing from the world of fine dining'. Menus include such delicacies as roasted black bass with parsley pesto, Petaluma chicken cacciatore, porcini-encrusted grass-fed beef, and whole-wheat spaghetti pomodoro. All meals are free, and Googlers bring their families into work to feed them rather than going out to restaurants. This is clever psychology: excellent food gratis is worth commuting for, and knowing that it's there helps workers relax when they're at their workstations. We're programmed by nature to be nervous about getting enough food, and if that worry is removed it's far easier to concentrate. According to Olivia Wu, one of five executive chefs that Google employs to give its café chefs direction, 'providing food for our employees supports our general desire to fulfil the basic needs of Googlers. We also believe that the free, healthy and delicious food options make for happier Googlers, and happier Googlers are more productive.'

Dotcom employers also sugar the pill by running private commuter-bus services. More than 35,000 Silicon Valley workers are collected from San Francisco every morning by fleets of luxury coaches with blacked-out windows, recliner seats and top-of-the-range broadband. They're reminiscent of army trucks, albeit very much more sumptuous, and count as a perk among employees. However, they compete for space on the roads with school and municipal bus services, and people who live along their routes but who don't get free gourmet food at their workplaces think of them as the equivalents of the club railway carriages of Victorian robber barons. According to an op-ed in the *San Francisco Chronicle*, 'San Franciscans feel resentful about the technology industry's lack of civic and community engagement, and the

Google bus is our daily reminder.' It seems unfair that some people should have fun commuting, while others are packed together in havens for exotic bacteria.

The companies that run the buses point out that each one takes fifty or so cars off the road, and so alleviate jams rather than causing them. Employees who commute on them are also ready to speak up for their benefits to the community and indeed the planet. A 'software engineer for a major internet company', speaking anonymously to the *Guardian*, pointed out that commuters like him inside the buses were spearheading a global battle against evil and ignorance: 'We feel what we're doing helps make the world a better place. Helping people share information is a force of empowerment for individuals.' Make way for the saints. Finally, the bus drivers are also in favour. Rick Fuch, who drives for Bauer, the major provider of services, thinks that they perform 'a kind of symphony on wheels' with the municipal bus drivers, and that there's respect on both sides. He also likes his passengers. They don't shoot up heroin like people used to do when he drove a public bus in Portland, nor do they attack or abuse him. His present daily load consists of peaceful, serious people, who try to get the most out of commuting: 'We have like the really, really geeky. I'm sure they are all on their devices and not talking because they are so socially inept; they don't know how to talk to the person next to them, and they want to write some code on the way home.'

Although tech-sector employers preach the benefits of real commuting for the sake of more noodling, they also have practical reasons for encouraging or enforcing it. The Achilles heel of teleworking is data security. You can't keep secrets once you're outside the office network and on the information superhighway, and who knows where in the virtual world a remote employee might be passing time? Indeed, companies find it difficult enough to keep information leaking from their head offices, where it seems that employees have taken a leaf out of their employers' books and started outsourcing too. The scale of the problem is highlighted by the case of 'Bob', the pseudonymous hero of an investigation by Verizon, the online security experts. Bob, a 'mid-40's software developer' who worked for a large US critical infrastructure company, described as a 'family man, inoffensive and quiet. Someone you wouldn't look at twice in an elevator', commuted to the office every day where he spent his time watching videos of cats, trading on eBay, and reading Reddit* stories, while subcontractors in China did his programming for him. He'd sent them his ID fob by FedEx so that they could tap into his employer's system. His ingenuity was only uncovered when a routine scan of the company's VPN logs 'showed him logged in from China' while he was 'right there, sitting at his desk, staring into his monitor'.

Bob's resourcefulness was of the type celebrated by author Timothy Ferriss in *The 4-Hour Workweek* (2007), a bestselling lifestyle guide that encourages people to outsource not just their work, but also their leisure, and to have fun while doing so. 'Have someone in Bangalore or Shanghai send emails to friends as your personal concierge to set lunch dates or similar basics.' Converts should 'find something to do other than let your brain fester in the

---

* Reddit is an entertainment, social-networking and news service.

inbox. Fill the void'. Bob's example showed how telecommuting has amazing potential for those individuals who don't want to give up commuting in the flesh, by allowing them to enjoy the pleasures of rush hour, of sitting at a desk nine to five and sharing coffee breaks while outsourcing their work to teleworkers elsewhere. But it also showed how employees trying to have the best of both worlds might compromise their employers even within the office, let alone outside it.

Data security is not the only problem associated with tele-commuting. Its green credentials are fading. While people may save on fuel and cut down on emissions by working from home, the energy used by the IT sector to enable them to do so is prodigious, and growing at a mind-boggling rate. It now uses 10 per cent of the world's electricity, and 50 per cent more energy than the entire aviation industry. In America, 'over $1 trillion of the economy is associated with the ecosystems of information and data – moving bits… This is more than twice the share of the GDP associated with transporting people and stuff… counting everything from vehicle manufacturing to FedEx and all transportation services'.

On a smaller scale, it's been estimated that using a smartphone to videoconference for an hour per week devours twice as much energy in a year as a refrigerator. Although the electricity needed to run the device itself is negligible, the power used by the data centres that store the information the phone accesses, together with the communications networks that distribute it, is considerable. Data centres are 'the factories of the 21st century information age'. An average one uses as much energy as a small town; a large one has the same requirements as 180,000 homes. And data-centre operators are paranoid about their power supplies. According to a 2012 *UK and European Data Centre Barometer Survey*, about two-thirds of 'IT decision-makers and datacentre managers rank power supply as their number one consideration' when choosing where to site a new installation. Their anxiety derives from the unwritten first premise of the internet: that it can't fail. Even if it's virtual, it must also be constant and perpetual. Data must be available on demand, or an operator's reputation will be lost and customers switch to a different server. Some have quintuple-redundant power sources: mains electricity, back-up generators, flywheels, batteries, maybe the odd wind turbine out the back, and solar panels on the roof. In consequence, not only do they use vast amounts of energy, they're also incredibly wasteful. 'This is an industry dirty secret, and no one wants to be the first to say *mea culpa*,' an insider told the *New York Times*. 'If we were a manufacturing industry, we'd be out of business straightaway.' When, for example, a Microsoft data centre in Quincy, Washington state, faced a penalty payment on its power supply contract with the local utility, because it had been running its back-up diesel generators rather than drawing hydroelectric power from the grid, it switched on giant heaters simply to waste millions of watts of electricity and threatened to continue to do so in a 'commercially unproductive' way until the penalty was erased.

The prodigious demand of data centres for power has excited diverse bodies. Both American Coal and Greenpeace have studied it, the one as a business opportunity, the other as a horror story. Both are bullish on growth. According to the industry study *The Cloud Begins With Coal*, US mobile traffic increased by 400 per cent between 2010 and 2012, and '*Hourly* internet traffic will soon exceed the annual' rate of the year 2000. The digital universe is expanding at a pace not seen since the astrophysical version of Big Bang, when our universe was born in the blink of a photon and occupied space beyond conception almost instantaneously. No one in the IT industry talks in kilobytes anymore. According to Oracle, we'll shortly be in the zettabyte era. A zetta = 1,000,000,000,000,000,000,000, or 10^{21}, 'a zetta stack of dollar bills would reach the sun and back – one million times'. As a result, everyone everywhere will need more and better data centres, and in the opinion of American Coal, electricity from coal-fired power stations should be their fuel of choice.

Greenpeace's 2012 study of the same phenomenon, *How Clean is Your Cloud?*, anticipates that demand will grow precipitously, and finds the prospect frightening: if the IT sector were a country in its own right, it would already be the fifth-highest user of electricity in the world, ahead of India, Germany, France and the UK. In its opinion, in order to stop the planet boiling over or humanity choking on its own emissions, data-centre providers should use their bargaining power with utility companies and insist that every volt of electricity that entered their premises had been sustainably sourced. Greenpeace names and shames: Amazon, Apple and Microsoft 'are all rapidly expanding without adequate regard to source of electricity, and rely heavily on dirty energy to power their clouds'. It hopes that this news will inspire people everywhere to rise up and demand that all their apps and texts come from green data centres, and, if not, reject them all.

However, if data centres continue to gobble power at an accelerating rate, and are forced to rely on inefficient green sources, it may soon be more efficient, from an energy usage point of view, to commute to an office and speak face-to-face than to stay at home and videoconference. Real travel also beats virtual because it's a charm against outsourcing. It's better to waste an hour or so a day for the sake of being there and connecting, than to be someone wearing a silly hat on a webcam doing a job an Indian with a good degree would do for £80 for a sixty-hour week. The threat is real and imminent. According to Roy, the godfather of Indian outsourcing, 'the first phase was just arbitrage and substitution'. There's no reason, barring antiquated restrictive practices, that lawyers or accountants (or most of the rest of the white-collar workforce) couldn't be outsourced like call-centre workers – for similar savings. From this perspective the willingness to commute looks more like a survival instinct than a misguided devotion to an outmoded way of life.

♦ ♦ ♦ ♦ ♦

CHAPTER XIV

All Change

> Democratic nations care but little for what has been,
> but are haunted by visions of what will be; in this
> direction, their unbounded imagination grows and
> dilates beyond all measure.
>
> Alexis de Tocqueville, *Democracy in America*, 1835

If even the tech industry, which has made remote working a possibility instead of a dream, is insisting its workers are physically present on corporate premises, it seems there is little chance of commuting vanishing in the near or distant future. Even in the absence of compulsion, there are good reasons to expect it to persist. It empowers people to separate their work and home lives, and both require face time to function. Unless and until we evolve into creatures that have no such needs, and have erased the desires to hunt and gather from our nature, there will be a Clapham omnibus, or its latter-day equivalent, ferrying people between their places of labour and rest. Unless, of course, we won't have to work in the future, or companionship goes out of fashion after, say, a deadly global pandemic. Would we then commute for nostalgia, or even pleasure? Has commuting worked its way so deep into our culture that we'd find it hard to give up absolutely?

Or would we frown on it, as we do slavery and burning witches, as belonging to an ignorant, violent and primitive past?

People have been predicting both the imminent demise and the perpetual rise of commuting almost since it started. There was a fad for futurology in the late Victorian era when a multitude of utopias and dystopias were formulated to titillate readers with visions of the future. Many authors chose the twentieth century as their location in time, though some went forwards by millennia. Most envisaged the persistence of both work and commuting. As we've seen, in 1901 H. G. Wells anticipated that the world would soon be driving motorcars to work. He also predicted a few advanced forms of transport that didn't – or haven't yet – become reality, such as giant motorized walkways that whizz pedestrians around in rush hour, and he was wrong about aviation. The fad for making predictions has continued more or less unabated since Wells's day, and when aeroplanes did appear, flying cars quickly became a staple of futurological commuting. It was thought self-evident that as soon as the roads filled up people would take to the air and go further and faster when travelling to work. The first aerial automobiles to be imagined after both cars and aeroplanes had been invented appeared in the July 1924 issue of *Popular Science* magazine, which featured 'An Expert's Visionary Picture of Motor Travel in the Future' and predicted that there would be 'Flying Autos in 20 Years'. Eddie Rickenbacker, the expert in question, foresaw a 'combined automobile-airplane' that would be smaller and more streamlined than a conventional car, and equipped with folding wings that were extended manually before flight. The artist's impressions that accompany the article might have been the inspiration for *Chitty Chitty Bang Bang*. As soon as a driver reached a straight stretch of road, or could pull over into a level pasture, he or she could spread their wings and take to the air. Aerial cars wouldn't be engineered for stunt flying, but might enable the suburbanites that Rickenbacker had in mind as first-users to 'live several miles further away from the heart of the city and spend less time going to work'. They might also inspire municipalities to regulate for a uniform building height and bridge over the gaps in between so as to 'form one vast landing field in the center of each city for flying machines'.* Rickenbacker had been America's Ace of Aces in the First World War with twenty-six kills to his name, and he seems to have been as charismatic in life as he appears in his photographs. He founded automobile and airline companies, owned and ran the Indianapolis Motor Speedway for a dozen years, survived a plane crash, wrote comics, spent nearly a month drifting around the Pacific in a life-raft eating seagulls and lived to see his prediction of flying autos fail by nearly thirty years when he died in 1973.

A similar confidence over the imminence of changes to commuter travel was afoot in Britain where Winston Churchill, writing for *The Strand Magazine* in December 1931, thought nuclear-powered fuel cells would be key. In 'Fifty Years Hence', he predicted that 'transport by land, water and air would take unimaginable forms' by 1981. His inconceivable vehicles would be propelled by something like 'an engine of 600 horsepower, weighing 20 lb and carrying fuel for a thousand hours in a tank

---

* Flying cars similar to those envisaged by Rickenbacker also featured in the film *Metropolis* (1927), Fritz Lang's paean to futurism.

the size of a fountain-pen'. Thanks also to simultaneous advances in telecommunications, the world would become a giant suburb:

> *The congregation of men in cities would become superfluous. It would rarely be necessary to call in person on any but the most intimate friends, but if so, excessively rapid means of communication would be at hand... The cities and the countryside would become indistinguishable. Every home would have its garden and its glade.*

Churchill wasn't alone in believing that fuel cells were just over the horizon. In 1959, a spokesman for the Ford Motor Company predicted that its models of the 1980s would be propelled on their wings through American skies by atomic power plants the size of shoeboxes.

Money as well as words have been wasted on the future of commuting. There've been some spectacular losing bets made in the past on how people were going to travel to work in the future. In 1985, for instance, not long after the concept of the electronic cottage appeared, a new commuter vehicle made its debut which was likewise expected to sort out rush hour once and for all. On 10 January of that year, in the depths of a cold and wet winter, Sir Clive Sinclair unveiled his 'C5' in a televised ceremony at the Alexandra Palace. The C5 was a recumbent tricycle, with a white plastic body and a small electric motor capable of propelling it at speeds of up to 15 mph along flat ground. Sinclair was the patron saint of miniaturization in British consumer electronics at the time. The archetypal boffin, with oversized glasses and a wispy ginger beard, he had introduced cheap word processors and portable televisions to an appreciative public and a supportive press. Prior to its launch, the media had swallowed Sinclair's publicity and then whipped itself into raptures over the C5: this 'completely new concept in personal transportation' was touted as the potential saviour of British industry, and an example of national ingenuity on a par with Sinclair pocket calculators and the bouncing bomb. It was anticipated that the C5 would be embraced by both urban commuters and rail travellers who had to drive to their stations, and predicted that it would sell millions in both domestic and overseas markets. Soon British dockyards would be piled high with shiny white* C5s en route to join the rush hour on at least four continents, while the roads at home would carry stately parades of these swan-like vehicles travelling at an even 15 mph, ferrying their owners between their beds and desks.

The C5 was assembled in a Hoover factory in Wales. An Italian manufacturer of washing-machine engines built its motor. It was for sale only by mail order. I saw one in the flesh a few weeks after its launch, and can still feel the disappointment. It was difficult to imagine an adult wanting to sit in one, or anyone over ten years old getting a thrill out of driving one. But I was wrong about the thrills: people who got theirs from being frightened loved the C5. In busy traffic the view at eye level was composed of bumpers and exhaust pipes. It was underpowered and underbraked, and far harder to steer out of trouble than a bike.

---

* It only came in white.

It looked and felt as fragile as an eggshell. One could imagine the world going Humpty Dumpty very quickly.

The media back-pedalled once they'd seen a C5 in all its glory. Not only did it look unsafe and feel unsafe, it also failed to perform to its very limited specification. In June 1985, *Which* magazine noted that 'performance, range and comfort do not compare with the better mopeds', which effectively banged a nail in the coffin of the expected revolution in commuter transport. Mopeds were for spotty adolescents or hairdressers. No true 1980s yuppie in a loud suit and bright red braces would be seen dead on one. In hindsight, the C5 didn't do too badly. In total there were 17,000 sold, which made it the bestselling electric passenger vehicle of all time until the Nissan Leaf overtook its record in 2010.

Latter-day rivals to the C5 in the field of personal transportation – small, slow vehicles whose inventors believe that they might somehow persuade people to give up large, powerful, climate-controlled cars – have since appeared, although none, as yet, have had much impact on rush hour. The Segway Personal Transporter, for instance, an electric scooter with two parallel wheels, that is ridden standing up, is touted by its manufacturers as the ideal replacement for an automobile for short-distance driving. The blurb for its i2 Commuter model emphasizes the pleasure and convenience it offers to motorists who are sick of being stuck in jams: 'sail past gas stations and lines of stopped traffic... getting to work has never been more fun!' However, Segways have been around for nearly a decade, and have yet to make any sort of dent in automobile sales. When Jeff Bezos of Amazon was shown a prototype, he made the prescient observation to its inventor that 'you have a product so revolutionary, you'll have no problem selling it. The question is, are people going to be allowed to use it?' The answer in many places has been no. Pedestrians don't want Segways on the pavements, cyclists don't want them in their lanes, and there are safety concerns about their use on the roads. The Segway is, after a fashion, a victim of its own originality. If a place could be found for it in the infrastructure – widened cycle lanes, perhaps – it would be an ideal vehicle for short-hop, fair-weather commuting. A similar niche is being explored by the RYNO, a self-balancing single-wheeled electric scooter, invented by Chris Hoffmann in Oregon and described by its creator as a 'transitional vehicle' that 'goes most places where a person can walk or ride a bike' and by the *Daily Mail* as 'a cross between a Segway and a unicycle'. It's small enough to take on a train, or in the lift at work, so as well as being a commuting vehicle in itself, it could replace cars for those who drive to railway stations as part of a multi-legged commute. It's chasing the same market as the C5, but looks a lot more fun.

Although many of the recent innovations in commuter transport have focused on finding a substitute for them, the next twenty years of commuting will still be all about motorcars. Anyone hoping that people will abandon their cars for recumbent tricycles or their latter-day equivalent is deluded. Most commuters in the developed world travel on four wheels. The figure ranges from 87 per cent in America to 39 per cent in Japan. Over two-thirds of Britons commute by car, and only 16.4 per cent of them use public transport, with the remainder walking, cycling or riding motorbikes. Even in London, which introduced congestion charging in 2003 to deter drivers, 29.8 per cent of its commuters travelled by car in 2013, which is more than on any other single form of transport.* This isn't simply because of perverse desires to expend hydrocarbons and cook the planet: driving, more often than not, is the only way. Here's an example from life. I live in Bishop's Waltham, a medieval market town in Hampshire. It was once the seat of the Bishops of Winchester, in whose palace Henry V prepared himself before leaving for France and the Battle of Agincourt, and where Queen Mary I waited for King Philip of Spain to arrive in the country for their wedding. It's now something of a commuter-shed serving the nearby cities of Winchester, Portsmouth and Southampton. Its railway station was closed in the Beeching cuts of the 1960s, and the nearest surviving station at Botley is four miles away along a twisting country road that has several crosses, with bunches of flowers scattered around them, where recent fatal accidents have occurred. There's a limited bus service, which takes forever to go anywhere. There are no designated cycle paths. The only way for 90 per cent of the people who live in Bishop's Waltham to get to work is by driving, even if it's just driving to Botley station as part of a longer commute. There aren't any plans to re-open the railway, or otherwise improve public transport. Moreover, there's no recognition of this reality at the national level. Road and petrol taxes trend up, as do policies favouring cycling and electric cars designed for carrying urbanites short distances, neither of which are relevant to commuting out of Bishop's Waltham. Like suburban Americans with their Hummers, we're wedded to our Mondeos and Golfs out of circumstance.

---

* 'Light rail services', which include the Underground network, came second with 21.8 per cent.

This is a lesson to policymakers everywhere: you can't wish motorcars away, especially if there's no viable alternative. Moreover, policies intended to reduce car use may not only be counterproductive, but also malevolent. Dr Alan Pisarski, guru of American commuting, who publishes a five-yearly analysis of the practice with data culled from the National Census, lambasted those in Washington who would have people give up their cars before there was any other option, and 'who think that if we just don't build any roads and let things get worse then we will induce more people into using transit. This is a theory that says if we make life miserable enough for 90 percent of travelers some of them might switch modes to work.' Pisarski also noted that forcing people out of cars had the unintended side effect of victimizing minorities, for whom car ownership was an important step towards achieving economic equality. Penalizing auto-commuters in the hope of compelling them to use public transport also overlooks the pleasure they get from driving. In the words of Brad Edmondson, former editor of *American Demographics*, 'planners who dream of a future where average Americans abandon their cars at home and switch to public transportation or carpooling are being unrealistic. This will not happen in our lifetime. People love the freedom, solitude, and choice they get from their personal cars, and they are not about to give them up.'

Auto-commuting is set to grow on a global basis over the next few decades. In China, for example, which didn't get its millionth car until 1992, a figure America reached in 1912, annual registrations now exceed 15 million. OPEC predicts that by 2035 China will have more than 380 million cars, and has increased its forecast of demand for crude oil to 108.5 million barrels per day to allow for the growth in what it terms 'fuel based transportation'. China is already preparing the highways for its auto-commuters of the future. According to its twelfth five-year plan for transportation, it will spend US$787.4 billion on building roads between 2011 and 2015, or about the same as the GDP of Holland.

While commuting by motorcar looks set to stay for the foreseeable future, there may be significant changes in the way it's carried out. Although more and more people will be using cars to get to work, it may be as passengers rather than drivers. Driverless or autonomous vehicles have been on futurologists' radars for longer than telecommuting. The first recorded example was the Achen Motor Company's 'phantom motor car', which it promised to drive around the streets of Milwaukee by radio control in December 1926. The *Milwaukee Sentinel* waxed lyrical over the 'ghost': 'Driverless, it will start its own motor, throw its clutch, twist its steering wheel, toot its horn, and it may even "sass" the policeman at the corner.'

Whether the phantom actually appeared or not is unknown. The next examples of autonomous autos materialized at General Motors' Futurama exhibition at the 1939 New York World's Fair, which proclaimed that the teardrop-shaped model vehicles that streamed along its miniature highways would communicate with each other and the environment via radio waves, and would be partially autonomous, in the sense that they would be controlled by a traffic management system as well as by their drivers. The prediction was repeated in Futurama II (also sponsored by GM) at the 1964 New York World's Fair. In addition to clearcutting the rainforests to build model cities, mining the moon and turning the oceans into fish farms (all using GM vehicles), Americans of the not-too-distant future would build avant-garde houses on hilltops and commute vast distances to giant metropolises, where all traffic would be 'electronically paced'. The phrase was not explained, but the exhibit showed evenly spaced autos peeling off fourteen-lane continental highways and maintaining perfect headway right into the heart of the city.

Driverless cars were trialled as well as modelled. In 1960, the British Transport and Road Research Laboratory at Crowthorne, Berkshire, modified a Citroën DS so that it was capable of driving itself and tested it over eight miles of custom-built track. A film from the period shows the then Leader of the House of Lords, Viscount Hailsham, reading a newspaper at its wheel. Magnetic sensors that followed a rail buried beneath the track guided the car, which was electrically controlled.

Indeed, many of the early prophets of driverless vehicles assumed that the phantoms might not just be guided by electricity, but powered by it too. The chance to compete with fossil fuels on the roads as well as the rails excited power generation companies. In 1957, for instance, the Central Power and Light Company of Texas published an advertorial that proclaimed, 'Electricity may be the driver! One day your car may speed along an electric super-highway, its speed and steering automatically controlled by electronic devices embedded in the road. Travel will be more enjoyable. It will be made safe – by electricity! No traffic jams… no collisions… no driver fatigue.' The picture that accompanies the blurb shows a family of four playing dominoes in a car with a pod-shaped interior, a torpedo nose and tail fins, which is hurtling along a freeway while no one inside is looking at the road ahead. Even though the futuristic promise of electric cars was heightened when three electric Lunar Roving Vehicles were set loose on the moon by the *Apollo 15, 16* and *17* missions of 1971 and 1972, enthusiasm for them, and for driverless cars in general, died out over the next few decades as car manufacturers engaged in an arms race involving ever larger and more powerful conveyances, to appease either the paranoid or saurian parts of their customers' brains: he or she who crashes in the biggest car wins.

When transit operators started taking drivers out of trains, auto-makers didn't rush to follow suit. Their business model relied on people loving driving themselves, if nothing else for the freedom it offered, and they were happy to let the idea of driverless vehicles sleep. However, it was revived by the American military after the 2003 Iraq War. Why send a soldier as well as a vehicle through a minefield? The Defense Advanced Research Projects Agency (DARPA), part of the US Department of Defense – hoping to inspire the creation of autonomous vehicles that might have martial applications – staged the DARPA Grand Challenges of 2004 and 2005, and the Urban Challenge of 2007, which offered million-dollar prizes and grants to teams who could create effective driverless cars. Various universities built entries, and while none met the challenge in 2004, four succeeded in 2005 and there were as many winners in the urban event. The grand challenges advanced autonomous technology by leaps and bounds, and also created a pool of engineering expertise, eager to take the concept further.

The potential that the DARPA challengers had demonstrated revived commercial interest in driverless cars. Companies including Nissan, GM, Lexus, Google, Mercedes Benz, Ford, Skoda, Audi and Volvo are now researching or building vehicles with varying degrees of autonomy. Volvo, for instance, will offer a self-parking system on its new XC90. It's eerie to watch a prototype in action. The driver gets out of the car then texts it a message from his mobile, telling it to go and park. It seeks out a space, dodging other vehicles and pedestrians all the while, and then reverses into a slot between two other cars. Its movements are incredibly smooth: although robotics is doing the driving, there's none of the jerkiness we usually associate with artificial life. But there's no one at the wheel and, since it's natural to seek eye contact with other drivers when we interact with them, the void beyond the dashboard is disturbing. If a car had a mind of its own, would it be evil? Volvo cites safety as the motivation behind its R&D in driverless technology. Its stated aim is that no one should die or get badly injured in a Volvo built after 2020. It is a noble ambition. The World Health Organization estimates that 1.3 million people die in traffic accidents every year, and a further 50 million are maimed or crippled. Most accidents are caused by human error. If motorcars could detect each other, could communicate among themselves, and might be programmed to avoid collisions, then rush hours would be far safer.

Google, which is leading research in autonomous vehicles, is also motivated by safety. Its informal corporate motto is 'Don't be Evil', and it believes that driverless cars will end the global carnage on the roads that claims more victims each year than warfare.

In the same speech in which CFO Patrick Pichette dismissed telecommuting, he also stated that, in an ideal world, 'nobody should be driving cars... Look at factorial math and probabilities of everything that could go wrong, times the number of cars out there... That's why you have gridlock... It makes no sense to make people drive cars.'

Google's ambitions for autonomous vehicles reach beyond safety: Its lead developer Sebastian Thrun, a veteran of the DARPA '05 Grand Challenge, sums them up as:

(1) *We can reduce traffic accidents by 90%.*
(2) *We can reduce wasted commute time and energy by 90%.*
(3) *We can reduce the number of cars by 90%.*

Although if you began with objective (3) you'd probably also succeed with (2) and (1) by default, progress the other way isn't so simple. Testing has started nonetheless: Google's initial fleet of ten driverless cars have clocked up over 300,000 miles between them. A human sits by the wheel ready to take control should the car's computers crash. They've had three accidents, the most serious of which – a minor rear-end collision with a Prius – occurred when a human was driving.

The company's next step has been to introduce a prototype of a truly autonomous vehicle, which made its debut on YouTube in May 2014. It's the antithesis of a Hummer, with only two seats, a tiny electric engine, a top speed of 25 mph, and no controls for its human passengers bar start and emergency stop buttons. It looks as if it was designed by a cartoonist and even has a friendly face on its foam front. Indeed, Google's first car is reminiscent in both shape and conception to Herbie, the four-wheeled star of Disney's *The Love Bug* (1968). Herbie, a modified Volkswagen Beetle, had a mind of his own, and very human emotions. Although he bore grudges, and sometimes wrecked other cars, his usual disposition was sunny and his behaviour altruistic. Although the film did not explain precisely how Herbie had become autonomous, it hinted that a combination of technology and attention had worked the change. As Tennessee Steinmetz, the film's guru figure, explains to Jim Douglas, Herbie's owner: 'We take machines and stuff 'em with information until they're smarter than we are. Take a car. Most guys spread more love and time and money on their car in a week than they do on their wife and kids in a year. Pretty soon, you know what? The machine starts to think it *is* somebody.'

Google don't pretend their prototype is about to develop feelings. It's comfortable, if utilitarian, inside, with only two cup-holders. It's shown carrying pensioners, children and a blind man around a closed circuit, all of whom are enthusiastic about the ride and its potential to extend their ranges. It's intended to ferry people between the towns and the suburbs rather than ambling along the highways.

Driverless cars are now partially legal in California, Nevada and Florida. According to their advocates, these are merely the first of many places that will approve them soon, and they'll be all over the roads before we know it. In the opinion of Chunka Mui, an innovations strategist writing for *Forbes* magazine, 'the issue is when, not if – and when is sooner than you think'. Nissan has promised the world affordable autonomous cars by 2020. Google will have a hundred of its Google-bugs on Californian test tracks, and possibly roads in 2014; the University of Michigan is building a 32-acre model village to test self-driving 'connected cars'; Volvo, in conjunction with the city of Gothenburg, has announced a pilot scheme scheduled to commence in 2017, in which a fleet of a hundred of its driverless cars will be set loose on an initial thirty miles of public roads described as 'typical commuter arteries'. Meanwhile the British city of Milton Keynes has plans to introduce a fleet of self-directed 'pods' in 2015, which will run along a dedicated track from its centre to its railway station.

Even accountants are getting fired up over autonomous vehicles: the multinational firm KPMG has quantified the potential benefits that might flow from letting computers and servomotors do the driving. As well as fewer accidents, lower insurance premiums and all the other safety-related savings, auto-commuters could work in their cars on the way to the office instead of having fits of road rage; hundreds of thousands of acres of car parks could be freed up for development; highway-building programmes could be cut since lanes could be narrower and there would be no need for signs or traffic lights; and road usage could rise significantly. At present, unless they're gridlocked in rush hour, cars occupy a surprisingly small percentage of the surface of the asphalt they're travelling over. Fearful human drivers leave larger gaps between their vehicles than would be necessary in an automated, driverless environment. We slow down faster than we speed up, resulting in a 'caterpillar effect' whereby traffic moves in fits and starts, alternately compressing and expanding, and we're also erratic in our spacing because we're preoccupied about things like families and hangovers as well as the road.

Autonomous vehicles, in contrast, wouldn't have lives beyond the ambit of their coding. In theory they could form themselves into 'platoons' that travelled inches apart at high speeds. Every car behind the leader would benefit from 'drafting' (slipstreaming) and cut its fuel use by a quarter. Traffic density could double or treble in rush hour, without creating the need to build any new roads. The vehicles could be fun to ride in, too. Instead of a row or two of forward-facing seats, there'd be space for beds, chandeliers, mini-bars, workstations, or a croupier and a roulette wheel. Commuting would become an adventure, or a form of luxury travel once again. Self-driving cars will also be wonderfully easy to use – the ultimate taxi service. You'll be able to text for one, anywhere, anytime. Those with handicaps, alcoholics, and other classes of people currently disbarred from driving would also be empowered by the hands-free revolution. Elderly people who, whether through sight loss or growing immobility, are unable to drive themselves, will not have to lose the freedom to ride in a car that they have enjoyed all their lives.

Apparently we're ready for change. KPMG think that Americans are all set to slip their emotional bonds with autos. They divide the population of the USA into four generations: Baby Boomers (anyone over 45); Generation X (35–45 years old); Generation Now (15–34) and Digital Natives (younger than 15). Whilst Baby Boomers and X-ers were in love with cars and got their licences young – in 1978, for instance, 75 per cent of American seventeen-year-olds had theirs – Generation Now aren't quite so obsessed. In 2008, only 49 per cent of their age cohort had passed their driving tests by the age of seventeen. If a machine does it for them, they won't care. They're happy to limit their driving experiences to *Grand Theft Auto*. Even auto-makers have spotted the growing indifference towards wheels. In the opinion of Catherine Lovazzano, senior manager for consumer trends at Chrysler, the motorcar is no longer 'the iconic freedom machine that it might have been for a baby boomer'. Generation Now, together with the Digital Natives in the age cohort beneath them, make up nearly half the population of America, and if the Natives are as apathetic as the Nows, then self-driving cars will have a giant market. A similar lack of interest in driving among the young is apparent throughout the West. In a 2012 feature, 'Seeing the back of the car', the UK news magazine *The Economist* noted that 'All over the rich world, young people are getting their licences later than they used to... in Britain, Canada, France, Norway, South Korea and Sweden' as well as in America. 'Even in Germany, car-culture-vulture of Europe, the share of young households without cars increased from 20% to 28% between 1998 and 2008.'

If coming generations don't want and might not need to drive cars, they may not wish to own them either. The thrill of possession, the old Deadly Sin of covetousness – of wanting something, buying it, maybe in instalments, then cherishing it forever, seems to be diminishing. Generation Nows are used to upgrading rather than making do and mending. Taxi or rental companies might own fleets of driverless cars that would emerge each dawn from underground bunkers like ants from their nests and stream out through cities and suburbs picking up and delivering commuters and schoolchildren in the mornings and evenings, and serve as taxis and shopping trolleys in between. When not in use they could take themselves away to refuel. If electric, they'd be able to draw power from the grid outside times of peak demand, so could make the best of intermittent sources of energy like wind and solar. They might even be surfaced with solar panels and left to bask in the sun whenever there was a gap in their busy schedules. Best of all, they could offer a 24/7 go-anywhere service for a fifth of the price of owning and running a car. A study by Lawrence D. Burns and William C. Jordan at Columbia University's Earth Institute Program on Sustainable Mobility, concluded that a handful of emergent technologies would not only make driverless feasible, but would lower the expense of travel in the same way that innovation had done for telecommunications. In their opinion, 'it is now possible to supply better mobility experiences at radically lower cost to consumers and society'. The 'better mobility experiences' would consist of shared driverless cars that communicated with the environment as well as with each other, and would be powered by 'advanced propulsion systems', by which Burns and Jordan mean electric engines. The fuel cells and mini-nuclear reactors imagined by the Ford Motor Company, Winston Churchill and the *Jetsons* cartoon series as the power sources of the future are still fifty years away – unless there's a eureka moment in between.

It would be ironic if the digital revolution was trumped by a similar shake-up in transportation, and the cost of conveying people or things fell back below that of carrying data. Commuting would be so cheap and painless that people might take pay cuts so as to get jobs that let them commute, simply for the pleasure of having separate lives at work and home. They'd also be able to commute more than once each day. Tales of 'The Man who went to London Four Times in One Day' would circulate. Siestas might become universal.

There are fortunes at stake on driverless auto-commuting: The American car market alone is worth \$2 trillion per annum. There will be losers as well as winners. According to KPMG: 'the implications would also be profoundly disruptive for almost every stakeholder in the automotive ecosystem'. The list of potential losers is long, and headed by the existing automobile industry in its entirety. Those that persist with the old business model of making dream chariots for men in grey flannel suits will fold. There will be collateral damage: if car crashes, which cost America \$400 billion a year, stop, then the people who make a living from them will be that much poorer. Losers in the private sector will include casualty-ward workers, undertakers, insurance companies, lawyers, garages and manufacturers of spares. The public sector, meanwhile, will lose revenue on parking fines, speeding tickets and petrol and road taxes.

If this all seems too good to be true, one must remember that many of the assumptions of the driverless lobby are wishful thinking. Would a platoon of, say, 200 autonomous vehicles, travelling at 150 mph a foot or so apart pass the Swedish *Undanmanöverprov*, or 'moose test'? The Swedes are paranoid about moose on their roads in autumn. An adult moose can weigh up to 110 stone, and be seven feet tall at the shoulders. When a car hits one head-on, the moose tends to drop through the windscreen and – if it is not dead – to kick out and thrash around in panic. Before any new car is allowed on Swedish roads it is tested on a short slalom course: turn sharp right, sharp left, and make an emergency stop in front of an imaginary moose, represented by a line on the road. Although the element of surprise is allowed for in current driverless testing programmes – Mercedes, for instance, have a 'washing machine test': 'Something suddenly falls off a truck ahead of the car. Can the system react faster and better than a human?' – reacting better than a human may not be good enough. There is still the possibility of non-human errors. Dr Ralf Herrtwich, a leader on the Mercedes programme, thinks that a completely autonomous car is 'maybe more than a decade away'. There's a long list of unknowable unknowables, like the effect of solar storms on guidance systems, or viruses in onboard computers that might send platoons of hundreds of driverless cars across intersections at speeds forbidden to human drivers – and into a mixture of gridlock and Armageddon.

Driverless cars will therefore need several levels of (theoretically) redundant safety features. They'll have to be stronger and more moose- or washing machine-proof than existing cars. They'll have to convince legislators and indeed passengers that travelling nose to tail at high speeds without being physically connected, and bobbing and weaving through traffic whilst generating sensational g-forces is perfectly safe. Indeed, simple human factors like fear might prevent them from realizing their true potential. Even strengths – like being able to see in the dark without headlights (as Google cars already can), so saving energy and cutting down on light pollution – may turn out to be liabilities rather than benefits: the experience of being whisked around in pitch darkness will probably trigger vertigo in some passengers.

Perhaps, too, instead of programming code, playing strip poker, or lining up shots while on their way to or from work, commuters will have to wear crash helmets and be strapped in with a web of belts, and their robot cars will refuse to move until they submit.

And what if their demand for electricity – together with that of the vast number of data centres required to manage them – was so great that they crashed the power grid and ended up requiring more hydrocarbons to be burned than the gas guzzlers they replaced, while simultaneously pushing up the price of electricity for other users? Although full autonomy may be years rather than decades away, in the immediate future there'll be more people commuting on American roads in Hummers, possibly with an automated parking function, than there will be in driverless pods.

It is possible, however, that autonomous autos might be adopted first in countries that don't have giant road networks or a driving culture already in place. Africa may have them by the platoon before they're common in California, or indeed Bishop's Waltham. According to Chunka Mui, 'The driverless car might… save developing countries from ever having to replicate the car-centric infrastructure that has emerged in most western countries.' In the same way that many developing nations went from having no telephones to mobiles, leapfrogging landlines altogether, so countries that are building new towns or highways for the first time could go straight to driverless.

What, then, of the future for commuters on public transport? Will there be seats for all and inexpensive, punctual services by 2050, or indeed, 2020? Unfortunately, comfort and convenience don't seem to inspire policymakers and transport planners, who think instead of speed and distance, of competing with commercial airlines rather than alleviating crush loading. In Britain, for instance, this bias has been rampant since the end of the Second World War. Money was poured into inter-city lines between nationalization in 1948 and privatization in 1997, while the average link between suburbs and centre was left to run with decrepit and overcrowded stock – if it wasn't axed by the Beeching cuts. The latest manifestation of the bias towards grand projects is High Speed 2 (HS2), a new line that's planned to run between London and the north of England and whose first phase is projected to enter into service in 2026. Its expected cost has been rising steadily since the Labour administration introduced the project in 2010, according to former business minister Peter Mandelson as an electioneering ruse. It was felt that a 'bold commitment to modernization' would 'paint an upbeat view of the future' to voters even if its costings were 'entirely speculative'. It's now projected to cost £46.2 billion, and its high-speed trains will shave a mere thirty minutes off current journey times between London and Glasgow. The science writer and Conservative peer Matt Ridley has suggested that British politicians, who do 40 per cent of their travel between Westminster and their constituencies on the trains, 'live in a rail bubble', and has suggested half a dozen smaller projects that would have the same total price but would achieve far more.

A similar love affair with grand designs and a general neglect of commuters prevail elsewhere in Europe. Although it may be scant consolation, British commuters might enjoy a little *Schadenfreude* when they learn that their equivalents in Germany also travel on old, dirty trains, which likewise are delayed by wet leaves or the wrong sort of snow on the tracks, while the Bundestag fire-hoses billions of euros at trans-European links. In France too, whose TGV trains (*Trains à Grande Vitesse*, i.e. high-speed trains) are a matter of national pride, funded by billions of government-guaranteed bonds, commuters are treated like the country's pre-revolutionary peasantry. In 2012, Guillaume Pepy, president of the state-owned railway company SNCF (Société Nationale des Chemins de fer Français), told the French National Assembly that its conventional train system, which included its commuter lines, had 'reached the end of its life'. Some of its locomotives were forty years old, and the stations on the Paris RER commuter system were literally falling apart. According to Carole Matlack, writing for *Bloomberg Businessweek*, commuters at Auber station, adjacent to the Paris Opera House, have to 'dodge chunks of falling plaster and buckets that catch water which drips through the ceiling on rainy days' in order to board their ramshackle trains. Although the French government promised to spend 400 million euros on upgrading the network in 2013, this was still less than half the sum budgeted for TGV lines.

It may be, however, that HS2 and its continental equivalents aren't being ambitious enough. If displacing aeroplanes is the aim, then why not build an elevated Maglev, such as was imagined by Cesare Marchetti in 1994, running from the Channel tunnel to Aberdeen? It's only 438 miles, which a Maglev travelling at conservative speeds, and stopping at London Heathrow, Birmingham, Manchester and Edinburgh en route, could manage within an hour. With a few feeder lines it might extend the 'commuter-shed' of all these places for dozens of miles in every direction. And since safety would be de rigueur at such high velocities – passengers would need to strap in, and trains follow split-second moving block schedules – commuters could be sure that the services would be punctual, and that they would always get a seat.

Precisely this kind of meta-solution has been proposed in California, where building work on a high-speed commuter train service between Los Angeles and San Francisco looks set to commence after years of wrangling. The California High Speed Rail (CHSR) is budgeted at US$68 billion and projected to be in operation by 2029. The journey time between its headline destinations will be about three hours. Its locomotives and carriages will be painted in the California state colours of blue and gold. The project, however, has had a spoke thrown in its wheels in the form of a counterproposal by Elon Musk, a forty-two-year-old South African-born entrepreneur, who co-founded PayPal and is now CEO of both Tesla Motors and SpaceX. Tesla is the first-ever electrical car manufacturer to turn a profit, and SpaceX the first private company to deliver supplies to the International Space Station. Musk's success is down to flair and lateral thinking. When he started Tesla, most electric car manufacturers were building small autos for eco-warriors (who'd rather not be seen on wheels at all), or making wolves in sheep's clothing – SUVs with large petrol and small ancillary electric motors – in order to take advantage of grants for green vehicles. Musk instead went for comfort and performance. The Tesla Model S does 0 to 60 mph in 4.2 seconds, tops out at 130 mph, and has more boot room and better safety standards than a Volvo. Musk's ambition is to retire to Mars. His counterproposal to the CHSR is the 'Hyperloop', a part pneumatic, part electromagnetic and part solar-powered system, which he claims could fly pods of commuters through elevated steel tubes between San Francisco and LA in about half an hour for a tenth of the price of building its rival.

However, the Hyperloop's costings have been shown to be out by a factor of several hundred per cent, and it's been labelled by Alon Levy, a respected transportation commentator, as a 'barf ride' on account of the emetic g-forces it would generate when accelerating, decelerating, or travelling on inclines or round corners. Other experts have attacked its safety – if there was an accident it would apparently have the same 'wow! factor' as 'Concorde hitting a mountain' – yet it does have its merits, being an innovative combination of speculative and road-tested technologies. Pneumatic railways, for instance, date back to the 1840s and even competed with steam trains for a short period. The South Devon Railway Company built a stretch of pneumatic track in 1847, designed by Isambard Kingdom Brunel, which carried its passengers in a silent, smoke-free atmosphere at a peak speed of 70 mph between Exeter and Newton Abbot. Unfortunately, rats ate holes in its leather bellows and the sea air corrupted its metal fittings and it was abandoned the next year. Similarly, the low-pressure tubes through which the Hyperloop might run have their precedents in 'vactrains', or vacuum tube trains, which have existed in theory and as models since 1909. Finally, not even its critics doubt that the Hyperloop's electromagnetic propulsion system would work, and it has also been simulated by the best available transport modelling software, which has given it the thumbs up – in principle. Its pods may need skis on the roof as well as the floor but otherwise it looks viable.

It's possible, however, that even the Hyperloop isn't radical enough. Although, in theory, it's quicker and cheaper than CHSR, it will carry fewer passengers. Perhaps what is needed are stacks of Hyperloops that use support pylons to carry tubes upon tubes, like a fibre optic cable in cross section. Why not bundle up transport like telecommunications? Some of the tubes in the roll could be feeder hypoloops, and others provide roadways for driverless cars. There would be arrivals and departures at each station every second, and ramps on and off at every road intersection. Auto-commuting and rapid transit would be yin and yang – two parts of the same unity. Perhaps a golden age of commuting is on its way. Unfortunately, it's doubtful that it will be with us before Elon Musk retires to Mars.

If basic comforts are unlikely to appear on public transport before Generation Now turn into pensioners, might it not be better to wish for, and work towards, an end to commuting altogether? If it can't be perfect, then why have it at all? Two distinct schools of thought have prophesied the death of rush hour in centuries to come. Both think that this will be because of population growth, although their opinions as to what counts as too many humans are far apart. Neo-Malthusians, who wring their hands at the present total of 7 billion on the planet, and shudder at the prospect of it growing to nine, would like us to take a step backwards from the Industrial Revolution, reduce our energy use and numbers, and revert to living in small communities, where no one need ever commute.

The opposing school, in contrast, predicts that no one will be able to commute in the future because – eventually – we will be too many, rather than fewer. But there's no need to fear 9 billion, or indeed 9,000 billion. In a 1964 essay, 'How Many People Can the World Support?', John Heaver Fremlin, an English physicist, argued that limitations on human population growth were determined by physics rather than biology. Barring catastrophes such as a meteorite strike, an apocalyptic war or a deadly global pandemic; and assuming that the entire surface of the planet, 'land and sea alike', was covered with 2,000-storey buildings; that people ate their dead and their sewage; that both the north and south poles had been melted on purpose; and there was absolute and eternal world peace; then mother earth could carry up to 60,000,000,000,000,000 (sixty thousand trillion) people by around the year 2964. Any more, however, would be pushing the laws of physics.

Fremlin's thirtieth-century humans wouldn't get the chance to commute. The best they might hope for would be socializing – 'occasional vertical and random horizontal low speed vehicular or moving-belt travel over a few hundred meters would be permissible', but nothing more. Immobility would have its consolations: 'one could expect some ten million Shakespeares and rather more Beatles to be alive at any one time, and that a good range of television entertainment should be available'. Best of all, super-dense-crush-loaded living wouldn't require any radical cultural changes: 'the extrapolation from the present life of a car-owning, flat-dwelling, office-worker to such an existence might well be less than from that of the Neolithic hunter to that of the aforesaid office-worker.' It is here, however, that Fremlin's argument fails. Flat-dwelling office-workers own cars because they need to satisfy a genetic propensity to hunt and gather. We must first exterminate this urge from the gene pool before we can dream of a commuter-free planet. After ten thousand years of agriculture, and a few decades of the information age, we've scarcely dented it. Call it clockwork wanderlust, commuting is here to stay – even if it means postponing the chance to go forth and multiply until we're limit up.

I started this book when I was commuting to London on the 07.01 in January of 2011. Botley, where the railway leg of my journey began, was close to the spot from which the political reformer William Cobbett set out on his rural rides in the 1820s. Agricultural England seemed to be dying at the time. Farm workers lived in abject poverty, and Cobbett wanted to see their condition for himself. He was a nostalgic man at heart, who would rather the country remained rural and reverted to the plenty – as he perceived it – of the prior century, than embraced industrialization and an uncertain future. He wanted rights rather than progress. While the country lanes along which Cobbett travelled on horseback ran through a landscape that had altered little since feudal times, my daily journey to Waterloo took me past mementos of all the stupendous changes that have happened since. The tracks sliced across strawberry fields, cut through oak forests, plunged into elliptical Victorian tunnels with brick vaulting, slid under motorways, passed derelict coal bunkers, water tanks in sidings and other relics of the age of steam locomotion, and ran through miles and miles of suburbs with their patio gardens and satellite dishes, before even reaching the outskirts of London. As we grew close to our destination, there were views of 1950s tower blocks and Battersea Power Station, and we braked beside the defunct Eurostar platforms, which had seemed so futuristic when they were opened in 1994, but are now covered in grime and pigeon droppings. Ironically, they sit on top of the remnants of the Necropolis Line, Waterloo's first dedicated passenger service, which opened in 1854 to carry corpses and their mourners from the capital to Brookwood Cemetery in Surrey, a monster graveyard created by speculators who advertised for new tenants in the papers and promised a parkland setting where these might enjoy eternal repose when their time came.

Waterloo, too, was a lesson in change. It covers what were once meadows and marshes. The people who lived there were outcasts, paupers and fugitives. Simon Forman, the Elizabethan 'Black Inchanter', told fortunes, 'haleked' maidens, and held seances with angels good and evil on the site of the points just outside the station. He died on the day and in the manner he predicted when he drowned on 12 September 1611 in the middle of the Thames. A storm arose immediately after his last breath. The station now serves over 200,000 passengers each day – more than the entire population of Hampshire when Cobbett rode around it, although this has since risen, with the help of commuting, by nearly 800 per cent. There are fast-food stands, mobile franchises and a W. H. Smith selling the present-day equivalents of the nineteenth-century railway libraries on Waterloo's concourses. Giant screens stream news and adverts above the ticket barriers. There are even very expensive public toilets, whose colloquial name – 'loo' – may have arisen as a diminutive of a popular Victorian brand of cistern christened Waterloo, like the station itself, after the famous British victory of 1815.

My daily trip on the 07.01 was a journey through all the progress we've made since commuting began, including technological, cultural and physical changes. Rush hour has been responsible, directly and indirectly, for many of them. Commuting has required us to revise our conventions of how to mix with strangers; has dictated the growth and form of cities; and has been both proving ground and marketplace for new technologies. Its impact from a humanitarian point of view, moreover, has been overwhelmingly positive. For the last century and a half it has given countless people the opportunity to improve their lives. Essentially, it has given them freedom of movement. Notwithstanding its petty vexations, and frequent discomforts, commuting is a positive part of our lives. If it sometimes feels like limbo, it's also full of optimism, for, in the words of Robert Louis Stevenson: 'Little do ye know your own blessedness; for to travel hopefully is a better thing than to arrive.'

♦ ♦ ♦ ♦ ♦

Notes

Crossing No Man's Land

page 2   For Viking smoothing boards see: http://www.euppublishing.com/doi/pdfplus/10.3366/gas.1994.19.19.109.

9   'To prepare a face to meet the faces that you meet', T. S. Eliot, 'The Love Song of J. Alfred Prufrock'.

CHAPTER I
The Man who Went to London Twice in One Day

12   'The late Dr. Arnold, of Rugby', Samuel Smiles, *Lives of the Engineers*, London, John Murray, 1862, p. 274 (on Project Gutenberg: http://www.gutenberg.org/files/27710/27710-h/27710-h.htm).

12   'The office is one thing and private life is another', Charles Dickens, *Great Expectations*, 1867 edition, from Project Gutenberg: http://www.gutenberg.org/files/1400/1400-h/1400-h.htm.

14   'there is only one privy', James Phillips Kay, *The Moral and Physical Condition of the Working Classes employed in the Cotton Manufacture in Manchester*, 1832, p. 24: https://archive.org/details/moralphysicalcon00kaysuoft.

15   'ran at twice the level', Christian Wolmar, *Fire & Steam: How the Railways Transformed Britain*, London, Atlantic Books, paperback edition, 2008, p. 55.

15   'Napoleon of Coaching', Dorian Gerhold, 'Chaplin, William James (1787–1859)', *Oxford Dictionary of National Biography*, Oxford University Press, 2004.

16   'amid the shrieks of the female portion', Sam Fay, *A Royal Road: Being the History of the London & South Western Railway, from 1825 to the Present Time*, Kingston-on-Thames, W. Drewett, 1882, p. 32.

17   'no other panic was more fatal to the middle class', Wolmar, *Fire & Steam*, p. 105.

18 'Spoil our Shires and ruin our Squires', Matthew Engel, *Eleven Minutes Late: A Train Journey to the Soul of Britain*, London, Pan, 2010, p. 60.

19 'one of the most unsightly objects ever constructed', Jack Simmons, *The Victorian Railway*, London, Thames and Hudson, 1991, p. 165.

19 'what else will it be fit for when every railway', Simmons, *Victorian Railway*, p. 167.

20 'Grave plodding citizens will be flying around like comets', Fay, *A Royal Road*, p. 28.

20 'The whole system of railroad travelling', John Ruskin, *The Seven Lamps of Architecture*, Chapter IV, The Lamp of Beauty, 1849, from Project Gutenberg, p. 117. http://www.gutenberg.org/ files/35898/35898-h/35898-h.htm.

22 'upon the South-western line a new town, called Kingston-upon-Railway', *The Year-Book of Facts in Science and Art*, London, Tilt and Bogue, 1841.

22 'gentlemen of business, who daily visit', David Norman Smith, *The Railway and its Passengers: a Social History*, London, David & Charles, 1988, p. 98.

22 'It is now not unusual', Dionysius Lardner, *Railway Economy: A Treatise on the New Art of Transport, its Management, Prospects and Relations*, London, 1850, p. 35. http://quod.lib.umich.edu/m/moa/ aes9701.0001.001/35?page=root;size=100;view=image.

23 For season tickets, see Simmons, *Victorian Railway*, pp. 326–27.

23 Bromley, Kent, 1871 Enumerator's return. J. M. Rawcliffe, 'Bromley: Kentish market town to London suburb, 1841–81', in F. M. L. Thompson (ed.), *The Rise of Suburbia*, Leicester University Press, 1982, p. 86.

24 'Sir – I live with thousands of others down the Mid Kent Railway', *The Times*, 15 January 1864.

25 'We are all railway travellers now', 'The railway calamity', *Saturday Review*, 29 August 1868, p. 281.

27 'The great bell of St Paul's strikes ONE', Henry Booth, *Uniformity of Time: Considered Especially in Reference to Railway Transit and the Operations of the Electric Telegraph, in a Letter to the Right Hon. Edward Strutt, Chairman to the Railway Commissioners*, J. Weale, 1847.

28 'fell down dead on the platform of a railway station', 'Trains, technology and time-travellers: how the Victorians re-invented time', Ralph Harrington: http://www.artificialhorizon.org/essays/pdf/time.pdf.

28   For Victorian railway phobias, see George Frederick Drinka,
      The Birth of Neurosis, Myth, Malady and the Victorians, New York,
      Simon and Schuster, 1984, pp. 108ff.

29   'consume their own smoke', Railways Clauses Consolidation Act 1845
      CXIII.

30   'Coffin No. 2', Simmons, *Victorian Railway*, p. 78.

31   'on French or Russian police ordinances', Simmons, *Victorian Railway*,
      p. 259.

31   'Why should half a dozen persons, each with minds to think and
      tongues to express', *The Railway Traveller's Handy Book*, 1862, pp. 75–76.

31   'the acquaintance begotten in the railway carriage', *The Railway
      Traveller's Handy Book*, p. 78.

32   'two pots of ale', James A. Secord, *Victorian Sensation: The
      Extraordinary Publication, Reception, and Secret Authorship of Vestiges
      of the Natural History of Creation*, Chicago and London, University
      of Chicago Press, 2000, p. 32.

32   'readers' emotions were being heightened by gripping narratives at
      the same time', Secord, *Victorian Sensation*, p. 28.

33   'secret travelling lavatory', Engel, *Eleven Minutes Late*, p. 133.

34   'workmen's trains from Edmonton and Walthamstow for 2d return',
      Wolmar, *Fire & Steam*, p. 134.

35   'pneumatic caoutchouc', *The Railway Traveller's Handy Book*, p. 74.

35   'the most wealthy and influential merchants', Simmons, *Victorian
      Railway*, p. 320.

36   'stale sponge-cakes that turn to sand in the mouth', Charles Dickens,
      'Chapter VI: Refreshments for Travellers', in *The Uncommercial Traveller*
      (1860), from Project Gutenberg: http://www.gutenberg.org/dirs/
      etext97/unctr10h.htm

36   'the real disgrace of England', quoted in Simmons, *Victorian Railway*,
      p. 355–6.

37   'fossil sandwiches', Simmons, *Victorian Railway*, p. 355.

37   'hot eels, pickled whelks, fried fish', Henry Mayhew, *London Labour and
      the London Poor*, London, Vol. 1, George Woodfall & Co., London, 1851.

39   'Keep us watching and refiring / With full pressure on', R.C. Richardson,
      'The "Broad Gauge" and the "Narrow Gauge": Railways and Religion in
      Victorian England', in *The Impact of the Railway on Society in Britain:
      Essays in Honour of Jack Simmons*, Aldershot, Ashgate, 2003, p. 109.

CHAPTER II
Suburbanization

40 'New forces, new cravings, new aims', John Richard Green, *A Short History of the English People*, London, The Macmillan Company, 1874, ch x.

40 'only around 27,000 daily rail commuters entering London in the mid 1850s', Roy Porter, *London: A Social History*, London, Penguin, 2000, p. 275.

41 'rising real incomes, the expansion of white-collar occupations', Porter, *London*, p. 76.

42 'It is better, morally and physically, for the Londoner', in Donald J. Olsen, *The Growth of Victorian London*, London, B. T. Batsford Ltd, 1976, p. 187.

43 'such as *The Builder's Practical Director, The Gentleman's House*', Listing Selection Guide, *Domestic 3: Suburban and Country Houses*, English Heritage, October 2011.

43 'the origin, through mutation and debasement', Thompson (ed.), *The Rise of Suburbia*, p. 9.

44 'a villa miraculously transported from the Lago', Olsen, *Growth of Victorian London*, p. 23.

45 For class anxiety, see Lara Baker Whelan, *Class, Culture and Suburban Anxieties in the Victorian Era*, London, Routledge, 2009.

46 'sound principle and sound knowledge, firmly grounded in the Christian faith', Nathaniel Woodard; see: http://www.woodard.co.uk/nathaniel_woodard.htm.

47 For suburbs and omnibuses, see Alan A. Jackson, *Semi-Detached London*, Oxford, Wild Swan Publications, 1991.

47 'Reserve bickerings and disputes for the open field', *The Times*, 30 January 1836.

47 'long after the working classes were at work', Porter, *London*, p 271.

48 'sixty years ago even the hill was as secluded and rural,' George Rose Emerson, *London: How the Great City Grew*, London, 1862. Quoted in Porter, *London*, pp. 266–7 and in Olsen, *Growth of Victorian London*, p. 193.

49 'a non-gregarious animal…', quoted in Olsen, *Growth of Victorian London*, p. 20.

49 '80 per cent of building firms had six or fewer houses under construction', Porter, *London*, p. 285.

49 'enough fur to knock down a bullock', T. M. Thomas, 'A Suburban Connemara', *Household Words*, 8 March 1851, p. 562.

50 'a large hill... in the vicinity of small suburb cottages', Richard Horne, 'Dust, or Ugliness Redeemed', *Household Words,* 13 July 1850, pp. 379–84. See also 'The Builder's House and the Bricklayer's Garden by an Eyewitness and Sufferer', *Household Words*, 22 February 1851, pp. 513–16.

50 For various breeds of rag-pickers, see Henry Mayhew, *London Labour and the London Poor*, Vol. 2, London, Griffin, Bohn and Company, 1862.

51 'unless one has a really large place', Jane Elizabeth Panton, *Suburban Residences and How to Circumvent Them*, London, Ward & Downey Ltd., 1896, p. 4.

51 'I look upon those pitiful concretions of lime and clay', John Ruskin, *The Seven Lamps of Architecture*, Chapter VI, The Lamp of Memory, 1849, from Project Gutenberg.http://www.gutenberg.org/files/35898/35898-h/35898-h.htm.

52 Wilkie Collins, *Basil*, 1852, Oxford, Oxford University Press, 1990.

52 'a tale of criminality, almost revolting from its domestic horrors', *The Athenaeum*, 4 December 1852, pp. 1322–23.

53 'absolutely disgusting', quoted in Norman Page (ed.), *Wilkie Collins: The Critical Heritage*, London, Routledge, 2002, p. 5.

55 'sardine box railway', *Punch* magazine 1863, see: http://www.ltmcollection.org/resources/index.html?IXglossary=Public+transport+in+Victorian+London:+Part+Two:+Underground.

55 'clerks and artisans', who 'stampeded in at the rate of 100 per week', Porter, *London*, p. 282.

56 'Monotonous streets and lines of villas' were 'fast encircling', quoted in Olsen, *Growth of Victorian London*, p. 197.

57 'Go where we will – north, south, east or west of this huge Metropolis', quoted in Porter, *London*, p. 281.

57 'the life of the suburb without any society', quoted in Olsen, *The Growth of Victorian London*, p. 213.

57 'atheism was the religion of the suburbs', G. K. Chesterton, *The Everlasting Man*, 1925, from Project Gutenberg: http://gutenberg.net.au/ebooks01/0100311.txt.

58 Emily Eden, *The Semi-detached House*, London, Richard Bentley, 1859.

58 George Grossmith and Weedon Grossmith, *Diary of a Nobody*, 1898, Ware, Wordsworth Editions Ltd., 1994.

59 The 'funniest book in the world', Evelyn Waugh, see https://sites. google.com/site/petermortonswebsite/home/grossmiths-diary-of-a-nobody/evelyn-waugh-s-annotations-to-his-copy-of-the-diary.

59 'improvised concerts', François Cellier & Cunningham Bridgeman, *Gilbert and Sullivan and Their Operas; With Recollections and Anecdotes of D'Oyly Carte & Other Famous Savoyards*, Boston, Little, Brown and Company, 1914, p. 131.

59 'the opinion of the bald-headed man at the back of the omnibus', Walter Bagehot, *The English Constitution,* 1867, from Project Gutenberg: http://www.gutenberg.org/files/4351/4351-h/4351-h.htm.

61 'the outer circlet of, say, half-a-mile', James Cantlie, F.R.C.S., '"Degeneration Amongst Londoners": A lecture delivered at the Parkes Museum of Hygiene, 27 January 1885', London, Field & Tuer, The Leadenhall Press, 1885.

61 'I should be very sorry indeed to allow any respectable female', quoted in Smith, *Railway and its Passengers*, p. 105.

62 'railway companies have on the whole done more than was required of them', Smith, *Railway and its Passengers*, p. 105.

63 'having regard to the urgent necessity which exists of', H. J. Dyos, *Exploring the Urban Past: Essays in Urban History*, Cambridge, Cambridge University Press, 1982, p. 93.

63 'celebrated writer on working-class housing problems', Dyos, *Exploring the Urban Past*, p. 93.

65 'I am quite sure that the remedy for the great disease of over-crowding is not be found', Dyos, *Exploring the Urban Past*, p. 87.

CHAPTER III
Snakeheads and Gourmands

66 'In the United States nature and domestic life are better than society and the manners of towns', Andrew Jackson Downing, quoted in Milette Shamir, *Inexpressible Privacy: The Interior Life of Antebellum American Literature*, University of Pennsylvania Press, 2005, p. 190.

66 'Space is killed by the railways and we are left with time alone',
    Heinrich Heine, quoted in Wolfgang Schivelbusch, *The Railway
    Journey: The Industrialization of Time and Space in the 19th Century*,
    Berkeley, University of California Press, 1986, p. 38.

66 'charmingly rural region', Lawrence Grow, *On the 8:02: An Informal
    History of Commuting by Rail in America*, New York, Mayflower
    Books, 1979, p. 27.

67 'enter into such an agreement by calling on an agent of the company',
    Grow, *On the 8:02*, p. 28.

67 'The foundation of our free institutions', Revd William G. Eliot
    Jnr, quoted in Kenneth T. Jackson, *Crabgrass Frontier: The
    Suburbanization of the United States*, Oxford, University Press, 1985,
    p. 48.

68 'A man is not a whole and complete man', Walt Whitman, quoted
    in Jackson, *Crabgrass Frontier*, p. 50.

68 'in the morning there is one incessant stream of people', Whitman,
    quoted in Jackson, *Crabgrass Frontier*, p. 28.

68 'Property is continually tending from our city to escape', *New York
    Tribune* 21 January 1847, quoted in Jackson, *Crabgrass Frontier*, p. 28.

70 'on, on, on – tears the mad dragon', Charles Dickens, *American Notes
    For General Circulation*, 1842, from Project Gutenberg:
    http://www.gutenberg.org/files/675/675-h/675-h.htm.

70 'and the train had gone but a few miles when a "snakehead"',
    Anthony J. Bianculli, *Trains and Technology: The American Railroad
    in the Nineteenth Century: Track and Structures*, Newark, University
    of Delaware Press, 2003, p. 88.

71 'Things are in the saddle / And ride mankind', from 'Ode to
    William H. Channing' in *The Early Poems of Ralph Waldo Emerson*,
    New York, and Boston, Thomas Y. Crowell & Company, 1899.

71 'five times a day, I can be whirled to Boston within an hour', Henry
    David Thoreau, quoted in Shamir, *Inexpressible Privacy*, p. 190.

71 'the main distinction between which', Dickens, *American Notes*.

71 'well stuffed, and covered with a fine plush,' quoted in John H. White
    Jr., *The American Railroad Passenger Car*, Baltimore, Johns Hopkins
    University Press, 1985, p. 373.

73 'We maintain in England our "lonesome stuffy compartments"',
    quoted in Olsen, *Growth of Victorian London*, p. 23.

75 'Their pleasantries, their growlings', quoted in Vincent F. Seyfried, *The Long Island Rail Road: A Comprehensive History, Part Two: The Flushing, North Shore & Central Railroad*, 1963. http://en.wikisource. org/wiki/The_Long_Island_Rail_Road:_A_Comprehensive_History,_ Part_Two:_The_Flushing,_North_Shore_%26_Central_Railroad.

77 'Thousands of the best citizens of New York are not citizens', Gustav Kobbé, *The Central Railroad of New Jersey*, 251, Broadway, New York 1890. https://archive.org/stream/centralrailroado00kobb/central railroado00kobb_djvu.txt.

78 'who, after listening to the evidence of these intelligent, competent and able bodied witnesses', see 'The Untold Delights of Duluth': http://collections.mnhs.org/MNHistoryMagazine/articles/34/ v34i02p067-078.pdf.

79 'favourite resort for literary and religious people', Grow, *On the 8:02*, p. 163.

81 'one of the most famous and horrible railroad slaughters', Charles Francis Adams, *Notes on Railroad Accidents*, New York, G.P. Putnam's Sons, 1879.

82 'a continuous lesson in equality and fraternity', quoted in Schivelbusch, *Railway Journeys*, p. 72.

82 'pulled along by a machine like a piece', quoted in Schivelbusch, *Railway Journeys*, p. 65.

82 'a railway library that will provide only interesting volumes', Eileen S. De Marco, *Reading and Riding: Hachette's Railroad Bookstore Network in Nineteenth-Century France*, Bethlehem, Lehigh University Press, 2006, pp. 40–41.

84 'I'll never forget my trip to Paris in a third-class carriage', quoted in Schivelbusch, *Railway Journeys*, p. 77.

85 'There was roast fowls, hot and cold', Charles Dickens, Andrew Halliday, Charles Collins, Hesba Stretton, and Amelia B. Edwards, *Mugby Junction* in the Extra Christmas Number of *All the Year Round*, 1866, London, Chapman and Hall, 1898.

86 'the new France fitting into the space of the old Ile-de-France, or its equivalent', quoted in Schivelbusch, *Railway Journeys*, p. 35.

86 'where a hundred clock faces began marching together in 1890', Peter Galison, 'Einstein's Clocks: The Place of Time', *Critical Inquiry*, vol. 26, no. 2, winter 2000, pp. 355–89.

CHAPTER IV
Automobility

89 'highly mobile conveyance capable of travelling', H. G. Wells, *Anticipations of the Reaction of Mechanical and Scientific Progress upon Human Life and Thought*, 1901, p. 10, from Project Gutenberg: http://www.gutenberg.org/files/19229/19229-h/19229-h.htm.

90 'cheap and practical substitute for the horse and other animals', *The State of Wisconsin 2007–2008 Blue Book*, Wisconsin Legislative Reference Bureau, Madison, 2007, p. 148.

90 'prototype of the modern automobile', John B. Rae, *The American Automobile*, Chicago, University of Chicago Press, 1965, p. 7.

90 'a luxury for the few', Rae, *American Automobile*, p. 1.

91 '"fairly howling" for automobiles', James J. Flink, *The Car Culture*, Cambridge, Massachusetts, MIT Press, 1975, p. 19.

91 'Imagine a healthier race of workingmen', Flink, *Car Culture*, pp. 39–40.

91 For 'that no man making a good salary', see: http://www.thehenryford.org/research/henryFordQuotes.aspx.

93 '2.5 million pounds of manure', Flink, *Car Culture*, p. 34.

93 For 'often waited for the corpses to putrefy so they could more easily be sawed into pieces and carted off', Eric Morris, 'From Horse Power to Horsepower', see: http://www.uctc.net/access/30/Access%2030%20-%2002%20-%20Horse%20Power.pdf.

93 'The improvement in city conditions by the general adoption', Flink, *Car Culture*, p. 39.

94 'It is hard now to imagine the difficulty of learning to start,' John Steinbeck, *East of Eden*, London, William Heinemann Ltd in association with Octopus Books, 1976, p. 730.

95 For chauffeurs in New York and reactions to the Callan Automobile Law, see Frederick H. Elliott, 'Working Out New Auto Law In New York', *New York Times*, 16 October 1910. http://query.nytimes.com/mem/archive-free/pdf?res=F00E11FB345D16738DDDAF0994D8415B808DF1D3.

95 'local landmarks and a source of community pride', Jackson, *Crabgrass Frontier*, p. 256.

96 'Raymond Hood-esque phallus in miniature', see: http://forgottenchicago.com/articles/chicago-motor-club-building/.

98   'the steady decline in railway passenger traffic since 1920', Hoover Committee, 1929.

98   'a car in every garage', Herbert Hoover 1928 campaign slogan.

99   'General Motors Did Not Assist the Nazis in World War II', Edwin Black, 'Hitler's Carmaker: How Will Posterity Remember General Motors' Conduct?', History News Network: http://hnn.us/article/38829.

100   'I thought that what was good for the country was good for General Motors', Charles Erwin Wilson, Confirmation hearings before the Senate Armed Services Committee (1952), responding to Sen. Robert Hendrickson's question regarding conflicts of interest. Quoted in William Safire, Safire's Political Dictionary, New York, Random House, 1978.

100   'as they cling to self-respect', quoted in Flink, Car Culture, p. 155.

100   'no factor in American life that does so much for the morals of the public', quoted in Flink, Car Culture, p. 157.

104   'Before the Roman came to Rye or out to Severn strode,' G. K. Chesterton, 'The Rolling English Road', 1913.

104   'bare, open, shadeless and shameless', quoted in Joe Moran, On Roads: A Hidden History, London, Profile Books, 2009, p. 31.

105   'was commonly viewed as marking an economic dividing line between the middle classes', Sean O'Connell, 'The Social and Cultural Impact of the Car in Interwar Britain', Ph.D. submission, Centre for Social History, University of Warwick, 1995, p. 14.

106   'cultivate technical aesthetic or snobbish appeal', O'Connell, 'Social and Cultural Impact of the Car', p. 25.

106   'it was an interesting exercise in consumer preference', O'Connell, 'Social and Cultural Impact of the Car', p. 21.

107   'one of the "baby" cars amply meet their needs', 'The Olympia Motor Show', British Medical Journal, 17 October 1931, p. 718.

107   'important occupational tool' et seq., O'Connell, 'Social and Cultural Impact of the Car', p. 15.

107   'among the 12,000 workers in the Ford works', O'Connell, 'Social and Cultural Impact of the Car', p. 51.

108   For average speeds in London in 2011, see 'London Streets, Performance Report', Transport for London, Quarter 1 2011/12.

108   'By-pass Variegated' et seq., Osbert Lancaster, Pillar to Post, London, John Murray, 1938, p. 68.

109 'Come, friendly bombs, and fall on Slough! / It isn't fit for humans now', 'Slough' (1937), from *John Betjeman's Collected Poems*, London, John Murray, 1958, p. 22.

CHAPTER V
The Spaces in Between

110 'The city is doomed' he declared; and 'We shall solve the city problem by leaving the city', quoted in Jackson, *Crabgrass Frontier*, p. 175.

111 'decentralization is taking place. It is not a policy', quoted in Jackson, *Crabgrass Frontier*, p. 190.

111 'the garage has become a very essential part of the residence', Jackson, *Crabgrass Frontier*, p. 252.

112 'organized into neighborhoods of about 1,200 homes', Herbert J. Gans, *The Levittowners: Ways of Life and Politics in a New Suburban Community*, New York, Pantheon Books, 1967 (third printing), p. xvii.

113 'commuting seems to influence the marital relationship', Gans, *The Levittowners*, p. 224.

113 'a hotbed of participation', William H. Whyte Jr, *The Organization Man*, New York, Doubleday, 1956, quoted in Robert D. Putnam, *Bowling Alone: The Collapse and Revival of American Community*, New York, Simon & Schuster, 2000, p. 209.

114 'motor vehicle registrations had outstripped the parking space available', Jackson, *Crabgrass Frontier*, p. 257.

115 'the largest pedestrian shopping mall east of the Mississippi', Jackson, *Crabgrass Frontier*, p. 258.

116 'the most important variable in determining the direction', Jackson, *Crabgrass Frontier*, p. 268.

118 'styling changes', quoted in Flink, *Car Culture*, p. 174.

118 'What Makes a New Car New', see: http://ucapusa.com/classic_car_commercials_ford_23.htm#.

120 'intermediate sized cars, like the Ford Fairlane and Oldsmobile F-85 [were] larger than the full-sized Ford of 1949', Flink, *Car Culture*, p. 195.

120 'does a 105-pound woman have to drive 4,000 pounds of car', 'Long Shot Gambler on Short Cars', *Life* magazine, 24 March 1958.

120 On Mitt Romney, see: http://thinkprogress.org/climate/2012/08/28/
744811/romney-opposes-fuel-efficiency-standards-actually-moving-
us-toward-energy-independence/.

121 'full jump start' *et seq.* quoted in John Keats, *The Insolent Chariots*,
Philadelphia and New York, J. B. Lippincott & Co., 1958, p. 102.

121 'as selling dreams of speed, luxury', Keats, *Insolent Chariots*, p. 98.

121 'it would no more occur to Detroit', Keats, *Insolent Chariots*, p. 103.

122 'For literally nothing down… you too can find a box of your own',
John Keats, *The Crack in the Picture Window*, Boston, Houghton
Mifflin, 1956, p. 7.

122 'a multitude of uniform, unidentifiable houses', quoted in Jackson,
Crabgrass Frontier, p. 244.

123 'in 1960 not a single one', Jackson, *Crabgrass Frontier*, p. 241.

123 For Detroit and blockbusting, see Scott Martelle, *Detroit:
A Biography*, Chicago, Chicago Review Press, 2012, pp. 191–92.

125 'a city of flowing arteries and veins', Moran, *On Roads*, p. 180.

126 'automatic radio control' *et seq.*, see *To New Horizons* at:
http://archive.org/details/ToNewHor1940.

127 'a lobbying front second only to that of the munitions industry',
Jackson, *Crabgrass Frontier*, p. 248.

127 *The Freedom of the American Road*, 1955, see: http://www.youtube.
com/watch?v=6wniXPj7vwM.

128 'organized predominantly on the basis of the universal availability',
Rae, *American Automobile*, p. 1.

CHAPTER VI
Bowler Hats and Mini Coopers

130 'we were absolutely snookered', Norman Longmate, *How We Lived
Then: History of Everyday Life During the Second World War*, London,
Pimlico, 2002 edition, p. 296.

131 'dramatization of events that occurred' *et seq.*, Cecil McGivern,
Junction X, London, War Office, 1944. Available online at: http://
freespace.virgin.net/neil.worthington/jx/theworks.htm.

133 'socialized industries' *et seq., Let Us Face the Future*, 1945, http://www.
labour-party.org.uk/manifestos/1945/1945-labour-manifesto.shtml.

133 'about a million passengers per week more than in 1938', Wolmar, *Fire & Steam*, p. 263.

134 'dingy railway stations', quoted in Engel, *Eleven Minutes Late*, p. 195.

134 'would bring a blush of shame to the', quoted in Engel, *Eleven Minutes Late*, p. 196.

134 'lion on a unicycle', quoted in Wolmar, *Fire & Steam*, p. 275.

134 'sorely neglected', quoted in Wolmar, *Fire & Steam*, p. 271.

135 'I'm paid by the buffet at Didcot', John Betjeman, quoted in Engel, *Eleven Minutes Late*, p. 197.

135 'In one carriage there would be four men,' quoted in David Kynaston, *Austerity Britain, 1945–51,* London, Bloomsbury Publishing, 2007, p. 403.

138 'is this what is really necessary here and now?', quoted in Engel, *Eleven Minutes Late*, p. 225.

138 'bikes and buses provide the memorable images of town traffic', quoted in Kynaston, *Austerity Britain*, p. 403.

140 'over 300 million passengers a year over 256 route miles', Colin G. Pooley and Jean Turnbull, 'Commuting, transport and urban form: Manchester and Glasgow in the mid-twentieth century', *Urban History*, vol. 27, no. 3, 2000, Cambridge, Cambridge University Press, 2000, p. 373.

141 'arguably the most emblematic bus route', Kynaston, *Austerity Britain*, pp. 403–4.

141 'you could tell where you were on the No. 8 route' and 'The buses were always full of workmen', see http://birminghamhistory.co.uk/forum/showthread.php?t=8.

142 'the biggest "Please-do-not-touch" exhibition', *Daily Express* 1948, quoted in Kynaston, *Austerity Britain*, p. 301.

142 'well into the 1950s a horse and cart', quoted in Kynaston, *Austerity Britain*, p. 403.

142 'effect on the industrial, commercial and community life will be electric', see: http://news.bbc.co.uk/ onthisday/hi/dates/stories/may/26/newsid_ 2502000/2502691.stm.

143 'I got a car... because to travel to [work]', Pooley and Turnbull, 'Commuting, transport...', p. 381.

144 For 'better to lose honourably', see: http://www.motorsports halloffame.com/Hall-of-Fame-Members/Bio.aspx?q=Stirling %20Moss.

145 'the size of the road itself so far transcends', quoted in Moran, *On Roads*, p. 26.
145 'the *Daily Herald's* man clocked up 130 mph', Moran, *On Roads*, p. 27.
146 'For the first time, the fact of unrestrained growth', 'Olympic Britain: Social and economic change since the 1908 and 1948 London Games', House of Commons Library, 2012, p. 135.
147 'middle classes should not "pull up the ladder"', quoted in Moran, *On Roads*, p. 207.

CHAPTER VII
Two Wheels Good

149 'a completely Italian product, such as we have not seen since the Roman chariot', quoted in 'Viva Vespa', by Janice Kirkpatrick, *Design Week*, 22 August 1996.
151 'ill-repaired bomb site manned by semi-starved workers', Correlli Barnett, *The Lost Victory: British Dreams, British Realities 1945–1950*, London, Macmillan, 1995, p. 392.
154 'It is smooth like the enamel of an automobile', Lewis H. Siegelbaum, *Cars for Comrades: The Life of the Soviet Automobile*, Ithaca, New York, Cornell University Press, 2008, p. 135.
155 'a commission of specialists evaluated the car', Tracy Nichols Busch, *A Class on Wheels: Avtodor and the 'automobilization' of the Soviet Union, 1927–1935*, Washington, Georgetown University, 2003.
159 'young, low-skilled workers, occupying positions requiring low qualifications', quoted in 'Suburbanisation, employment change and commuting in the Tallinn Metropolitan Area' (2005), Institute of Geography, University of Tartu: http://epc2006.princeton.edu/papers/60516.
163 For Japan and the Honda Super Cub, see Jeffrey W. Alexander, *Japan's Motorcycle Wars: An Industry History*, Vancouver, UBC Press, 2008.
164 For Thai government survey of commuting, see R. Choiejit and R. Teungfung, 'Urban Growth and Commuting Patterns of the Poor in Bangkok', 2004: http://geography.wincoll.ac.uk/pages/PreU/files/3A1/80_Bangkok/bangkok%20-%20migration,%20commuting%20and%20growth.pdf.

166 For the switch from motorcycles to cars, see 'China's urban transport development strategy: proceedings of a symposium in Beijing, November 8–10, 1995': http://documents.worldbank.org/curated/en/1997/01/695034/chinas-urban-transport-development-strategy-proceedings-symposium-beijing-november-8-10-1995.

167 'bicycles made up 27.7 per cent', Andrew Neather, *London Evening Standard*, 30 June 2011.

168 'the fatigue of the sanctimonious', David Barter, *Obsessive Compulsive Cycling Disorder,* lulu.com (paperback edition), 2013, p. 157.

CHAPTER VIII
Crush Loading

170 'travellers routinely find themselves subjected to levels of overcrowding that are not simply uncomfortable, but positively frightening', House of Commons Transport Committee, *Overcrowding on Public Transport, Seventh Report of Session 2002–03*, London, The Stationery Office, 2003

172 'arboreal life calls for keen vision' *et seq.*, Edward T. Hall, *The Hidden Dimension* (1966) New York, Anchor Books, 1990, p. 39.

175 'Interviewer: Can you say how much unity', John Drury, Chris Cocking, Steve Reicher, 'The Nature of Collective Resilience: Survivor Reactions to the 2005 London Bombings', *International Journal of Mass Emergencies and Disasters*, vol. 27, March 2009, pp. 66–95.

175 'governments should treat them as the "fourth emergency service"', Drury et al., 'The Nature of Collective Resilience'.

176 'we used to think that the hard part of the question', Paul Bloom, 'First Person Plural', *The Atlantic*, November 2008.

176 For 'The Girl Fetish' and comments following, see Alisa Freedman, *Tokyo in Transit: Japanese Culture on the Rails and Road*, Redwood City, CA, Stanford University Press, 2010.

179 'ventral denial', see Joe Navarro, *What Every BODY is Saying*, New York, HarperCollins, 2008.

180 For 'got a rush from dirtying their school uniforms', see: http://en.rocketnews24.com/2012/08/24/japanese-man-arrested-for-squirting-mayonnaise-on-unsuspecting-high-school-girls/.

181 'trains, subways or at stations in Tokyo', Daniel Krieger, 'Why Women-

Only Transit Options Have Caught On', *The Atlantic*, 8 February 2008.

181 'I feel sorry for them', Krieger, 'Why Women-Only Transit…'.

181 'we decided to have women-only cars to protect women from gropers,' Krieger, 'Why Women-Only Transit…'.

182 For 'old age smell' *et seq.*, see http://en.rocketnews 24.com/2012/11/12/ break through-deodorizing-underwear-can-make-your-farts-silent-and-not-deadly-also-eliminates-an-array-of-body-odors-fast/.

184 For Mumbai Suburban Railway, see *Bombay Railway: Pressures*, BBC 4 http://www.bbc.co.uk/programmes/b007t30p.

187 For behaviour architecture, see Samanth Subramanian, 'Mind games to stop death on the tracks', *live mint & The Wall Street Journal*, 6 January 2010: http://www.livemint.com/Home-Page/PGOJwDyboNbejam6 1mpotL/Mind-games-to-stop -death-on-the-tracks.html.

187 'brain activity – and hence alertness – peaks during short silences', Mitzi Baker, 'Music moves brain to pay attention, Stanford study finds', Stanford School of Medicine, 1 August 2007:http://med.stanford.edu/ news_releases/2007/july/ music.html.

188 For 'Eve teasing', see: http://archive.indianexpress.com/news/69-- jump-in-cases-of-eveteasing-men-entering-ladies-compartments-in-2012/1061111/0.

189 'strumming an imaginary banjo', David Wilkes, *Daily Mail*, 7 March 2012.

189 For 'experienced unwanted sexual attention', see: http://www.endviolence against women.org.uk/news/20/4-in-10-young-women-in-london-sexually-harassed-over-last-year.

190 For 'I was really scared when I first heard about these balls,' see: http://www.bbc.co.uk/news/world-asia-16596181?print=true.

CHAPTER IX
Road Rage

193 'This is ridiculous, it is like a bad joke', David Williams, *London Evening Standard* and *Daily Mail*, see: http://www.dailymail.co.uk/ news/article-39965/Stay-M25-rush-hour.html#ixzz2xIOIXWcH.

194 'roads cause traffic', Gilles Duranton and Matthew A. Turner, 'The Fundamental Law of Road Congestion: Evidence from US Cities', *American Economic Review*, vol. 101, no. 6, 2011, pp. 2616–52.

195 'the car is a prized and symbolic possession', 'Aggressive Driving: Three Studies', AAA Foundation for Traffic Safety, Washington, March 1997 (AAA study): https://www.aaafoundation.org/sites/default/files/agdr3study.pdf.

196 'bodily harm… by wanton or furious driving', Offences Against the Person Act 1861, Section 35.

197 'a problem that police, motoring organisations and psychologists say is sweeping the country', Moran, *On Roads*, p. 91.

197 For 'Three years ago, road rage… was unheard of in Utah' see: http://commdocs.house.gov/committees/trans/hpw105-34.000/hpw105-34_0.HTM.

198 'resulted in at least 218 murders and another 12,610 injury cases', AAA, Foundation for Traffic Safety, study, 1997.

198 'He practically ran me off the road – what was I supposed to do?', Paul Eberle, *Terror on the Highway*, Amherst, New York, Prometheus Books, 2006.

198 For 'No one cuts in front of me and gets away with it!', see the statements in: http://caselaw.findlaw.com/oh-court-of-appeals/1410080.html.

200 'rate themselves almost perfect in excellence as a driver', Dr Leon James and Dr Diane Nahl, 'Dealing with Stress and Pressure in the Vehicle. Taxonomy of Driving Behavior: Affective, Cognitive, Sensorimotor', in J. Peter Rothe (ed.) *Driving Lessons: Exploring Systems That Make Traffic Safer*, Edmonton, University of Alberta Press, 2002.

200 'repeated episodes of aggressive, violent behaviour', *Diagnostic and Statistical Manual of Mental Disorders*, American Psychiatric Association, Fifth Edition, 2013.

201 'Tension tends to build up when the body is physically restricted and constricted', James and Nahl, 'Dealing with Stress and Pressure in the Vehicle'.

202 For 'Anger builds on anger; the emotional brain heats up', and 'rage rush', see D. Goleman, *Emotional Intelligence*, New York, Bantam Books, 1995, p. 62.

202 'we're looking at everyone's rear', Jack Katz, *How Emotions Work*, Chicago, University of Chicago Press, 1999, p. 25.

203 For 'if you add a lag time of 23 years', Rick Nevin (2000), see: http://www.ricknevin.com/uploads/Nevin_2000_Env_Res_Author_Manuscript.pdf.

203 'Drivers grow up being socialized', James and Nahl, 'Dealing with Stress and Pressure in the Vehicle'.

205 'armoured cars for the battlefield', Sheldon Rampton and John Stauber, 'Trading on Fear', *Guardian*, 12 July 2003.

206 For 'Rushkoff: What about the environment?', see: http://www.one-country.com/052rapaille2.html.

207 For 'I commute every other day from New Jersey', see the Hummer forum: http://www.elcovaforums.com/forums/archive/index. php/t-38591.html.

207 'combine road rage with congealed traffic', Don Nelson, 'New meaning to the term "road hog"', *San Francisco Business Times*, 25 April 1999.

207 For 'crash incompatibility', see: http://cta.ornl.gov/cta/Publications/ Reports/Analysis_of_Impact_of_SUVs_in_US.pdf.

208 For 'online disinhibition effect', see Daniel Goleman and Clay Shirky, 'Web Rage: Why It Happens, What It Costs You, How to Stop', *CIO*, 28 June 2007: http://www.cio.com/article/121550/Web_Rage_Why_ It_Happens_What_It_Costs_You_How_to_Stop.

210 'Don't offend: "be a cautious and courteous driver"', 'Road Rage: How to Avoid Aggressive Driving', AAA Foundation for Traffic Safety, Washington, 2013: https://www.aaafoundation.org/sites/default/files/ RoadRageBrochure.pdf.

210 'Go forth down the road and be yourself, with compassion towards others', Steve Albrecht, DBA, 'The Psychology of Road Rage', in *Psychology Today*, 2013. See: http://www.psychologytoday.com/blog/ the-act-violence/201301/the-psychology-road-rage.

210 For road rage in the Dalai Lama's place of exile, see Sanjay Yadav, *The Times of India*, 10 July 2012.

211 'I used to laugh and say that everyone driving slower', *Hindustan Times*, 4 August 2012.

212 For sacred cowboys, see Jeremy Kahn, 'Urban Cowboys Struggle With India's Sacred Strays', *New York Times (New Delhi Journal)*, 5 November 2008.

215 For 'Such impudence, especially accompanied by unlawful actions', see: http://en.rian.ru/russia/ 20101201/161578641.html.

216 'encourage *hansei* (self-reflection)', Howard Tsang, 'Drivers' Education in Japan: Personality tests and "Road Rage"?', *Asia Pacific Memo*, 24 May 2012.

216 For 'their reaction to verbal abuse and physical confrontation', see *Herald Scotland*, 28 December 2001: http://www.heraldscotland.com/sport/spl/aberdeen/rac-calls-for-road-rage-test-for-new-drivers-anger-control-should-be-part-of-motoring-exam-1.163653.

217 'the biggest cause of road rage in Britain', *Daily Mail*, 9 February 2013.

CHAPTER X
Quo Vadis?

221 'For too long, we seem to have surrendered', Robert F. Kennedy, quoted in 'GDP: One of the Great Inventions of the 20th Century,' *Survey of Current Business*, January 2000.

222 For Day Reconstruction Method (DRM), see Daniel Kahneman and Alan B. Kruger, 'Developments in the Measurement of Subjective Well-Being', *Journal of Economic Perspectives*, vol. 20, no. 1, winter 2006, pp. 3–24. (Also summarized in Daniel Kahneman, *Thinking, Fast and Slow*, Penguin, 2012, pp. 393–94.)

222 For OECD Well-being Index, see: http://www.oecd.org/statistics/howslife.htm For Denmark see: http://www.oecdbetterlifeindex.org/countries/denmark/.

223 'strain of commuting is associated with', Alois Stutzer and Bruno S. Frey, 'Stress That Doesn't Pay: The Commuter Paradox', Institute for Empirical Research in Economics, University of Zurich, Working Paper Series ISSN 1424-04599, Working Paper No. 151, August 2004.

224 'the ideal commute time is something greater than zero', Lothlorien S. Redmond and Patricia L. Mokhtarian, 'The Positive Utility of the Commute: Modeling Ideal Commute Time and Relative Desired Commute Amount', *Transportation*, vol. 28, no. 2, 2001, pp. 179–205, http://www.uctc.net/papers/526.pdf.

225 '45 per cent of American drivers agreed with the statement', Brad Edmondson, 'Personal Travel: The Long and Short of It', New Ideas For Tracking Travellers, Transportation Research Circular E-C026, p 22.

226 'even said that they liked commuting a great deal', Martin Turcotte, 'Like commuting? Workers' perceptions of their daily commute', Statistics Canada, Catalogue No. 11-008: http://www2.canada.com/vancouversun/news/extras/commuting.pdf.

227 For 'It's unbelievable, nearly all trains offer internet access, but you can't take a pee,' see: http://www.worldcrunch.com/dutch-train-company-solves-toilet-fiasco-emergency-pee-bag/culture-society/dutch-train-company-solves-toilet-fiasco-with-emergency-pee-in-a-bag/c3s4040/.

228 'directed attention', Adam Alter, 'How Nature resets our minds and bodies', *The Atlantic*, 1 April 2013.

228 For green spaces, see Mathew P. White, Ian Alcock, Benedict W. Wheeler and Michael H. Depledge, 'Would You Be Happier Living in a Greener Urban Area? A Fixed-Effects Analysis of Panel Data', *Psychological Science*, published online 23 April 2013, DOI:10.1177/ 0956797612464659.

229 For 'Stall Luft', see: http://metro.co.uk/2011/03/ 04/cow-fart-cans-offers-authentic-smell-of-countryside-642451/.

230 'free up sufficient equity to fund', Sophie Chick, Savills, 'Value in the commuter zone', 19 February 2013: http://www.savills.co.uk/research_articles/141560/144657-0. See also *Insights, Commuting Trends Review*, Autumn 2010, Blue Door Media Ltd., for Savills.

231 'quintessential unity of travelling instincts around the world', Cesare Marchetti, 'Anthropological Invariants in Travel Behaviour', *Technological Forecasting and Social Change*, vol. 47, no. 1, 1994, p. 88.

232 For the Hadza tribe of Tanzania, see Michael Finkel, 'The Hadza', *National Geographic* magazine, December 2009. http://ngm.national geographic.com/print/2009/ 12/hadza/ finkel-text.

234 For 'it's worth it to me to come home', Dave Givens talking to Andrea Seabrook of NPR, 14 June 2008, see: http://seattletimes.com/html/nationworld/2002970862_commute04.html.

234 For 'better option', see: http://www.bbc.co.uk/news/magazine-25551393.

236 For 'more than half of America's schoolchildren', see: http://www.americanschool buscouncil.org/issues/environmental-benefits.

CHAPTER XI
Limbo Rules

238 For upper-class dislike of telephones, see Alan S. C. Ross, 'Linguistic class-indicators in present-day English', *Neuphilologische Mitteilungen* (Helsinki), vol. 55, 1954, pp. 113–49.

239 'when we talk in person,' Dan Goleman and Clay Shirky, 'Web Rage: Why it Happens, What it Costs You, How to Stop', *CIO*, 28 June 2007. http://www.cio.com/article/121550/Web_Rage_Why_It_Happens_ What_It_Costs_You_How_to_Stop.

243 For 'A colleague told me today that the man sitting next to her', see: http://www.mumsnet.com/Talk/_chat/a2032406-Man-watching-porn-on-train-WWYD.

244 'To guard against the baneful influence', James Frazer, *The Golden Bough*, 1922 edition, from Project Gutenberg: http://www.gutenberg. org/files/41082/41082-h/ 41082-h.html.

245 For bacteria on public transport, see Aston University Press Release, 26 July 2013: 'Aston involved in Mission for Health Campaign'.

246 For bacteria on the New York subway, see Roxanne Khamsi, 'Subway Freeloaders', *New York* magazine, 3 November 2013: http://nymag. com/news/intelligencer/topic/subway-bacteria-2013-11/.

246 '60 per cent of emerging human pathogens are zoonotic', S. J. Cutler, A. R., Fooks, W. H. van der Poel, 'Public health threat of new, reemerging, and neglected zoonoses in the industrialized world', *Emerging Infectious Diseases*, January 2010, 16 (1): http://www.ncbi. nlm.nih. gov/pubmed/20031035.

248 Arnold Palmer, *Movable Feasts: Changes in English Eating Habits*, Oxford, Oxford University Press, 1984 paperback edition.

249 'The automobile changed our dress, our manners,' Keats, *The Insolent Chariots*, p. 13.

250 'it can be quite therapeutic to act like a yelling maniac', Annika Mengisen, 'How's My Driving? A Q&A With the Author of Traffic', Freakonomics.com, 6 May 2008: http://freakonomics. com/2008/06/05/hows- my-driving-a-qa-with-the-author-of-traffic/.

250 'ran a simulation where people drove under the assumption', Elizabeth Landau, 'Can you believe this traffic? Health consequences of a long commute', CNN, 24 November 2012: http://edition.cnn. com/2012/11/19/health/driving-traffic-commute-consequences/.

252 For Datamonitor, see 'Food Service at the Service Station Channel in Europe', July 2012: http://www.datamonitor. com/store/Product/toc. aspx? productId=CM00083-005.

253 'an exciting new channel', *British Baker* magazine, 2012.

254 'More than any other sense,' odours 'affect driving ability', BBC News 2

June 2005: http://news.bbc.co.uk/1/hi/uk/4604869.stm.

255 'the traffic bulletins really are about collective solace', Moran, *On Roads*, p. 185.

257 'frequent and explicit', see: http://digital.library.unt.edu/ ark:/67531/ metadc1641/ m1/116/.

257 'mass-marketing of outrage', Gene Lyons, 'Profiting from political road rage', *Salon*, 20 January 2011: http://www.salon.com/2011/ 01/ 20/gene_lyons_road_rage/.

CHAPTER XII
Controlling the Flow

261 'It was a Monday morning rush hour at an underground station', Anonymous [attempted suicide], *Guardian*, 27 January 2012. http://www. theguardian.com/lifeandstyle/2012/jan/27/i-threw-myself-under-a-train.

263 'many passengers have been dragged to their deaths', Robert Griffiths, *Mind the Doors! Tales of a Tube train driver, since 1966*, Kettering, Northants, Silver Link, 2002, p. 28.

263 For 'Next time you might find it easier to wait until the doors are open', see: www.goingunderground.net.

264 'From 7 o'clock until 9, swarms of them emerged', Magnus Mills, *The Maintenance of Headway*, London, Bloomsbury, 2009, p. 67.

265 'like sheep', Episode 6, *The Tube*, BBC TV documentary, 2012.

266 'symptomatic of authoritarian government', *On Roads*, Moran, p. 63.

267 'brash reminders of an aesthetically impoverished age', Moran, p. 67.

267 For Hewlett Packard and brain activity amongst commuters, see Andrew Clark, 'Want to feel less stress? Become a fighter pilot, not a commuter', *Guardian*, 30 November 2004.

267 For seat acquisition strategy, see Brendan Nelson, 'Do you want to sit down on the Overground during rush hour? Then prepare for war', 4 October 2011, on www.brelson.com.

268 'I firmly believed that if a bus was destined', Mills, *The Maintenance of Headway*, p. 126.

269 'to be a bit of a babysitter... turn into mummy and daddy sometimes', Jane Oakes, Episode 6, *The Tube*, BBC TV documentary, 2012.

270 'No eye contact – Penalty £200', *Daily Telegraph*, 11 October 2012.

271 '@centralline : A good service has resumed on the line', Central-line twitter feed 31 March 2014.

271 'allows us to talk to people in a manner', David Lee, 'Handling the London Waterloo rush hour on Twitter', BBC News 27 July 2013.

273 For West Ashfield Station, see Ian Mansfield, 'London Underground's "secret" tube station', 9 July 2010: http://www.ianvisits.co.uk/blog/2010/07/09/london-undergrounds-secret- tube-station/.

274 'You can't swerve to avoid someone', *Guardian*, 11 October 2000: http://www.guardian.co.uk/society/2000/oct/11/guardiansocietysupplement2.

274 For the psychological effects of suicides on drivers, see Richard Farmer, Troy Tranah, Ian O'Donnell and Jose Catalan, 'Railway suicide: the psychological effects on drivers', *Psychological Medicine*, vol. 22, no. 2, 1992, pp. 407–14. doi:10.1017/S003329170003035X.

274 'a high-risk occupation', Professor M. A. J. Kompier, 'Bus drivers: Occupational stress and stress prevention', Working Paper CONDI/T/WP.2/1996, International Labour Office, Geneva, 1996.

276 'to adopt an attitude whereby the passengers are regarded as freight', Kompier, 'Bus drivers', p. 9.

277 'surrounded by a black slick of trodden-in chewing gum', Edward Simpkins, 'What a way to run a railway', *Daily Telegraph*, 2 December 2001.

279 For Claudio Andrade 'Eliminating human factor interference', see: http://metroautomation.org/wpcontent/uploads/2012/12/PTI_2011_6.pdf.

CHAPTER XIII
Virtual Journeys

282 'We are entering an era of electronically extended bodies', William Mitchell, *City of Bits: Space, Place and the Infobahn*, Cambridge, Mass., MIT Press, 1994; http://mitpress2.mit.edu/ebooks/City_of_Bits/Getting_to_the_Good_Bits/1994Telepresence.html.

283 'enable employees of large organizations', Jack Nilles, 'Telecommunications and Organizational Decentralization', *IEEE Transactions on Communications*, vol. COM-23, no. 10, October 1975.

285 For 'A new civilization is bursting into being in our midst!', Alvin Toffler, 'The Electronic Cottage', 14 October 1981, see: http://www.embedded.com/print/4319730.

288 'counting teleworkers is like measuring a rubber band', Lars Qvortrup quoted in Paul J. Jackson and Jos M. van der Wielen (eds), *Teleworking: International Perspectives. From Telecommuting to the Virtual Organisation*, London, Routledge, 1998, p. 21.

289 'In the late '90s my favorite line at the beginning of a presentation', Ruth David, 'The Father of Indian Outsourcing', *Forbes*, 29 May 2007: http://www.forbes.com/2007/ 05/21/outsourcing-raman-india-oped-cx_rd_0522raman.html.

291 'Tell an American that your name is Raja', Chris Walker and Morgan Hartley, 'The Culture Shock of India's Call Centers', *Forbes*, 16 December 2012: http://www.forbes.com/sites/morganhartley/2012/12/16/the-culture-shock-of-indias-call-centers/.

291 'I don't know what Wales is', *Daily Mail*, 28 April 2014: http://www.dailymail.co.uk/news/article-2270536/Wales-heard-What-Welsh-BT-customer-told-spoke-centre-worker-India.html.

292 For 'IBM was one of the first global companies', see: http://www.ibm.com/ibm/environment/climate/commuting.shtml.

292 For IBM headcount secrecy, see: http://www.computerworld.com/s/article/9169678/IBM_stops_disclosing_U.S._headcount_data.

293 For IBM headcount statistics, see: http://www.ieeeusa.org/calendar/conferences/stem/ 2012/presentations/HIRA.pdf.

293 For 'presumably because it does not want unemployed Americans', see: http://blogs.timesofindia.indiatimes.com/Tech-a-tete/entry/if-cognizant-is-indian-so-are-ibm-and-accenture.

294 For 'we believe there are significant tangible and intangible benefits', see: http://allthingsd.com/ 20130225/survey-says-despite-yahoo-ban-most-tech-companies-support-work-from-home-for-employees/? utm_source=dlvr.it&utm_medium=twitter.

294 For 'The surprising question we get', see: http://www.smh.com.au/it-pro/business-it/do-as-we-say-not-as-we-do-googlers-dont-telecommute-20130218-2eo8w.html.

297 'trampling on the future', James Surowiecki, 'Face Time', *The New Yorker*, 18 March 2003.

297 'There's a ton of abuse at Yahoo', Nate C. Hindman, *Huffington Post*,
26 February 2013: http://www.huffingtonpost.com/2013/02/26/
marissa-mayer-memo-yahoo-home_n_2764725.html.

298 'a remote-access future possible', see Surowiecki, 'Face Time'.

298 'helmed by its own chef', Tanya Steel, 'Inside Google's Kitchens',
Gourmet Live, 3 July 2012: http://www.gourmet.com/ food/
gourmetlive/2012/ 030712/inside-googles-kitchens?printable=true.

299 'San Franciscans feel resentful', Rory Carroll, 'Why people hate the
Google Bus', *Guardian*, 26 May 2013.

300 'software engineer for a major internet company', Carroll, 'Why people
hate the Google Bus'.

300 'a kind of symphony on wheels', Justine Sharrock, 'What's it like to
drive the "Google Bus"', *BuzzFeed*, 24 July 2013: http://www.buzzfeed.
com/justinesharrock/what-its-like-to-drive-the-google-bus.

301 For 'mid-40's software developer', Andrew Valentine, Verizon,
see: http://www.verizonenterprise.com/security/blog/index.
xml?postername=Andrew %20Valentine.

301 'Have someone in Bangalore or Shanghai', Timothy Ferriss, *The
4-Hour Workweek*, London, Vermilion, 2011 edition, p. 131.

302 'the factories of the 21st century information age', 'How Clean is
Your Cloud?' Greenpeace International, April 2012.

303 'This is an industry dirty secret', James Glanz, 'The Cloud Factories,
Power, Pollution and the Internet', *New York Times*, 22 September 2012.

304 '*Hourly* internet traffic will soon exceed the annual', Mark P. Mills,
CEO, Digital Power Group, 'The Cloud Begins with Coal – Big Data,
Big Networks, Big Infrastructure, and Big Power, An Overview of the
Electricity used by the Global Digital Ecosystem', August 2013.

CHAPTER XIV
All Change

311 'you have a product so revolutionary', Steve Kemper, *Code Name
Ginger: The Story Behind Segway and Dean Kamen's Quest to Invent
a New World*, 2003. See: http://www.stevekemper.net/disc.htm.

312 For UK commuting statistics 2011, see: http://www.ons.gov.uk/ons/
dcp171776_227904.pdf.

314 'who think that if we just don't build any roads', Alan Pisarski, 'Forcing Drivers Off the Road Won't Solve Virginia's Traffic Woes', *The Virginia News Letter*, vol. 76, no. 1, January/February 2000.

314 For US commuter statistics, see 'Commuting in America III: The Third National Report on Commuting Patterns and Trends', Transportation Research Board of the National Academies, 2006; and Alan E. Pisarski, 'Commuting in the 21st Century', Final Data, 29 June 2011.

314 'planners who dream of a future', see Brad Edmondson, 'Personal Travel'.

314 'fuel based transportation', *Financial Times*, 7 November 2013: http://www.ft.com/cms/s/0/1edaf8f6-479a-11e3-9398-00144feabdc0.html#axzz2k4AdHGQz.

315 'Driverless, it will start its own motor', *Milwaukee Sentinel*, 8 December 1926.

319 'Google's first car on YouTube: http://www.youtube.com/watch?v=CqSDWoAhvLU.

319/326 For Google and Mercedes driverless cars, see Dan Neil, 'Driverless Cars for the Road Ahead', *Wall Street Journal*, 27 September 2013.

320 'We take machines and stuff 'em with information until they're smarter than we are', International Movie Database online: http://m.imdb.com/title/tt0064 603/quotes?qt=qt0375405.

320 For Chunka Mui and driverless cars, see: http://www.forbes.com/sites/chunkamui/.

321 'typical commuter arteries', Chris Knapman, 'Large-scale trial of driverless cars to begin on public roads', *Daily Telegraph*, 2 December 2013: http://www.telegraph.co.uk/motoring/news/10484839/Large-scale-trial-of-driverless-cars-to-begin-on-public- roads.html.

321 For KPMG and driverless cars, see 'Self-driving cars: the next revolution': https://www.kpmg.com/US/en/IssuesAndInsights/ArticlesPublications/Documents/self-driving-cars-next-revolution.pdf.

326 'Something suddenly falls off a truck ahead of the car. Can the system react faster', Dan Neil, 'Driverless Cars'.

328 A 'bold commitment to modernisation', Jim Pickard, 'Mandelson fears HS2 will prove an "expensive mistake"', *Financial Times*, 2 July 2013.

328 'live in a rail bubble', Matt Ridley, 'Hadrian's wall was a marvellous mistake; so is HS2', 26 July 2013: http://www.rationaloptimist.com/blog/hadrian%27s-wall-was-a-marvellous-mistake-so- is-hs2.aspx.

329 For 'reached the end of its life', see: http://www.businessweek.com/
articles/2013-07-12/french-wreck-reveals-hidden-danger-in-its-
vaunted-train-system.

331 For 'barf ride', see: http://pedestrianobservations.wordpress.
com/2013/08/13/loopy-ideas-are-fine-if- youre-an-entrepreneur/.

333 For population estimates and the world's carrying capacity, see
World Population Monitoring 2001, United Nations, Department
of Economic and Social Affairs, Population Division, New York,
2001, pp. 31ff.

333 'occasional vertical and random horizontal low speed vehicular or
moving-belt travel', John Heaver Fremlin, 'How Many People Can
the World Support?' *New Scientist*, no. 415, 1964, pp. 285–87.

336 'Little do ye know your own blessedness', Robert Louis Stevenson,
Virginibus Puerisque, 1881.

Bibliography

AAA Foundation for Traffic Safety, 'Aggressive Driving: Three Studies',
Washington, March 1997.

Adams, Charles Francis, *Notes on Railway Accidents*, New York, G.P.
Putnam's Sons, 1879.

Alexander, Jeffrey W., *Japan's Motorcycle Wars: An Industry History*,
Vancouver, UBC Press, 2008.

Bagehot, Walter, *The English Constitution*, 1867, Project Gutenberg edition.

Barnett, Correlli, *The Lost Victory, British Dreams, British Realities 1945–
1950*, London, Macmillan, 1995.

Barter, David, *Obsessive Compulsive Cycling Disorder,* lulu.com (paperback
edition) 2013.

Betjeman, John, *John Betjeman's Collected Poems*, London, John Murray, 1958.

Bianculli, Anthony J., *Trains and Technology: The American Railroad in
the Nineteenth Century: Track and Structures*, Newark, University of
Delaware Press, 2003.

Busch, Tracy Nichols, *A Class on Wheels: Avtodor and the 'automobilization' of the Soviet Union, 1927–1935*, Washington, Georgetown University, 2003.

Cantlie, James, 'Degeneration Amongst Londoners: A lecture delivered at the Parkes Museum of Hygiene, January 27, 1885', London, Field & Tuer, The Leadenhall Press, 1885.

Cellier, François, & Cunningham, Bridgeman, *Gilbert and Sullivan and their Operas; with recollections and anecdotes of D'Oyly Carte & Other Famous Savoyards*, Boston, Little, Brown and Company, 1914.

Chesterton, G. K., *The Everlasting Man*, 1925, Project Gutenberg edition.

Choiejit, R., and R. Teungfung, 'Urban Growth and Commuting Patterns of the Poor in Bangkok', Ratiporn, 2004.

Collins, Wilkie, *Basil*, 1852, Oxford, Oxford University Press, 1990.

Dahl, Roald, *Someone Like You*, New York, Alfred Knopf, 1953.

De Marco, Eileen S., *Reading and Riding: Hachette's Railroad Bookstore Network in Nineteenth Century France*, Bethlehem, Lehigh University Press, 2006.

Dickens, Charles,

American Notes For General Circulation, 1842, Project Gutenberg edition.

The Uncommercial Traveller, 1860, Project Gutenberg edition.

Mugby Junction: being the Extra Christmas Number of *All the Year Round*, 1866, London, Chapman and Hall, 1898.

Great Expectations, 1867, Project Gutenberg edition.

Drinka, George Frederick, *The Birth of Neurosis, Myth, Malady and the Victorians*, New York, Simon and Schuster, 1984.

Drury, John, Chris, Cocking, Steve, Reicher, 'The Nature of Collective Resilience: Survivor Reactions to the 2005 London Bombings', *International Journal of Mass Emergencies and Disasters*, vol. 27, March 2009.

Duranton, Gilles and Matthew A. Turner, 'The Fundamental Law of Road Congestion: Evidence from US Cities'. *American Economic Review*, 101(6).

Dyos, H. J., *Exploring the Urban Past: Essays in Urban History*, Cambridge, Cambridge University Press, 1982.

Eden, Emily, *The Semi-detached House*, London, Richard Bentley, 1859.

Emerson, George Rose, *London: How the Great City Grew*, London, 1862.

Emerson, Ralph Waldo, 'Ode to William H. Channing', *The Early Poems of Ralph Waldo Emerson*, New York and Boston, Thomas Y. Crowell & Company 1899.

Engel, Matthew, *Eleven Minutes Late: A Train Journey to the Soul of Britain*, London, Pan, 2010.

Farmer, Richard, Troy Tranah, Ian O'Donnell, and Jose Catalan, 'Railway suicide: the psychological effects on drivers'. *Psychological Medicine*, Vol.22, no.2, 1992.

Fay, Sam, *A Royal Road: Being the History of the London & South Western Railway, from 1825 to the present time*, Kingston-on-Thames, W. Drewett, 1882.

Ferriss, Timothy, *The 4-Hour Workweek*, expanded and updated edition, London, Vermilion, 2011.

Flink, James J., *The Car Culture*, Cambridge, Mass., MIT Press, 1975.

Frazier, James, *The Golden Bough*, 1922, Project Gutenberg edition.

Freedman, Alisa, *Tokyo in Transit: Japanese Culture on the Rails and Road*, Redwood City, CA, Stanford University Press, 2010.

Fremlin, John Heaver, 'How Many People Can the World Support?', *New Scientist*, no. 415, 1964.

Galison, Peter, 'Einstein's Clocks: The Place of Time', *Critical Inquiry*, vol. 26, no. 2, 2000.

Gans, Herbert J., *The Levittowners: Ways of Life and Politics in a New Suburban Community*, New York, Pantheon Books, 1967.

Goleman, Daniel, *Emotional Intelligence*, New York, Bantam Books, 1995.

Griffiths, Robert, *Mind the Doors: Tales of a Tube train driver, since 1966*, Kettering, Northants, Silver Link, 2002.

Greenpeace International, 'How Clean is Your Cloud?' April' 2012.

Grossmith, George, and Grossmith, Weedon, *Diary of a Nobody*, 1898, Ware, Wordsworth Editions Ltd, 1994.

Grow, Lawrence, *On the 8:02: An Informal History of Commuting by Rail in America*, New York, Mayflower Books Inc., 1979.

Hall, Edward T., *The Hidden Dimension*, 1966, New York, Anchor Books edition, 1990.

Harrington, Ralph, *Trains, technology and time-travellers: how the Victorians re-invented time*, www.artificialhorizon.org.

Horne, Richard, 'Dust, or Ugliness Redeemed', *Household Words*, 13 July 1850.

House of Commons Library, *Olympic Britain: Social and economic change since the 1908 and 1948 London Games*, 10 July 2012.

Jackson, Alan A., *Semi-Detached London*, Oxford, Wild Swan Publications, 1991.

Jackson, Kenneth T., *Crabgrass Frontier: The Suburbanization of the United States*, Oxford, Oxford University Press, paperback edition, 1985.

Jackson, Paul J. and Jos M. van der Wielen (eds), *Teleworking: International Perspectives: From telecommuting to the Virtual Organisation*, London, Routledge, 1998.

James, Leon and Diane, Nahl, 'Dealing with Stress and Pressure in the Vehicle. Taxonomy of Driving Behavior: Affective, Cognitive, Sensorimotor', in J. Peter Rothe (ed.), *Driving Lessons: Exploring Systems That Make Traffic Safer*. Edmonton, Canada, University of Alberta Press, 2002.

Kahneman, Daniel, *Thinking, Fast and Slow*, Penguin, 2012.

Kahneman, Daniel, and Alan B. Kruger, 'Developments in the Measurement of Subjective Well-Being', *Journal of Economic Perspectives*, vol. 20, no. 1, Winter 2006.

Katz, Jack, *How Emotions Work*, Chicago, University of Chicago Press, 1999.

Kay, James Phillips, *The Moral and Physical Condition of the Working Class employed in the Cotton Manufacture in Manchester*, 1832.

Keats, John, *The Insolent Chariots*, Philadelphia and New York, J. B. Lippincott Company, 1958.

Keats, John, *The Crack in the Picture Window*, Boston, Houghton Mifflin, 1957.

Kobbé, Gustav, *The Central Railroad of New Jersey*, 251, Broadway, New York, 1890.

Kompier, Professor M. A. J., 'Bus drivers: Occupational stress and stress prevention', Working Paper CONDI/T/WP.2/1996, Geneva, International Labour Office, 1996.

Krieger, Daniel, 'Why Women-Only Transit Options Have Caught On', *The Atlantic*, 8 February 2008.

Kynaston, David, *Austerity Britain, 1945–51*, London, Bloomsbury Publishing, 2007.

Lancaster, Osbert, *Pillar to Post*, London, John Murray, 1938.

Lardner, Dionysus, *Railway Economy: a Treatise on the New Art of Transport, its Management, Prospects and Relations*, London, 1850.

Longmate, Norman, *How We Lived Then: History of Everyday Life During the Second World War*, London, Pimlico, 2002.

Marchetti, Cesare, 'Anthropological Invariants in Travel Behaviour', *Technological Forecasting and Social Change'*, vol. 47, no.1, 1994.

Martelle, Scott, *Detroit: A Biography*, Chicago, Chicago Review Press, 2012.

Mayhew Henry, *London Labour and the London Poor*, Vols 1 and 2, London, 1851 and 1862.

McGivern, Cecil, *Junction X*, London, BBC, 1944.

Mills, Magnus, *The Maintenance of Headway*, London, Bloomsbury Publishing, 2009.

Mills, Mark P. (Digital Power Group), 'The Cloud Begins with Coal – Big Data, Big Networks, Big Infrastructure, and Big Power, An Overview of the Electricity used by the Global Digital Ecosystem', August 2013.

Mitchell, William, *City of Bits: Space, Place and the Infobahn*, Cambridge, Mass., MIT Press, 1994.

Moran, Joe, *On Roads: A Hidden History*, London, Profile Books, 2009.

Navarro, Joe, *What Every BODY is Saying*, New York, HarperCollins, 2008.

Nilles, Jack, 'Telecommunications and Organizational Decentralization', *IEEE transactions on Communications*, vol. COM-23, no.10, October 1975.

O'Connell, Sean, 'The Social and Cultural Impact of the Car in Interwar Britain', Ph.D. submission, Centre for Social History, University of Warwick, 1995.

Olsen, Donald J., *The Growth of Victorian London*, London, B. T. Batsford Ltd, 1976.

Oxford Dictionary of National Biography, Oxford University Press, 2004.

Palmer, Arnold, *Movable Feasts: Changes in English Eating Habits*, Oxford, Oxford University Press, 1984.

Panton, Jane Elizabeth, *Suburban Residences and How to Circumvent Them*, London, Ward & Downey Ltd, 1896.

Pisarski, Alan E., 'Commuting in America III: The Third National Report on Commuting Patterns and Trends', Transportation Research Board of the National Academies, 2006.

Pooley, Colin G., and Jean Turnbull, 'Commuting, transport and urban form: Manchester and Glasgow in the mid-twentieth century', *Urban History*, vol. 27, no.3 (2000), Cambridge, Cambridge University Press, 2000.

Porter, Roy, *London: A Social History*, London, Penguin, 2000.

Putnam, Robert D., *Bowling Alone: The Collapse and Revival of American Community*, New York, Simon & Schuster, 2000.

Rae, John B., *The American Automobile*, Chicago, University of Chicago Press, 1965.

The Railway Traveller's Handy Book (1862), Oxford, Old House books & maps, Oxford, 2012.

Rawcliffe, J. M., 'Bromley: Kentish market town to London suburb, 1841–81', in *The Rise of Suburbia,* edited by F. M. L Thompson, Leicester, Leicester University Press, 1982.

Redmond, Lothlorien S., and Patricia L., Mokhtarian 'The Positive Utility of the Commute: Modeling Ideal Commute Time and Relative Desired Commute Amount', *Transportation*, vol. 28, no. 2, 2001.

Richardson, R. C., 'The "Broad Gauge" and the "Narrow Gauge", Railways and Religion in Victorian England', in *The Impact of the Railway on Society in Britain: Essays in Honour of Jack Simmons*, Aldershot, Ashgate, 2003.

Ross, Alan S. C., 'Linguistic class-indicators in present-day English', *Neuphilologische Mitteilungen* (Helsinki), vol. 55, 1954.

Ruskin, John, *The Seven Lamps of Architecture*, Chapter IV, The Lamp of Beauty, 1849, Project Gutenberg edition.

Safire, William, *Safire's Political Dictionary*, New York, Random House, 1978.

Schivelbusch, Wolfgang, *The Railway Journey: the Industrialization of Space and Time in the 19th Century*, Berkeley, University of California Press, 1986.

Secord, James A., *Victorian Sensation, The Extraordinary Publication, Reception, and Secret Authorship of Vestiges of the Natural History of Creation*, Chicago and London, University of Chicago Press, 2000.

Siegelbaum, Lewis H., *Cars for Comrades: The Life of the Soviet Automobile*, Ithaca, Cornell University Press, 2008.

Seyfried, Vincent F., *The Long Island Rail Road: A Comprehensive History, Part Two: The Flushing, North Shore & Central Railroad*, 1963.

Shamir, Milette, *Inexpressible Privacy: The Interior Life of Antebellum American Literature*, University of Pennsylvania Press, 2005.

Simmons, Jack, *The Victorian Railway*, London, Thames and Hudson, 1991.

Smiles, Samuel, *Lives of the Engineers*, John Murray, London, 1862.

Smith, David Norman, *The Railway and its Passengers: A Social History*, London, David & Charles, 1988.

Steinbeck, John, *East of Eden*, London, Heinemann, 1976.

Stevenson, Robert Louis, *Virginibus Puerisque*, Project Gutenberg edition, 1881.

Stutzer, Alois, and Bruno S., Frey, 'Stress That Doesn't Pay: The Commuter Paradox', Institute for Empirical Research in Economics, University of Zurich, *Working Paper Series* ISSN 1424-04599, Working Paper No. 151, August 2004.

Tammaru, Tiit, 'Sub-urbanisation, employment change and commuting in the Tallinn Metropolitan Area', Institute of Geography, University of Tartu, Estonia, 2005.

Thomas, T. M., 'A Suburban Connemara', *Household Words*, 8 March 1851.

Thompson, F. M. L. (ed.) *The Rise of Suburbia*, Leicester University Press, 1982.

United Nations, *World Population Monitoring 2001*, Department of Economic and Social Affairs, Population Division, New York, 2001.

Wells, H. G., *Anticipations of the Reaction of Mechanical and Scientific Progress upon Human Life and Thought*, 1901, Project Gutenberg edition.

Whelan, Laura, *Class, Culture and Suburban Anxieties in the Victorian Era*, London, Routledge, 2009.

White, John H. Jr, *The American Railroad Passenger Car*, Baltimore, Johns Hopkins University Press, 1985.

Whyte, William H. Jr, *The Organization Man*, New York, Doubleday, 1956.

The State of Wisconsin 2007–2008 Blue Book, Wisconsin Legislative Reference Bureau, Madison, 2007.

Wolmar, Christian, *Fire & Steam: How the Railways Transformed Britain*, London, Atlantic Books, London, paperback edition, 2008.

The Year-Book of Facts in Science and Art, Tilt and Bogue, London, 1841.

Acknowledgements

My love and gratitude to Ness, for her patience; my thanks to Ben Mason, for his help with the planning of this book, to Richard Milbank, for his guidance in its execution, to Paul Newton, for his assistance with the manuscript, and to Jeremy Latham, for putting me back on my feet.

Picture credits

Page 11: Passengers leaving the *Flying Scotsman* at King's Cross railway station, London, after their journey from Edinburgh, 1891; Getty Images.
Page 169: An aerial view of traffic congestion at the entrance to New York's Holland Tunnel, 1935; Getty Images.
Page 281: A test of an early Apollo spacesuit prototype taking place in one of the simulators; Getty Images.

Index